Holmberg

FOOTSORE 1

W9-DAX-917

Walks & Hikes Around Puget Sound

**By Harvey Manning/Photos by Bob & Ira Spring
Maps by Gary Rands/The Mountaineers • Seattle**

*Seattle • Puget Sound Trail from Tacoma to
Everett • Overlake Highlands and Sammamish
Valley • Issaquah Alps • Cedar and Green Rivers •
White River*

THE MOUNTAINEERS

Organized 1906

To explore and study the mountains, forests, and watercourses of the North-
west;
To gather into permanent form the history and traditions of this region;
To preserve by the encouragement of protective legislation or otherwise the
natural beauty of Northwest America;
To make explorations into these regions in fulfillment of the above purposes;
To encourage a spirit of good fellowship among all lovers of outdoor life.

First edition, December 1977
Copyright © 1977
Second Printing, November 1978

The Mountaineers
719 Pike St.
Seattle, Washington 98101

Manufactured in the United States of America

Published simultaneously in Canada by
Douglas & McIntyre, 1875 Welch St., North Vancouver, B.C. V7P 1B7

Library of Congress Catalog Card No. 77-23727
ISBN 0-916890-53-8

Book design by Marge Mueller

**Cover photo: Edmonds ferry dock from Brackett's Landing Park on
Puget Sound.**

INTRODUCTION I

Other guidebooks published by The Mountaineers direct the feet to high or distant areas where, to quote the 1964 Wilderness Act, "the earth and its community of life are untrammeled by man, where man himself is a visitor who does not remain." Quite different is the realm — Puget Sound City and outskirts — of the **Footsore** series. There man definitely does remain. He lives there. Works there. Fools around there. And trammels there — boy does he ever trammel. Yet his creations/destructions are not unrelieved; on the walks described in these pages tree green is more prominent than asphalt black, birdsongs than hornhonks, clean breezes than vile gases. If the routes traverse little pristine wilderness they're wild to a degree. Or wildlike in part. Or anyhow nice.

And they're close to home. Few **Footsore** paths lie more than a going-and-coming total of 2 automobile hours (many are less than 1 hour) from one or another major lump of Puget Sound City population, whether in Everett or Olympia, Bremerton or Bellevue. The Two-Hour Rule derives from this book's philosophical foundation (and those who reject it are invited to leap on their wheels and buzz off) that (1) walking, if not done to such silly extremes as the 50-Mile-Day mania of the early 1960s, is good-in-itself and good for you; (2) automobile riding in more than modest doses is devil's work and very bad for you. Walking is superb medicine for under-exercised bodies and over-stressed minds, but the knitting together of damaged flesh and spirit by a day on the trail can be unraveled by too long an evening battle homeward through the mobs of deranged children whose grim joy is playing war games on freeways and byways. If to gain for a day the sweet balm of Nature a person must suffer more than 2 or 3 hours of automobile trauma, he perhaps is better off spending the re-creation day home in bed.

Automobile ownership continues to be a prerequisite for full American citizenship and all its rights and privileges, including easy transport to trails. On some surveys for this book the thumb was employed, with varying success; other hitchhikers unquestionably would be picked up faster than was the surveyor, but being aged, crummy, and poor is not without compensations — a roadside display of youth, beauty, or wealth, particularly by a solitary thumber, is asking for it. Risks aside, hitchhiking nearly always adds time to a trip, maybe a lot. But as of 1977 it's legal on most roads in Washington. And if you don't get knocked on the head and dumped in the ditch it's cheap.

Then there's the bus. The text here notes walking routes reasonably accessible via Metro Transit as of Autumn 1977. For precise planning one must obtain current route maps and schedules (contact Metro Transit, 600 First Avenue, Seattle 98104); the notes are intended mainly to stimulate hikers to think bus — and bus managers to think hikers.

NO MONEYBACK GUARANTEE

The country of **Footsore** I is portrayed here as it was when surveyed in person (no fudging, no library "research") during the winter-spring of 1976-77. But that doesn't mean it'll be the same when you arrive. This lived-on, worked-on, fooled-around-on, trammeled land is ever changing, often radically and without notice.

The following "buyer beware" warnings are not aimed at forestalling complaints. To the contrary. Volumes in the **Footsore** series will be periodically revised, correcting errors, updating information, dropping trips that have been trammeled to death and replacing them with new ones. However, the series covers upwards of 2500 miles and the surveyor, who does not plan to walk every step every year, will gladly accept any help anybody cares to offer. And don't bother to be polite — if you've had a bad day trusting the golly dang guidebook, let the steam blow. The surveyor welcomes irate letters, solicits them, begs for them. He will be pleased as punch to receive your denunciations of his eyesight, intelligence, and character if in the process you provide news and comment on the current state of a route. Address your diatribes to the author c/o The Mountaineers, 719 Pike Street, Seattle 98101.

Several specific caveats must be made:

1. A great many **Footsore** trips cross private property where trespassing long has been tolerated and was at the time of survey. But a copy of this book in your hot little hand does not serve as a license to infringe on property rights. If the "No Trespassing" signs have gone up, you must obey. (And when you get home, write that hot little letter to the surveyor.)

The behavior of you and other **Footsore** readers in many cases will determine whether or not trespassing continues to be tolerated. Obviously you should not foul the path with body wastes or garbage — and in fact the modern thoughtful walker picks up and carries out garbage left by others, gaining a glow of virtue plus whatever cash the glass and metal earn at the recycling station. For further discussion of trespassing see the introduction to "Puget Sound Trail: Seattle to Tacoma."

2. Railroad rights-of-way are private property and the owners do not invite, approve or officially tolerate trespassing. Walking tracks is dangerous, as witness the annual death toll, for which railroads are not legally or morally responsible — the trespasser always is at fault. Though the rights-of-way have been multiple-used by walkers and trains since the beginning of the rail era and nothing short of a billion dollars in fences and armies of guards could evict feet, description of a traditional walking route in this book is not a recommendation that you go there and break the law and take risks. To report that tens of thousands of people annually trespass on Puget Sound area train tracks is not to encourage you to do so but simply to record a significant historical-sociological fact. You trespass of your own free will, at your own risk. (The railroads wisely try to ignore a situation fraught with peril for the existing definition of "private property," but if they were to speak up they might say, and the surveyor certainly does, that if you insist on a life of crime for gosh sake keep an eye over the shoulder, stay off trestles, and if a railroad employee commands you to depart, don't give him any sass about quasipublic land, traditional vested rights, common-law easement, revesting the Northern Pacific Land Grant, nationalization, or nyaa-nyaa-catch-me-if-you-can. Politely salute and get stepping.)

3. Vast expanses of **Footsore** country are in tree farms managed by the state Department of Natural Resources (DNR) and private landowners. Unlike national forests, where the Sustained Yield-Multiple Use Act places recreation on a parity with lumber and pulp, the laws of the state on DNR lands and the laws of economics on private lands give short shrift to any statistic not preceded by a $.

East Channel, Lake Washington

Let there not be assumed any hatred here of the $. And let us remember that you can't get beefsteak without hurting the cow nor boards for houses and paper for guidebooks without letting daylight into the swamp. Easy weepers ought to stay out of slaughterhouses. Tree farms demand some stiffness in the upper lip. A walk described as being through cool depths of a green tunnel may be, when you arrive, in sun-blasted bleakness of a raw new clearcut. You may not be able to find the route at all, out there in the stumps and slash.

4. Not merely man transforms the terrain. Nature, too, runs amok. Many **Footsore** routes are maintained, if at all, solely by the stomping boots and brushcrashing bodies of hikers who, should their attention wander briefly, soon lose the contest to rank greenery.

5. Some trips are so lacking in distinctive landmarks that you may be unable to follow the surveyor's confusing directions without map and compass, a higher order of routefinding skill than required in the North Cascades wilderness, and lots of luck.

To conclude these caveats, very little is firmly preserved, nearly everything is subject to change, in the realm of **Footsore**. A hiker setting out for a day is wise to have not one but several trips in mind. If you miss on the first try, keep swinging. And keep those vitriolic cards and letters rolling in.

Sailboats racing on Lake Washington

FOOTROADS

Were **Footsore** confined to protected footpaths the series would boil down to a skinny pamphlet. If you're going to do much walking in and around Puget Sound City you're going to walk a lot of roads. The question is, how much wheeled traffic can a pedestrian accept? The amount varies, of course, from person to person, situation to situation. Strolling the shore of Lake Washington one may be oblivious to a steady stream of Sunday drivers creeping along the adjacent boulevard. Deep in the wildwood a single snarling motorcycle may be a stomach-churning outrage.

The finest footroads have perfect wheelstops that convert them to de facto trails. Generally quite acceptable are ways traveled only by the occasional logging truck or other work machine. Meeting two or three recreation vehicles an hour may not critically aggravate the hypertension. A day-long parade of razzing motorcycles — well, you'd have better stood in bed.

The surveyor sought routes reasonably free of racket most of the time. Some routes were judged too scenicly splendid to be conceded to wheels; labeled "Never on Sunday," they are recommended for, say, stormy winter Wednesdays before school lets out. Some routes found serene by the surveyor may subsequently have been invaded, some perfect wheelstops breached by jeeper engineers, those good-deed-a-weekend latter-day Dan'l Boones; if you have a scarifying encounter with machines on a **Footsore** trip, please write that hostile letter. (And others to somebody in government and to some newspaper editor.)

HOW TO USE THIS SERIES OF BOOKS

Outdoor recreation professionals distinguish between "walks," short excursions on easy paths in forgiving terrain, requiring no special clothing or equipment and no experience or training, and "hikes," longer and/or rougher, potentially somewhat dangerous, demanding stout shoes or boots, clothing for cold and wet weather, gear for routefinding and emergencies, rucksack to carry it all in, and best done in company of experienced companions or eased into gradually, conservatively.

Footsore describes short walks in and around Puget Sound City, outings suitable for a leisurely afternoon or even a spring-summer evening, as well as long walks that may keep a person hopping all day. For any walk, equipment demands no more than a passing thought; as for technique, the rule is just to pick 'em up and lay 'em down and look both ways before crossing the street.

Hikes are another matter and the novice must take care, when choosing a trip, to be aware of the difference and to make appropriate preparations. On every hike where a shout for help might not bring quick assistance to the lost or injured or ill, each person should carry the Ten Essentials:

1. Extra clothing — enough so that if a sunny-warm morning yields to rainy-windy afternoon, or if accident keeps the party out overnight, hypothermia ("exposure" or "freezing to death") will not be a threat
2. Extra food — enough so something is left over at the planned end of the trip, in case the actual end is the next day
3. Sunglasses — if travel on snow for more than a few minutes may be involved
4. Knife — for first aid and emergency firebuilding (making kindling)
5. Firestarter — a candle or chemical fuel for starting a fire with wet wood
6. First aid kit
7. Matches — in a waterproof container
8. Flashlight — with extra bulb and batteries
9. Map. Travel directions herein assume the reader has the proper highway maps for driving to the trip vicinity, from where the text and sketch maps zero in on the trailhead. For the walks no other maps are necessary. However, for many of the hikes a person is risking not achieving the destination — and not returning to civilization until carried there by a search party — if he lacks the appropriate U.S. Geological Survey maps, available at map shops and some mountain shops, including (in Seattle) Recreational Equipment Inc.
10. Compass — with knowledge of use

Hiking isn't so complicated that a person needs a lot of instruction, but the same can be said of dying. To learn how to select and use the Essentials a novice lacking tutelage by a family member or friend may enroll in a course offered by an outing club, youth group, church, park department, or professional wilderness guide. Alternatively, one can buy a book; the surveyor is partial to **Backpacking: One Step At A Time** but if you don't like that manual there are hundreds of others on the market.

Some words about the information summary given for each trip:

The "round trip xx miles" and "elevation gain xxxx feet" tell a person if the trip fits his energy and ambition. Some hikers do 20 miles a day and gain 5000 feet without a deep breath, others gasp and grunt at 5 miles and 1500 feet. The

Wintery morning on the Tolt Pipeline Trail

novice will quickly learn his capacity. Note: the "elevation gain" is gross, not net; an upsy-downsy trail can gain hundreds of feet while going along "on the flat."

The "allow x hours" must be used with a personal conversion factor. The figures here are based on doing 1½ miles an hour on the flat (walking at a rate of 2 miles an hour but walking only 45 minutes in the hour) and an elevation gain of about 700 feet an hour, with added time for slow tracks — muddy, brushy, loggy. From these figures a hiker accustomed to doing 1 mile an hour or 3, or gaining 200 feet an hour or 2000, can calculate his own approximate travel time.

"High point xxxx feet" tells the knowing much about the vegetation and views to expect, as well as the probable amount of snow in any given month. The bottom line, the "all year" or "February-December" or whatever, attempts to spell this out. It does not suggest the "best time", which is a subjective judgment based on whether one likes spring flowers or fall mushrooms or what. The intent is to tell when, in an average normal year (whatever that is) a trail is probably sufficiently snowfree for pleasure walking, meaning less than a foot of snow or only occasional deeper patches.Several factors are involved. One is elevation. Another is distance from Puget Sound, whose large volume of above-freezing water warms winter air masses. In any locality, higher is generally snowier. But also, for identical elevations the farther from saltwater is generally snowier. And mountain valleys, acting like giant iceboxes, generally are snowier than nearby lowlands outside the mountain front. Finally, though south and west slopes get as much snow as north and east, they also get more sun (and also more sun than valley flats) and thus melt out faster.

These factors are taken into account, and eked out with guesswork, in coding the trips. To explain the code:

"All year" means the trail is always open — except during intervals when the snowline drops to sea level or near it.

"February-December" doesn't imply any prejudice against January, which may be no colder than adjacent months, but means an ordinary winter has maybe 4-8 weeks, from late December to late February, when the trail may be under more than a foot of snow. But it can be snowfree in a mid-January thaw or throughout a mild winter. And in a tough winter can be up to the knees from November to March.

"March-November" means a typical snowpack of several feet or so that begins piling up in November, early or late, and melts mostly out in March, early or late. Again, the path may be walkable in dead of winter. Or up to the crotch from October to May.

"April-November" means quite a deep snowpack that may begin accumulating in October (or December) and may melt in March (or June).

And so on. In short, the aim is to tell approximately how things usually have been, not predict what they will be.

ACKNOWLEDGMENTS 1-2

The primary debt owed by this and every other hiking guide to the Puget Sound region is to the tens of thousands of Mountaineers who have prowled the countryside for 70-odd years. Anyone setting out to survey the pedestrian pleasures of the territory starts, wittingly or not, from their group wisdom.

The debt to Janice Krenmayr and her famous **Footloose Around Puget Sound** is as obvious as the echo in **Footsore**. After a decade and three revisions she had enough, what with other projects demanding attention, and I was hired as replacement. That her one book grew into my multi-volume series may be explained partly by the fact I'm notoriously wordy, partly by a hope to stamp out the infestation of machines by flooding the countryside with feet.

Even before I met him I owed much to Stan Unger, who as a planner for King County played a key role in shaping the 1971 Urban Trails Plan. Reading that exhilarating document's schemes for future paths interlacing throughout the county and tying to networks of adjoining counties inspired many explorations described herein. Very early in my surveying I was fortunate enough to be introduced to Stan by Tom Eksten of King County Parks, another devout pedestrian and avid pathfinder and trail planner and promoter. At a first meeting Stan and Tom told me all manner of good places to walk. Stan himself had been mulling a guidebook; finding me already at work he graciously yielded the field and volunteered free access to his knowledge. In subsequent months he not only suggested trips but led me on several, demonstrating enviable form in crossing barbed-wire fences and indefatigable devotion to cleaning up routes and packing out litter. Finally, Stan and Tom read and criticized the entire manuscript that became **Footsore 1** and **2**.

If my expression of gratitude to others who helped on 1 and 2 is briefer it's solely because space considerations forbid proper thanks:

Don Campbell, Mt. Baker-Snoqualmie National Forest; Jack Mosby, Bureau of Outdoor Recreation; Dan Fryberger, Doug Bailey, and W. C. Alguard, U.S. Army Corps of Engineers; William A. Bush, Larry Kay, Bob Genoe, Don Malloy, Carl Nelson, Steve McBee, Bob Togstad, Jim Collins, Joe Cowan, and Monty Fields, Washington State Parks; Terry Patton and Joe Potter and Cassie Phillips, Washington Department of Natural Resources; W. M. Foster and Richard P. Wilson, Washington Department of Highways; Robert H. Barnard, Washington Department of Game; Gregory W. Lovelady, State Trails Coordinator in the Interagency Committee for Outdoor Recreation; Marjean Deach, Metro Transit; Bruce Finke, Seattle Office of Policy Planning; Larry E. Jones, Seattle Parks; Siegfried Semrau, Bellevue Parks; people in Mercer Island and Kent parks whose names I didn't catch; Pat Cummins, Green River Community College; Max Eckenburg, Camp Sheppard, and Dan Minzel, Camp Brinkley, of the Scouts; and in the Weyerhaeuser Company, James W. Crotts, Dave Mumper, and Howard Millan — the latter of whom was Senior Patrol Leader of Troop 324 when I was a Tenderfoot, **Footsore** thus providing a welcome excuse for a reunion on the trail with my Leader.

Expressing gratitude to the Literary Fund Committee and co-workers is superfluous (excepting my editor here, Verna Ness). However, the entertainment provided by walking the 1300 or so miles of I and II in the winter-spring of 1976-77 requires me to thank John Pollock, LFC chairman, and Ira Spring for dragooning me into becoming Janice's successor. Not that I see anything demeaning about production of guidebooks, the occupation of some of my best friends and one in which I myself have dabbled as editor or junior partner, but I'd never thought of soloing a text. What finally tipped the balance in convincing me to take this post as brush-beater was the acute withdrawal syndrome from quitting cigarettes; my IQ was cut in half, to 26, rendering me incapable of any intellectual effort greater than distinguishing flowers from birds, left boot from right, perfectly suiting me for guidebooks, which need not be written but must be walked — poetry be hanged but in the name of golly don't drylab and don't screw up at the forks in the trail. I've done my level best; only once did my directions send photographer Ira to the left when I meant right. Several times he didn't end up at the destinations specified in my text; however, he pretty well liked the places he did get to, wherever they may be, took nice pictures, and managed to get home okay.

So no harm done.

H.M.

White-crowned sparrow singing to hikers on Bridlecrest Trail

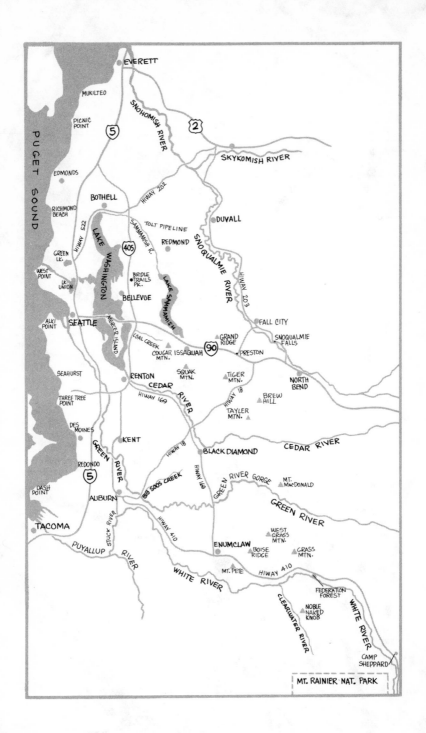

CONTENTS 1

Seattle's skyline from 10th Avenue South and South Snoqualmie

SEATTLE

As far as this book is concerned Seattle is an anomaly. First, unlike the provinces of other chapters it doesn't constitute an orderly drainage basin or unified upland; the landscape, already so scrambled by the Puget Glacier that 10,000-odd years since melting of the ice hadn't sufficed for streams to organize the terrain, has been so distorted by a century of man's fiddling that the only hope for geologic logic in the reasonably near future is a return of the ice or a rise in sealevel or birth of a new volcano. Second, despite myriad green nooks surviving amid the concrete, as a densely-inhabited, intensely-manipulated piece of real estate it scarcely seems a prime arena for the sort of wildland exercise that is the subject in hand.

This is not to disparage the opportunities for feet in Seattle. The system of parks was magnificently designed for the needs of 1910 and when, a half-century later, it had become too cramped for an enlarged population, a major expansion was made possible by the decision of the armed forces to abandon preparations for another First World or Spanish-American War. Further, a new generation of city planners, harking back beyond immediate predecessors to the wisdom of a past age, accepted as legitimate forms of recreation those requiring no equipment more complicated than a bicycle and/or two legs in working condition; thus began what may be called, for one of its early fruits, the "Burke Gilman Trail Era."

Finally, the sidewalks are in. Residents of the New Cities built on the Los Angeles Plan travel by foot near tract homes at their peril, confined by developers' penury and government's apathy to the middles of streets posted for 25 miles per hour but normally driven at 40 mph or tire-squealing speed, whichever is greater; should a suburbanite do something really bizarre, such as undertake an evening constitutional of several miles, much of his route probably will be on a highway shoulder inches removed from a roaring torrent of fume-spewing juggernauts. By contrast, a pedestrian can safely and pleasurably traverse virtually the entire length and width of old Seattle along rather quiet and peaceful, sometimes tree-shaded and flower-garden-brightened residential streets, and perhaps never once be accosted by police and asked to explain his suspicious behavior.

Throughout Seattle are attractive local walks known to residents of the various neighborhoods, plus lovely short strolls in small parks whose locations the stranger easily can find on a city map. In addition there are several long walks that rank with any in this book; if not as wild as some they are closer to home than most and the shorter confinement (or none) in the automobile gives an overall "wildness of the day" that may well surpass that of a hike requiring a lengthy before-and-after ordeal on freeways. The finest of these long walks, those having a regional interest as distinguished from local or neighborhood interest, are described here.

Should a patriot feel the metropolis is short-changed by so skimpy a chapter, be reminded that Janice Krenmayr's two **Footloose In Seattle** booklets, available at your bookstore, describe enough trips to keep the feet busy a year. Further, note that the two following chapters on the Puget Sound Trail are in large measure about Seattle and indeed feature some of the best parts.

USGS maps: Edmonds East, Seattle North, Kirkland, Shilshole Bay, Seattle South, Mercer Island

Beacon Ridge (Map - page 17)

A 200-foot-wide green lawn rolling up hill and down dale for miles, in broad views west to saltwater and Olympics, east to Lake Washington and Cascades. And if you don't bother them the Seattle City Light power lines won't bother you. The hike can begin and end at any number of places; the full tour, starting at the north end, will be described here.

Power line across Beacon Ridge

Park at or near Maple Wood Playground Park, Corson Avenue S and South Snoqualmie, in itself a nice little broad-view stroll around the greensward. Elevation, 200 feet.

Walk a long block north to the powerline lawn; here is a panorama over I-5 (which rules out any extension of the route westward) and the Duwamish industrial plain to Elliott Bay and downtown Seattle and Queen Anne Hill and Magnolia Bluff and Olympics.

Ascend the lawn 1 mile to the crossing of busy Beacon Avenue (good parking), just south of the Veterans Administration Hospital and Jefferson Park Golf Course. Here the lawn bends right to follow on or near the crest of Beacon Ridge. Streets (mostly quiet) are crossed and backyards merge into public lawn, but the walk-anywhere no-trail-needed strip is so spacious and calm (no motorcycles permitted) that despite the all-aroundness of Puget Sound City a person feels the green peace.

Ascending grassy knolls, dipping to hollows, the way offers looks south over Lake Washington to Renton and Rainier, up to jets sliding down to land, and east over Mercer Island to the Issaquah Alps. Beyond Empire Way the ridge assumes a rural air, often wildwooded on either side, pleasantly invaded by garden plots and orchards and horses pasturing and roosters crowing. And dogs barking. After crossing 51 Avenue S, the green lane drops a bit to fruit

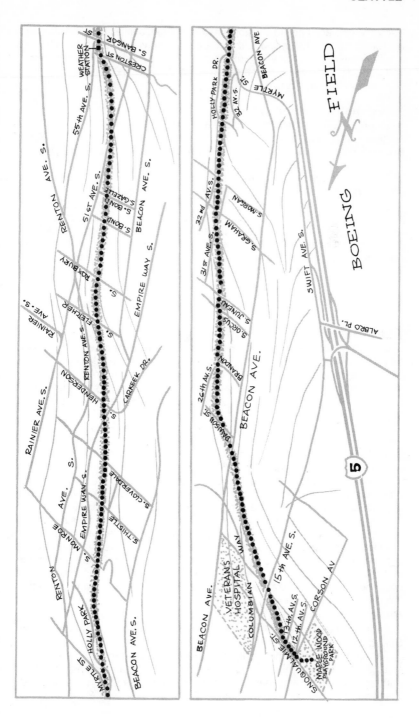

trees in a vale and rises to a hilltop weather station, 5 miles from the start and the recommended lunch spot and turnaround. The view extends back the full length of the route to the Veterans Hospital and beyond to downtown towers and Capitol Hill, as well as over the Duwamish Valley and Boeing Field to West Seattle and the Olympics.

Round trip 10 miles, allow 7 hours
High point 350 feet, elevation gain 800 feet
All year
Bus: Metro 3 and 31 and 48 to Beacon Avenue, 42 to Empire Way

The route goes on and has marvelous potential for a trail to Renton, connecting there to Interurban (Green River) and Cedar River Trails (which see) and golly knows what all. But in dropping from Weather Station Knoll the powerline leaves the wide lawn and the city and enters a grubby motorcycle hell which continues to Skyway, relieved only by the small oasis of Skyway County Park. The swath moreover is intruded by shopping center parking lots and private fences and garbage. Achieving the potential will take some effort.

Seattle Lakes Trail (Map - page 21)

In 1903, during the decade when Seattle established the bulk of what was to be its park system for the next 60-odd years, J.C. Olmsted designed for the city a magnificent park-and-boulevard network. A portion of the plan was implemented in those years before the automobile began to call the tune of urban development. To emphasize the unity and pre-freeway character, it might well be officially named "Olmsted Trail"; here, though, it is called the Seattle Lakes Trail, linking the city's three major lakes, traversing kempt-lawn parks, an arboretum containing thousands of native and exotic plants, and a virgin-forest wildland, passing beaches, bird-busy marshes, sailboats on blue waters, and broad mountain views.

To experience the oneness, on the survey trip the entire trail was hiked in a day: the car was parked at East Green Lake; Metro buses 16, 7 and 39 were taken to Seward Park, the total trip time 1½ hours; the trail was hiked back to the car, with the sustaining knowledge that if ambition failed or rain crushed the umbrella, always ready to rescue was Metro Transit. The hike is described here in the sequence of the survey; most people, of course, will prefer doing only short segments of the trail on any single excursion. (Had he not been inspired by a Larger Purpose, the surveyor would have felt it downright obscene to spend a mere hour in Seward Park and only half that rocketing through the Arboretum.)

Mile 0-2½: Seward Park

Park at the entrance, just off Lake Washington Boulevard South at Juneau Street.

The Seattle Lakes Trail properly begins by looping around Bailey Peninsula. Walk the shore in either direction, by fish hatchery and fishing piers, bathing beaches (on a hot day, break the hike for a dip) and views across Lake Washington to Mercer Island, south to Rainier.

Seward Park trail

Some Lake Washington facts: 210 feet is the deepest point; water level is now 20.0-21.85 feet above sealevel, having been lowered 10 feet in 1916; main tributaries are the Sammamish River and Cedar River, the latter diverted early in the century from the Green-Duwamish to the lake; former outlet was the Black River (now defunct) to the Green-Duwamish, present outlet is the Lake Washington Ship Canal.

The shore is not the sole attraction of 278-acre Seward Park. The peninsula spine features Seattle's largest virgin forest, close to 1 mile long and averaging ¼ mile wide. The old-growth Douglas firs are dazzlers, the maples are huge, and the supporting cast of native trees and shrubs forms a fine wild tangle. The forest trail system has entries around the peninsula; paths range from broad-flat to narrow-primitive. No map required. Just plunge in and explore. If lucky, get lost, thus making the wildland seem all the larger.

A basic introduction to Seward Park requires a 2½-mile shore loop plus a tour up and down the 1-mile-long peninsula; 4½ miles, 3 hours. For hikers intending to reach far points by day's end the short introduction is up either shore to the peninsula tip and back down the spine, a 2½-mile opening segment in the Lakes Trail.

Mile 2½-9: Lake Washington Boulevard
Parking is plentiful (not summer Sundays) the whole route.

Officially known as Lake Washington Park and Parkway, the entire length is along streets, but most of the walking path is a decent distance from car lanes, traversing this or that pocket park; machines are easy to ignore if eyes are pointed over the water to the mountains.

The first 3½ walking miles are trees and lawns and wall-to-wall ducks and coots and, in the reeds, redwing blackbirds. Some attractions, in order: pretty little Andrews Bay, enclosed by Bailey Peninsula; Japanese cherry trees; yacht moorage at Ohler's Island; dismal pits of Sayres Memorial Park; bathing beach at Mt. Baker Park, adjoined on the north by Colman Park; mountain views from Baker to Pilchuck to Index to Si to Issaquah Alps to Rainier.

For the next 1 mile the street changes name to Lakeside Avenue and is lined by private homes. But under Mercer Island Floating Bridge is public access to the water. For perhaps the best mountain views of the whole trip, walk up to the plaza and out on the bridge. While driving over the bridge one can't (shouldn't) enjoy the view, which includes one of the best Seattle looks at Glacier Peak.

At Leschi business district and yacht harbor the boulevard resumes; on the hillside are lawns and trees of Frink Park, on the water is Leschi Park. A little old ferry, now some sort of private enterprise, catches the sentimental eye, reminding of the pre-bridge era when this was the landing for the Mercer Island ferries. For a scant 1 mile the path is on the shore, passing the bathing beach of Madrona Park. (Ready for that swim yet?) Then private homes again pre-empt the water.

The final 1 mile leaves the lake and climbs the hill in a forest of private trees, plus the public trees of boulevard-side Howell and Viretta Parks. Not yet lost is the lake. Just down a deadend street is tiny Denny-Blaine Park. Note the handsome granite-block bulkhead, wonder why it is so high above the water — and realize that when built that's where the waves lapped. Above here the boulevard switchbacks through little Lakeview Park; dodge off the street in a secluded grassy hollow and climb a greensward knoll with a tree-screened look over the lake. Thence it's not far to East Madison Street and the Arboretum.

Mile 9-10: University of Washington Arboretum
Parking at Madison Playground at the south end, in several lots along the boulevard and "upper road", and at the north Broadmoor entrance at the north end.

The full official name is University of Washington Arboretum in Washington Park. In the 200 acres of city park managed by the University as a scientific arboretum are thousands of shrubs and trees and other plants, native and from all over the world, arranged in logical groupings, placed in artful land-scapings to exploit the natural terrain of ridges and valleys, marshes and ponds and creeks. Some 40 years of loving care and artistry are represented.

Attempting to summarize the Arboretum in this short space would be insulting. It needs to be visited plant by plant from one end to the other. When the tour is complete it's another season and the whole job has to be done over. The most cursory introduction requires four walk-throughs: along the valley of Lake Washington Boulevard (the main road), sidetripping in the Japanese Garden; along Arboretum Drive (the "upper road") on the ridge east of the

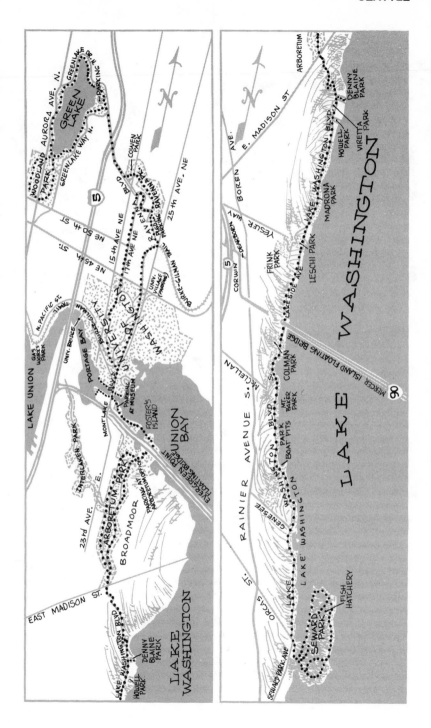

Lake Washington Ship Canal from Montlake Bridge

valley; along the broad green valley-bottom lawn of Azalea Way; and along the hillside trails between Azalea Way and Arboretum Drive, passing the Lookout, a shelter (refuge in the rain) with views down Azalea Way and out the valley north to the University District. Before starting, visit the Arboretum offices at the northeast corner, by the north Broadmoor entrance, for a brochure describing the flowering seasons and the plant groupings. Total cursory introduction 4 miles, 4 hours.

A lifetime is too short. The only justification for treating the Arboretum as a mere 1 mile on the Lakes Trail is to stress its connection to other good things.

Mile 10-11½: Foster's Island-Waterfront Trail-Montlake Bridge

One of which is coming right up.

Parking on the south at the north Broadmoor entrance, on the north at the Museum of History and Industry.

The concrete-and-thunder Evergreen Point Floating Bridge ripped off a fifth of the former acreage of the Arboretum, brutalizing Foster's Island and Union Bay marshes. But even the remnant is a wonderland. The damage could have been worse, and would have been, had not the "Save the Arboretum" campaign of the early 1960s halted the Thompson Expressway planned to blast down the middle of the Arboretum and across (or under) Union Bay; in Seattle, this battle was the start of something new.

From the parking lot at north Broadmoor entrance the path crosses a slough to Foster's Island. Lakeshore. Groves of water-loving trees. A passage under the concrete span of the bridge approach. Views of University stadium and campus, sailboats on Union Bay, Laurelhurst homes on the far shore, and mountains.

Here begins the Waterfront Trail built in 1968 through reeds, among a profusion of birds (and critters unseen), in cattails and bulrushes. The floating walkway has spurs to observation piers. (Incidentally, this marsh is not "primeval" but "new" — the area was all open lake until the water level was lowered to that of Lake Union in 1916.) Competing for attention with marsh texture is freeway geometry.

The Waterfront Trail ends at the Museum of History and Industry parking lot. However, the Lake Washington Ship Canal Waterside Trail, a project of the U.S. Army Corps of Engineers and Seattle Garden Club, carries on without a break, rounding the corner to Montlake Cut connecting Portage Bay of Lake Union and Union Bay of Lake Washington. Ships pass through, and yachts, and racing-shell crews practice. The trail goes under quaint old Montlake Bridge, built in 1925.

Before climbing the steps up to the bridge, sidetrip ¼ mile west to the end of the cut and the public park by the Seattle Yacht Club. Fine view of Portage Bay. Some Lake Union facts: maximum depth 50 feet; due to filling and building, present size is about half the original.

Mile 11½-13½: University of Washington

Parking, for a reasonable fee, on campus.

Montlake Bridge has grand views west and east over the lakes, down to water traffic. On the north side is another waterside walkway which the Corps of Engineers plans to extend.

There are three routes from here to Ravenna Park. For one, cross Montlake Boulevard to campus, hit the Burke-Gilman Trail (which see), follow it north 1½ miles to the vicinity of 25th Avenue, and there cut left to the park. For a second, at an unknown future date there will be a Union Bay Trail on the University campus, an extension of the Waterfront Trail leading near but not into wildlife sanctuaries, through a new arboretum, by water and marsh.

The third is through the campus, whose 600 acres offer miles and hours of strolling. Architecture from French Chateau to College Gothic to Concrete Brutal. Thousands of trees and shrubs, a veritable "other arboretum" and used as such by botany and forestry classes. Windows out to Olympics, Lake Washington and Cascades, and Rainier.

For purposes of the Lake Trail the shortest line may be taken: up Rainier Vista (so named for the view of The Mountain which provides the campus its central axis) to Frosh Pond and resident ducks and onward to the vast brickery

University of Washington campus

of Red Square, then up Memorial Way past the Astronomy Observatory and Washington State Museum, exiting from campus at NE 45 Street.

Turn right to reach the Burke-Gilman Trail. Alternatively, proceed north through Greek Row to Ravenna Boulevard and eastward down it to the lower end of Ravenna Park.

Mile 13½-15½: Ravenna and Cowen Parks

Street parking all around and at the lower end in Ravenna Playground.

A person can drive over (on bridges) the deep gulch of these parks and scarcely know they exist. But down in the dark hole, by the creek in big maples and firs, the city almost is silenced. Some ravine facts: before Seattle grew up this was the drainage of Green Lake to Lake Washington; the drainage continues but mainly underground in sewers and basements.

The ravine can be traversed along the bottom, on either sidehill, or by combinations; several trails interlace. Quiet semi-wild areas of native plants. Exotics, including a tangle of Himalaya berry thorny vines only beloved by birds and critters seeking a refuge from pussycats.

For 1 (walking) mile the ravine ascends from the level of Lake Washington to that of Brooklyn Avenue. At Brooklyn take tree-lined Ravenna Boulevard under I-5, by Boehm's Candy Kitchen, 1 mile to Green Lake, reached near the East Green Lake business district.

Mile 15½-18½: Green Lake

Parking on streets and lots all around.

You can't get your ticket punched as having done the Lakes Trail without one 3-mile lap around Green Lake. Lawns and trees, views of surrounding ridges and Rainier, resident mobs of waterfowl, who have their sanctuary, Swan (Duck) Island. Beware of buzzing swarms of bicycles and thundering herds of joggers; you could get knocked on the grass. Despite the popularity, many hours of many days the loop is peaceful.

Some Green Lake facts: maximum depth 29 feet; lowered 7 feet in 1911 to enlarge Green Lake Park; due to eutrophication (the "dying" which all lowland Puget Sound lakes are doing) was once guaranteed to give any swimmer daring the waters in summer a case of the "Green Lake Crud"; various attempts to clean up the lake by dredging and poisoning having failed, eventually science was consulted and Seattle City Water began diverting surplus water from the mountains, and this flushing keeps Green Lake cleaner than most.

By no means ignore the adjoining uplands of Woodland Park, one of Seattle's oldest (1890) and still among its largest. Though entirely kempt, with picnic grounds and rose gardens and zoo, it offers miles of serene green at certain times of year and week. For a basic introduction do a 2-mile perimeter loop, no guidebook or map required.

One-way trip 18½ miles, allow 12 hours
High point 250 feet, elevation gain 1000 feet
All year
Bus: Metro 39, Seward Park; 10, Colman Park; 27, Mercer Island Floating
    Bridge and Leschi Park; 2, Madrona Park; 11, 48, 4, Arboretum; 4, 7, 8,
    25, 30, 48, 76, 77, University; 7, 8, Ravenna-Cowen Parks; 16, 26, 48,
    East Green Lake; 6, West Green Lake

Burke-Gilman Trail (Map - page 27)

A succession of urban scenes, industrial, commercial, academic, and residential. Changing vistas of waterways from Salmon Bay to Lake Union to Lake Washington to the Sammamish River. A series of parks and connections to side trips and other major pedestrian arteries.

As of 1977 the abandoned railroad grade is officially open as the Burke-Gilman Trail, a cooperative enterprise of city and county, for 12 miles. Ultimately the route is planned for some 20 miles from Chitttenden Locks to Blythe Park in Bothell. Most walkers do partway trips, picking a suitable starting point and going as far as seems proper, then either doubling back or using a Metro bus return (this latter ploy making quite reasonable a complete one-way trip from the University to Bothell).

Chittenden Locks to Gasworks Park, 4 miles

From Chittenden Locks and the Puget Sound Trail (which see) the presently-unopened trail route follows Market Street into downtown Ballard and through the Ballard Avenue Historic District, where old buildings are being restored to their early-day appearance. Becoming industrial, the way goes from Ballard Avenue to 17 Avenue NW to Shilshole Avenue, then on NW 45 Street to cross under the Ballard Bridge (15 Avenue NW). Railroad tracks and/or Leary Way lead to a footpath along poplar-lined Lake Washington Ship Canal, with ships and yachts and ducks. Fremont Bridge is passed, and the old Fremont District, being cleaned up and made artsy-craftsy attractive. North 34 Street leads to Northlake Avenue, the final stretch to Gasworks Park.

The park (good parking) demands a tour. Inspect machinery of the plant which for decades generated gas from coal, walk the ¼ mile of frontage path on Lake Union. See tugboats, sailboats, police boats, climb the knoll for a view of downtown Seattle towering at the other end of the lake. Gulls, ducks, coots, crows, pigeons.

Gasworks Park to north end of University of Washington campus, 3 miles

The park is ¾ mile from the 1977 official trail start and is a superior place to begin, the parking usually better than at the NE Pacific Street and Latona Avenue NE commencement of maintained path. The Northlake Bikeway is the connection.

On abandoned railroad grade the Burke-Gilman crosses under the Freeway Bridge and University Bridge over the ship canal and passes through the new West Campus to the old Central Campus beginning at 15 Avenue NE. Metro bus stops make this a good place for hikers-busriders to start.

The campus is among the best parts of the whole route. Views to Lake Union and Portage Bay, up Rainier Vista to the campus center and out to The Mountain, and over Union Bay to Lake Washington and the Cascades. Plentiful parking east of Montlake Boulevard. An intersection with the Seattle Lakes Trail (which see) offers tempting sidetrips to campus and Aboretum. Eventually the University plans a nature trail through reconstituted natural areas on and around Union Bay, where for decades Seattle dumped its garbage.

At NE 45 Street the trail passes the tiny "University Wilderness" on the sidehill, crosses under the viaduct, and leaves campus. The traffic of students, professors, joggers, runners, strollers, bicyclers lessens.

University campus to Sand Point, 3 miles

On campus the trail is attractive and easy-on-feet (and easyriding) red cinders. The city has blacktopped the main path for bicycles but to save feet from pounding to putty has also provided a crushed-rock path. The county (see later) has omitted the latter.

From campus the way passes close to University Village (parking, Metro buses, food, restrooms), swinging inland from the present lakeshore to curve around the former bay. Mostly residential, partly commercial, the way blooms in season with park plantings and private gardens. Urban birds sing.

The trail returns to lake views at Sand Point.(For a sidetrip on NE 65 Street to Lake Washington beaches, see Warren G. Magnuson Park).

Sand Point to city limits at NE 145 Street, 4½ miles

Past Sand Point views are good over Lake Washington. At Thornton Creek are a Metro pumping station and a valley wildland of Himalaya berries penetrated by a path climbing the hill to a lake panorama.

A bit beyond is Matthews Beach Park. A sidetrip is mandatory out on the forested grassy knoll and down lawns to the shore to look over the waters to sailboats and mountains and fend off ducks and coots and gulls and crows that want your lunch.

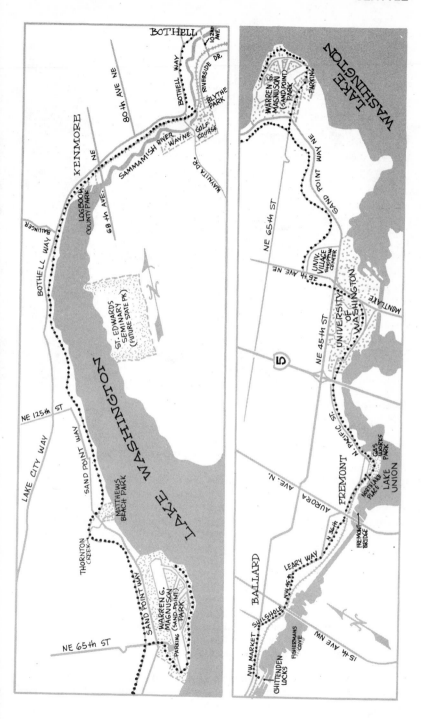

Ocean-going tugboat in Chittenden Locks

A final 3 miles through residential neighborhoods on the water conclude at Seattle city limits.

City limits at NE 145 Street to Kenmore Logboom Park, 2½ miles

With no change except in style of signs and the end of foot-saving crushed rock, the trail enters King County jurisdiction, proceeding by more lakeside homes (Sheridan Beach, Lake Forest Park) to the 1977 end at Logboom Park, on the edge of Kenmore at the north end of Lake Washington. Bothell Way and Metro buses and commercial services are handy.

Kenmore Logboom County Park invites a sidetrip to view old pilings, once used to assemble log rafts for downlake floats to sawmills, and the sagging pier, formerly jutting out 1000 feet for the unloading of logs from railroad cars. The 2000-odd feet of shoreline offer the trip's final lake views. The parking lot and next-door bus line make this a good start-end for Burke-Gilman hikes.

Logboom Park to Blythe Park in Bothell, 3 miles

The existing (1977) Burke-Gilman is left behind and the future general route is followed along railroad tracks beside Bothell Way through the Kenmore industrial area.

Then the tracks diverge from the highway and enter the narrow, pastoral valley of the Sammamish River. Views to neat greenery of Wayne Golf

Course. Sidetrips to river bridges for vistas up and down the duck-swimming lane.

The railroad tracks lead to a bridge over the river. The crossing is not safe for pedestrians and the hike thus must presently end, no matter how tempting the prospect of Blythe Park on the far bank, the connection (future) to the Sammamish River and Tolt Pipeline Trails (which see).

Sound-to-Mountain Trail hikers must (1977) detour north through downtown Bothell. (See Tolt Pipeline Trail.) A hiker who has come all the way from the trail start can return to square one by catching a bus on Bothell Way.

One-way distance from Chittenden Locks to Blythe Park 20 miles
One-way distance open 1977 (officially) 12 miles, allow 8 hours
High point 150 feet, minor elevation gain
All year
Bus: Metro 17 at Chittenden Locks; 15, 18, and 30 in Ballard; 26 and 28 in Fremont; 4, 7, 8, 22, 25, 30, 48, 76, and 77 in University District; 30 in Laurelhurst; 8 and 41 on Sand Point Way; 25 on 37 Avenue NE; 307 on Bothell Way

Warren G. Magnuson (Sand Point) Park (Map - page 27)

Eventually the enormous blacktop desert will be replaced by green fields and groves of trees and paths winding this way and that. But even in the year of establishment, 1977, and utterly lacking improvements, the 196-acre park is a pedestrian's delight, offering Lake Washington's longest waterside walk unmolested by machines.

From Sand Point Way turn east on NE 65 Street and follow signs to the parking area at the south end of the abandoned airplane runway. Elevation, 25 feet.

For maximum shorewalking start at the south boundary fence. Some of the way is on mowed lawn, some in tall grass; part of the shore is jungled by thickets forcing short detours inland. Before lowering of the lake Sand Point was much smaller and mostly marshy; in converting the flat to a U.S. Navy airfield all manner of trash was hauled in — years of work will be required to restore a natural-seeming beach. However, the views over the lake are fine, the sailboats pretty, and the birds numerous. On his initial tour the surveyor observed an ugly-tempered redwinged blackbird chase a heron clear to the other side of the lake, then harass a hawk out of the country, after which the surveyor himself was sent packing.

At 1 long mile from the south fence is another fence; Sand Point continues but the 116 acres north are reserved as a seaport for NOAA's ocean-going ships, which may or may not succeed in fighting through the legal tempests threatening to bar the voyage from their existing base on Lake Union.

For the return a walker can retrace the shore route or go inland for a tour through the fields — or until they are dug up, beside the landing strips, so vastly bleak as to be worth a visit for a thorough boggling of the mind.

An overview may be gained by ascending from the south fence to the hilltop. In the gravel pit below the crest was the "Boneyard," depository in War II for

Burke-Gilman Trail at Kenmore

scrap lumber and crashed airplanes and civilian workers, including the surveyor, found unemployable elsewhere. As park development proceeds and windows are opened in alder forests where stockpiled laborers used to idle away the days there'll be a grand panorama over the whole of Sand Point and out across Lake Washington. In mind's eye one can watch several generations of aircraft taking off and landing, in mind's ear hear the thud-a-thud-thud of machine guns in the gunnery practice range below the Boneyard.

Introductory round trip 3 miles, allow 2 hours
High point 100 feet, elevation gain 75 feet
All year
Bus: Metro 8 and 41

Sound-To-Mountains Trail

For many years hikers have discussed how splendid and fitting a trail would be from beaches of Puget Sound to the Cascade Crest. Routes have been proposed along the Nisqually River and Stillaguamish and Skagit.

The King County Urban Trails Plan published in 1971 proposed a route that would start in Seattle on Lakeside Avenue, cross the Mercer Island Floating Bridge, proceed to Bellefields Nature Park, Houghton, Bridle Trails State Park, and Marymoor Park, 15 miles to that point; thence via Evans and Patterson Creeks to the Snoqualmie River and parallel to Redmond - Fall City Road to Snoqualmie Falls, 20 miles; follow railroad tracks and river dikes to the Middle Fork Snoqualmie and thence on National Forest roads and trails to Dutch Miller Gap.

In 1972 a plan was published for the Lake Washington to Cascade Crest Ecology Trail, prepared by John Warth, who more than a decade before had drawn up the first boundary proposals for an Alpine Lakes Wilderness (at last achieved in 1976). Selected after 2 years of scouting trips, the Warth route traverses a great variety of ecosystems, thus being useful as (among other things) a laboratory for school instructional programs. His trail would go from Lake Washington up Coal Creek over the top of Cougar Mountain, cross Tibbetts Creek, Squak Mountain, Issaquah Creek, Tiger Mountain, East Fork Issaquah Creek, and Grand Ridge to the Snoqualmie River. It would then ascend Griffin Creek, go over the highland to the Tolt River at the forks, over another divide to Youngs Creek, climb Big Haystack Mountain, drop to the Proctor Trough, round the sides of Persis and Index, go through headwaters of the North and South Forks Tolt to Lennox in headwaters of the North Fork Snoqualmie, and proceed through the mountains to Lake Dorothy, down to the Middle Fork Snoqualmie, and up to Dutch Miller Gap. Wow.

Civilian hikers who long had applauded the dreams were startled in 1975 when the King County Division of Land Use Management suddenly brought forth a plan that was no distant vision but very near a reality. If it's not quite that, on August 20-24, 1975, Stan Unger hiked the whole 93 miles from West Point in Seattle to Snoqualmie Pass.

Pedestrians less determined than Mr. Unger are advised to wait for certain linkage problems to be solved and the trail officially opened, perhaps in the next several years, before setting out to do the complete trip. But most of the length is described in this book and can be walked now on separate jaunts.

As presently conceived the Sound-to-Mountains Trail commences at West Point in Discovery Park and goes northeast to Chittenden Locks (see Puget Sound Trail — Seattle to Everett), east and then north on the Burke-Gilman Trail (which see) to Blythe Park in Bothell. The way from there is the Tolt Pipeline Trail (which see) to the Snoqualmie River Trail (which see), this being followed to Snoqualmie Falls. The route then lies on abandoned railroad to Tanner, east of North Bend, and along the Middle Fork Snoqualmie road to the logging road up Granite Creek (which see). Up on the ridge above Granite Lakes the Trail hits trail in National Forest and proceeds along slopes of Defiance and across Pratt River headwaters to Denny Creek, from there following the old wagon road to Snoqualmie Pass.

Mr. Unger celebrated his inaugural tramp with "a nice tall beer" — whether for dry mouth or sore feet is not recorded in his published journal. When last heard from he was trying to recruit companion fanatics to scout an Alternate Sound-to-Mountains Trail that would traverse Cougar, Squak, Tiger, Taylor, Rattlesnake, and Washington, from there following the ridge between Cedar River and South Fork Snoqualmie to the Cascade Crest. Don't bet against him.

Anchor recovered from bay, Alki Beach

PUGET SOUND TRAIL — SEATTLE TO TACOMA

Having gotten devout pedestrians hysterical by proclaiming an unsuspected wonder, one must hasten to declare, "There is no Puget Sound Trail." Or rather, there always has been. When man first arrived in these parts 10,000 (?) years ago he quickly found his way to the clams. And for eons few local residents ever spent much time beyond the smell of saltwater, beside which were their homes. When European man arrived a century and odd decades ago he also leaned toward water-side living, and still does. If, between Seattle and Tacoma, a strip of shore is lacking houses it's usually due to (1) the steepness and instability of the wave-cut bluffs of morainal materials deposited by the Puget Glacier; (2) some speculator holding a chunk of land waiting for the price to go up.

Only in minor part is it due to the existence of public parks. There are a few of these, glory be, mostly in ravines of creeks whose slipping-sliding slopes frustrated builders until government awoke to the need. Government took its time. Upon attainment of statehood in 1889 all saltwater beaches in Washington were public property. But the selling commenced immediately and continued until the scandalously late date of 1969, when 60 percent of the beach length had been sold, including perhaps 99 percent of what anybody might want for residential purposes.

Is it, then, possible to wall off the public from Puget Sound? If the law says so, then "the law, sir, is a ass." As well attempt to wall off the sky. And indeed, many scholars of the law feel 10,000 years of continuous use have firmly established a public highway beside the water and there is no such thing on tidal beaches as completely private property.

But who wants to go hiking with his lawyer? We don't take to the trails to hassle and get hassled. We go walking for the peace, not the war. It therefore is the first commandment of this book that "Thou shalt not bug the people who live by the beach." If you want to argue philosophical and legal points about land ownership, go to court or write your legislators or organize a league or something. Don't do it on the beach. Go there to have a nice day.

The most any legal expert claims for the public is the right of passage, of walking through "private" property. Everyone agrees there is no right to dig clams or pick oysters, gather pebbles or driftwood, or to camp or build a fire or have a picnic lunch or even to sit down. Certainly there is no right to leave garbage or anything else.

Legal theory aside, no rational walker wants to get into a squabble. Thus the second commandment of this book is "Thou shalt instantly depart when somebody tells you to get off his property." With an apology. (To finish off the commandments, a third: "Thou shalt not trespass with thy dog, which shalt be left at home.")

If this treatise seems an apologia for trespassing, look again. It certainly is not. However, during the survey in the winter of 1976-77 many local residents were interviewed. Most are nature-sensitive folk; that's why they live on the beach. Most sympathize with other nature-sensitives and are apologetic about "owning" the beach. Even amid thickets of "No Trespassing" signs most say, "Oh, nobody minds if you walk their beach, as long as you don't make a nuisance." Whatever the property rights of beach residents they have human rights — the right to live in peace, not subjected to dumping of garbage in yards, to noisy picnics and wild night-time beach orgies; the right to sunbathe in privacy, not subjected to the stares of a thousand foreigners marching by.

Some of the signs say "Trespassing by Permission Only." And this is the key to the Puget Sound Trail: the beach traditionally has been walked by tacit permission — but permission that can be revoked by any property owner at any time he pleases. Interviews with local residents revealed some rules as to the times and places when such permission is least likely to be revoked, your presence least likely to be challenged.

Good days are bad. On weekends the year around and on fine evenings of spring and summer, stay away. At such times if you must go to the beach visit the public parks described here or (for reasons discussed in that chapter) walk the Puget Sound Trail north of Seattle.

Crowded beaches are the worst. If you see a mob of people walking past and ignoring "No Trespassing" signs, do not suppose there is safety in numbers. The numbers will just be infuriating residents, who will be calling the police.

Lighthouse on Alki Point

Walking off the ends of public park beaches onto private beaches is the most inviting to the ignorant — and to residents the most irritating.

The "wild" beaches, those with bluffs that keep houses at a distance from the water, are the most open to tolerated trespassing.

Low tide, when the "trail" lies at the water's edge far out from houses, is better than high.

When trespassing, be clean and quiet. No garbage. Carry a litterbag and use it. No shouting. No dogs. Don't come in gangs but alone or in small groups. Keep moving. Don't stare at the houses, fascinated though you may be by littoral architecture, like a burglar casing jobs. If challenged, politely apologize and retreat and go someplace else.

If you avoid built-up stretches (who wants to walk in a succession of front yards anyway?) in favor of wilder areas, and pick the off-seasons and off-days (a stormy Wednesday morning in December) you perhaps can walk from Seattle to Tacoma with no greeting from the locals but a friendly hello.

Advanced pedestrians, if permitted by residents, can walk the entire trail. Probably not on a single day. Aside from the many miles there are the tides. Unlike the trail north of Seattle there is no all-tides route provided by the railway. The surveyor was constantly running out of beach, waves lapping impossible tanglewood cliffy bluffs or residential bulkheads, and forced to return another day. And he constantly had to keep in mind the possibility of having his retreat cut off by an incoming tide. The long-distance walker must check the tide table before setting out.

The attractions of beach-walking probably need no praise here. But the importance of the Puget Sound Trail should be stressed. First, it is close to the homes of just about everybody — perhaps within a half-hour of 90 percent of Puget Sounders. Second, it's an all-year route, never blocked by snow except during the infrequent Ice Ages. Third, due to a partial rainshadow from the Olympics, combined with the air masses not yet rising to cross the Cascades and cooling, the weather is better than farther east in — say — the Issaquah Alps. Frequently when storms are chasing each other over the Northwest and the mountains and foothills never free themselves of one storm's murk before the next descends, "Blue Holes" open along the beach. These interludes are particularly superb for walking — clouds boiling around the Olympics, whitecaps gleaming in the sun, surf rattling the gravel, wind nipping the nose.

Of course, when the inland weather is sunny-blue, fogs may linger long on the water. But that's not a bad time for walking either, lonesome foghorns sounding, ghost ships sliding through mists, seagulls wailing at the mystery of it all.

USGS maps: Seattle South, Duwamish Head, Vashon, Des Moines, Poverty Bay, Tacoma North

Mile 0-5½: Pioneer Square-Duwamish River-Duwamish Head-Hamilton Viewpoint Park (Map - page 37)
Fanatics will want to walk the Trail to the last inch and thus must hoof it from Pioneer Square to the waterfront, south to Spokane Street, west over the Duwamish Waterways to West Seattle, and north to the start of open beach. The route is interesting to students of commerce and industry, though the best viewing of ships and docks and all is on a sidetrip to Harbor Island. (And opportunities for close study of a working beach are much better at the south end of the Trail in Commencement Bay.) However, this book is devoted to nature walks. Where man fits fairly unobstrusively into the landscape, well and good. Where he overwhelms it, that's terrain for some other guidebook.

Hamilton Viewpoint Park (with parking) on Duwamish Head is the best spot anywhere to watch marine traffic: Bainbridge Island ferries passing close, ships and barges and tugs to and from Duwamish Waterways, sailboats and motorboats to and from marinas. Views too of downtown Seattle, Queen Anne Hill, Magnolia Bluff, Winslow and Eagle Harbor on Bainbridge Island, the Olympics.

Mile 5½-8: Alki Beach Park-Alki Point Lighthouse (Map - page 37)
With plentiful parking and buses steps away, this may be the most popular beach walk in Seattle. A favorite time is winter storms, when aficionados come to see ocean-size breakers smashing against and over the seawall. The sidewalk is open at any tide; at low tide one can stroll the beach and there, below the wall, utterly forget the busy street a few yards off and the houses at the foot of the omnipresent bluff.

The entire strip beyond Duwamish Head is called Alki Beach Park. At the south end is the sandy bathing beach, where there is beach at even the highest tide, and the usual gangs of gulls and crows and pigeons and ducks

Black Brandt Geese near Alki Point

and blackbirds and sandpipers whose presence the rest of the route will not be further mentioned.

A stretch of private beach intervenes between bathing beach and the historic Alki Point Lighthouse. (Visiting hours on weekends and holidays, 1-4 p.m.)

Schmitz Park (Map - page 37)

An inland sidetrip from Alki Avenue the short way up SW Stevens Street or 59 Avenue S to Alki Recreation Center, which abuts the lower end of Schmitz Park. (Alternatively, drive up SW Admiral Way and at Stevens go down the park entrance road to the small parking area.)

Started from one of three gifts of land by Ferdinand and Emma Schmitz, this 50-acre park contains one of Seattle's few bits of genuine virgin forest — Douglas firs up to 5 feet in diameter and cedars even thicker, nurselogs supporting rows of hemlocks, and thickets of salmonberry, walls of swordfern.

The "birthplace of Seattle" monument close by (on Alki Point at 63 Avenue SW) causes one to reflect that when the schooner **Exact** landed the first settlers a century and a third ago this forested ravine was just about exactly as it is now. And this was what the country looked like all the way from the Sound to the mountains.

From Alki Recreation Center walk a blockaded old street, now a path, up the ravine, complete with a creek that here is not, as are most city streams, in a storm sewer. At the parking lot old street yields to old trail continuing up the ravine, definitely not city-park-kempt but natural-wild. The trail divides and redivides in a maze of paths down to and along the creek, up tributaries, along

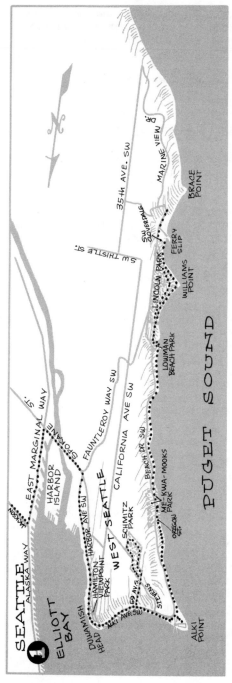

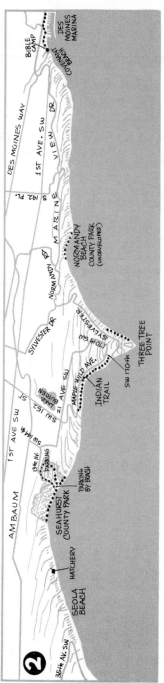

sidehills, by sandbanks, onto knolls. To fully sample the park ascend the ravine along one side to where it's about to enter residences, swing to the far side, and loop back down. Though small, the park contains nearly 2 miles of paths.

Sample round trip from beach 2 miles, allow 1½ hours
High point 250 feet

Mile 8-12: Me-Kwa-Mooks Park-Lowman Beach Park-Williams Point-Lincoln Park (Map - page 37)

South of Alki Point the bluff, which temporarily has receded inland, one of the few places on the route it is out of sight, returns to the beach. Also here is one of the few outcrops of non-glacial rock, sandstone ledges atop which rest glacial debris.

Immediately south of Alki Point homes are built on the beach. Then the beachfront drive prevents construction and permits public access for a bit. Walking is halted by pilings of Harbor West, a condominium built out on a dock. Cheek-by-jowl homes extend 2 miles south; even though in spitting distance of the water one can't see it.

Right in the middle, however, is a small opening. At Oregon Street is a 32-acre park, half a wooded upland on the base of the bluff, half shorelands. Another Schmitz gift, to avoid confusion it has been renamed from Emma Schmitz Memorial Viewpoint to Me-Kwa-Mooks ("entire Alki area"). The opening permits a walker to see the view has changed. Bainbridge Island is being replaced by Blake Island and the Kitsap Peninsula. Now prominent to the south is the green-and-white ferry shuttling from Fauntleroy Cove to Vashon Island.

Private beach ends at little Lowman Beach Park. From it a public alley-street leads behind homes to the beach at Lincoln Park. The next 1 mile of the Puget Sound Trail, through the park, requires separate treatment.

Lincoln Park (Map - page 37)

The best beach park in Seattle? Only Discovery Park can contest the claim. The 107 acres, served by buses and many parking lots, have been a favorite for generations.

For a basic introductory loop start from the parking area off Fauntleroy Avenue SW at Cloverdale Street. Head for the water, following steps or ramp down to the bulkhead walkway, which destroys the naturalness of beach but does permit high-tide walking. (At low tide one can walk natural beach.) The bluff, partly green jungle, partly gray sand cliff, rises 175 very vertical feet, topped by magnificent madrona groves. Smackdab on climactic Williams Point is Colman Pool, a good thing in the wrong place, reminding us that a sewage plant was built on West Point — and an aquarium was not built on Meadow Point, the people by then having learned to leave points alone.

Having walked 1 splendid mile north to homes, retreat to the first of three good (safe) paths that climb the bluff to the top. Walk the rim path, lawns and groves left, wild bluff right. Views over the water to Vashon ferry, Bainbridge ferry, Olympics.

Puget Sound and Olympic Mountains from Lincoln Park

For variations try other paths wandering inland to groves of trees native and exotic, to landscaped shrubbery and flower gardens, to wild places, to other parking areas.

Basic loop trip 2 miles, allow 1½ hours
High point 175 feet

Mile 12-16½: Fauntleroy Cove-Vashon Ferry Slip-Brace Point-Seahurst (Ed Munro) Park (Map - page 37)

Just south of Lincoln Park in Fauntleroy Cove is the Vashon ferry slip. Always worthwhile to a ferry fan is pausing to watch the docking. An excellent rest stop on a long-distance walk is a trip over to the island and back, gaining perspective on the mainland.

In the 3 miles south from the slip there is no formal and darn little informal access to the beach. Breaks in the bluff, such as on the flats of Brace Point and in the creek valleys of Arroyo Beach and Seola Beach, permit homes to be built by the water. But three strips of beach, each ¼ mile long, are kept wild by tall bluffs, the northernmost rising 300 steep feet from beach to top, a prominent feature of the shoreline as viewed from the Trail south.

The fourth and best wild stretch is in Seahurst Park, and this nearly 1-mile haven from **No Trespassing** signs must be treated separately.

Ed Munro Seahurst Park (Map - page 37)

Ed Munro Seahurst (King County) Park, 185 acres of woods and nearly 1 mile of beach, is reached from Ambaum Boulevard in Burien via SW 144 Street. Like most beach parks this consists of a creek valley that couldn't easily be built in; it thus remained wild until acquired in the 1960s.

The parking area by the creek mouth gives access to a unique combination of an upper concrete seawall protecting a picnic-area path usable at highest tides, a lower gabian wall atop which is beach walkable at middle tides, and the outside natural beach open at low tides. All this eventually ends, and in ½ mile north so does the park, at a row of homes. All the way is a fine high bluff. Park beach also extends a scant ½ mile south from the creek; beach wild but posted continues south.

To beach the park adds wildwoods. On the south side of the creek, by the bridge, an unmarked path climbs the bluff, then contours steep slopes, crossing above the large inland parking lot and diverging up a roadless tributary valley. The gulch is wild, the firs big, the bushes a green snarl. The way swings around the valley, crossing creeks, sidepaths branch this way and that, permitting quite a long trip. In the park are about 3 miles of trail, ranging from primitive to downright mean. For the introduction, loop down to the entry road and return on it to the beach.

Basic woods-walk loop trip 2 miles, allow 1½ hours
High point 300 feet

Mile 16½-23½: Three Tree Point-Normandy Park-Normandy Beach Park-Covenant Beach-Des Moines Marina (Map- page 37)

The ¼ mile south from Seahurst Park is below a tall wild sliding bluff, houses unseen atop, slumping trees hanging boughs over the sand. Homes begin and continue 2 miles to Three Tree Point (Point Pully).

Maplewild Avenue SW leads to the beach just south of Three Tree Point and the light — which is on private property and can't be visited. Parking here for a half-dozen cars and access to a short piece of apparently public beach.

The Indian Trail. Said to be part of an old Indian route, this 4-foot-wide public walkway extends about 1 mile north from the point. To find it (unmarked) turn off Maplewild at SW 170 Street, just by Three Tree Point Store. A street-end (which goes to the beach, providing public access) has parking for two or three cars. Off it, north, stairs lead up a path. The only signing is to forbid public use between sunset and sunrise. (Orgies were ruining the neighborhood.) The path goes north in backyards along the steep bluff, giving intimate glimpses of bluff-suited architecture and views through firs and madronas to the water and the Olympics. The trail ends at Maplewild — no parking at this end. A short bit south of the north end a public path drops to the beach, permitting a waterside return for a 2-mile loop. Don't do the Indian Trail on weekends or summer evenings; come on a winter morning. Don't park stupidly; park by the beach at the public spot or on a shoulder somewhere in the neighborhood in such a manner as not to block a street or driveway; if you can't find a good parking place, go away and return some other day.

From the above-mentioned public access just south of Three Tree Point, which is a landmark visible for many miles, new vistas open south, including

House built on steep hillside along the Indian Trail near Three Tree Point

Rainier. The next 1 mile the road is close by the beach, house-lined most of the way.

A wild bluff then rears up, marking the start of the Normandy Park area. The highway swings far inland and public accesses from here south are well-concealed from the public. However, for very long stretches nobody lives on the beach or even very close, up there atop the bluff. Moreover, the undeveloped Normandy Beach (King County) Park has 1000 feet of waterfront. Beach access is via obscure trails, not presently recommended for heavy public use.

For about 1 mile from the wild bluff, in a broad creek valley, habitations are by the beach but not many. The bluff rears up to protect wildness of the next ¾ mile. A little valley has a few houses, then comes ¼ mile of high wild lovely bluff, 200 nearly vertical feet from the shore, and no houses atop. For ¼ mile a marshy valley borders the beach; a house is situated inland and an unused road leads to the beach. A bluff then has several houses and after that is 1 mile with only a couple inhabited spots. This excellent stretch ends at a row of houses built on pilings at the foot of a cliff, the houses having only trail access at high tide, car access via the beach at low. This access is from the gulch occupied by Covenant Beach Bible Camp (proposed as a future park); a road leads to the entrance and the beach.

The last ½ mile of this segment is the huge pier (and public parking area) of Des Moines Marina, close by the town, where the highway at last returns near the water after a long absence. The marina is a good place for boatwatching. Great views over the water too.

Mile 23½-25½: Saltwater State Park (Map - page 43)

Due to solid barriers of private yacht club and then homes it is not practical to get off the Des Moines Marina onto the beach at the south end. But little matter; just 1½ miles south is Saltwater State Park.

From the marina the first ¾ mile is beach houses, there being virtually no bluff in the broad Des Moines valley. But the next 1 mile is something else — the bluff abruptly leaps up 150 feet and though homes are on top and some paths come down, the beach is quite wild because the bluff is exceptionally vertical, formed here of quite hard sandstones-shales and, atop a discontinuity, 90-degree-steep gravels. This fine long stretch of naked cliff is striking from miles away. Imbedded in foreset river gravels are large granite erratics dropped from icebergs. Layers of black, partly-carbonized wood are an early step toward coal. Tree clumps from the top of the bluff have slid to the bottom, there growing on the sand — until the next big storm makes driftwood of them.

The final ¼ mile of this segment is in Saltwater State Park, whose north end has a great big fence signed against trespassing.

Saltwater State Park (Map - page 43)

Because of the paucity of public beaches hereabouts, Saltwater State Park gets some 1,000,000 visitations a year. Quite a lot for 88 acres with just 1445 feet of public beach.

Reach the park from Marine View Drive SW, Highway 509, the route having many twists and turns but guided by signs leading to the park.

In addition to beach there is forest in the valley of Smith Creek. For the basic introductory loop, park near the beach. By the restroom on the south side of the parking lot, find the unmarked trail switchbacking up the bluff, then contouring the sidehill in big firs and hemlocks and maples, crossing little creeks. Pass under the highway bridge and climb to the plateau top, with views down to the creek. Amid a rather confusing maze of paths choose a route that turns up a tributary ravine nearly to private homes, contours past privies and campsites of the Youth Camp, then drops to the campground area, where two valleys join.

To do the loop, cross the two bridges over the two creeks just above their union, switchback to the plateau, hike through a fine conifer grove, descend to the valley, find a path ascending a tributary, pass under the highway bridge, on the opposite side of the valley from before, and hit the entrance road.

For a sidetrip, cross the road and walk out to a superb bluff-top viewpoint. Then return to the entry road and walk it down to the car.

Basic introductory loop trip 1½ miles, allow 1 hour
High point 125 feet

Mile 25½-27: Poverty Bay-Redondo Beach (Map - page 43)

A handful of homes abut Saltwater State Park to the south and signs sternly forbid trespassing. But in a very short distance begins a long stretch of mostly empty beach. For ½ mile a 125-foot cliff keeps houses respectfully at a vertical distance. Then there is a short strip of homes reached via a piling-protected

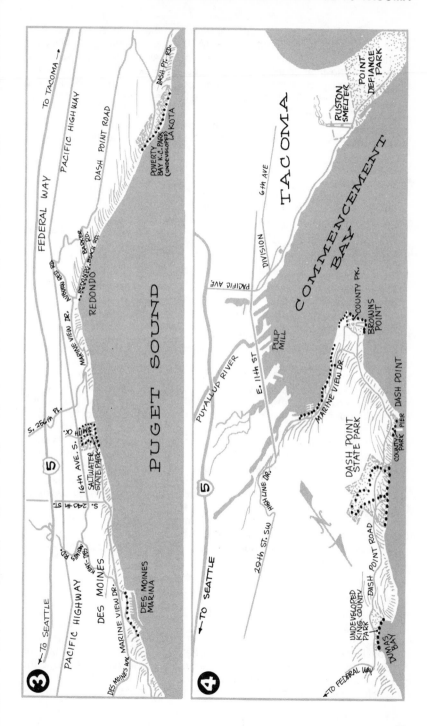

road along the water from Woodmont Beach on the south. At Woodmont a public road comes to the beach but PRIVATE signs bar parking and access.

The bluff is low, scarcely more than a bank, and houses are solid and water-close the final scant 1 mile to Redondo Beach. Here, north of the marina, is public parking and a moderately long public beach. (From Highway 509 just off Highway 99 in Federal Way, take Redondo Way down the ravine to Redondo Beach Drive and the marina.)

The views now are over the water to Maury Island, close across the here-narrow Sound; southward appears Point Defiance and the tall stack of the Tacoma Smelter; when south winds are blowing, sniff for it, but learn to distinguish between smelter stink and pulpmill stink, both of which are in the air.

Mile 27-31½: Poverty Bay Park-Dumas Bay Park-Dash Point State Park

Three parks. And many wild bits, many delights of bluff and beach, creeks and marshes.

For 1 mile south from Redondo Beach houses are at waterside, and half that distance the road is there too before veering uphill and away. After ½ mile of high bluff and wild beach, the ¼ mile of Adelaide valley is inhabited.

There is then ½ mile of wild bluff, partly occupied by undeveloped Poverty Bay (King County) Park. Present access to the beach is by obscure trails not presently recommended for heavy public use.

The wild bluff ends in a low bank and valley of densely-dwelt-in Lakota Beach, extending ½ mile to a point featuring huge granite boulders, houses on bulkheads, and the north boundary point of Dumas Bay.

Dumas Bay, about 1 long mile by shoreline from point to point, is quite unlike any other part of the Trail. At low tide the bay empties and the wide flat permits a shortcut across the mouth, far from shore. Three creeks enter, one of them through a deep green ravine, where two red houses catch the eye. There aren't many more houses than that, partly because the highway is at the bluff-lip part of the way; the cliff here is not a practical access to the beach.

But the main show is the unsigned and undeveloped, as of early 1977, Dumas Bay (King County) Park. Accessible (with limited shoulder parking) from Marine View Drive (Highway 509), and 44 Avenue SW, the park notably features a fine big beach-bordering marsh full of birds and other good things.

Dumas Bay ends in a bluff at the west point. Houses are atop at first but soon yield to wildwoods. In the next 1 mile are notably large granite erratics on the beach, the hulk of a beached barge, the **Biltgood,** and paths to the top of the bluff. Humanity then intrudes in the form of a dozen houses at the bluff base, accessible solely by trails hacked in the 150-foot cliff.

At the end of this intriguing neighborhood is Dash Point State Park and its long ½ mile of beach.

Dash Point State Park (Map - page 43)

The 297-acre park has 3500 feet of sandy beach beneath a 225-foot bluff of vertical clay and sand topped by forests. It also has, de rigeur, a ravine.

From Federal Way drive via SW 320 Street, then right on 47th and finally left on Dash Point Road, south to the park entrance. Descend the ravine to the parking lot upstream a bit from the beach.

One trail leads through a tunnel under the entry road to the beach. There, on

Saltwater State Park

the east side of the valley, look for a broad path ascending the bluff to a viewpoint and a second picnic area.

For the main trail, the boundary loop, find the path at the upstream end of the parking lot, going up the gorgeous valley in ferns and alders. Passing under the highway bridge and by a massive cedar stump, the way crosses the creek in a wide maple-alder flat, at ¼ mile from the parking lot reaching a Y.

Take the right fork, switchbacking to the plateau and park boundary. The trail proceeds across the upland in fir forest and alder-maple, marshes, delightful ravines, no sights or sounds of residences in the wildland. Ignoring minor sidepaths, at a major intersection with a road-trail turn left, soon joining the paved campground road. Turn left down the campground loop road to the bottom end of the camp and a sign, "Trail to Beach." Drop to the valley-floor Y, completing the loop, and return to the parking lot.

Boundary trail loop 2½ miles, allow 1½ hours
High point 250 feet

Mile 31½-40: Dash Point County Park-Browns Point County Park-Commencement Bay (Map - page 43)

Some ¾ mile along the beach from the state park is Dash Point proper. The absolute tip is a private home but short of it is Dash Point (Pierce County) Park, with parking, a public beach, and a long fishing pier the hiker should walk out on for northward views nearly to Three Tree Point (Point Robinson on Maury

Dash Point State Park

Browns Point Light

Island blocks it out), but mainly across the mouth of Commencement Bay (not yet quite seen) to Point Defiance — and the tall stack of the smelter. Also look across East Passage to points on Vashon-Maury Island and into Dalco Passage, leading to the west side of the island.

Beachside homes continue past the point ¼ mile; then a 175-foot cliff leaps up from the water. atop it being Marine View Drive, protecting wildness of the beach for ½ mile. At the outward bulge of Browns Point the bluff retreats inland, allowing solid houses the next 1½ miles around the point.

The road off the boulevard down to the lighthouse on Browns Point leads to the adjacent Browns Bay Improvement Club and Library, with public parking. Enclosing the lighthouse (beach access via the lawns) is Browns Point (Pierce County) Park. Picturesque lighthouse. Nice views, variations on those from Dash Point.

As the shore swings around Browns Point to turn easterly into Commencement Bay, a very short stretch of wild bluff 100 feet high provides a grand

47

viewpoint. Just by the boulevard is a small, unmarked parking area. Paths lead down to the beach and also out on the madrona-decorated promontory. For the first time on the Trail, here is a look directly into Commencement Bay, to the industrial waterway and across open waters to downtown Tacoma.

Now comes a long ¼ mile of homes on beach and bluff. But just as one expects increased urbanization, wildness rules. (The beach, not the view.) For nearly 1 mile the beach is guarded by a tall bluff atop which is Marine View Drive with many splendid viewpoints but apparently no paths down. For a bit the bluff is an amazingly vertical 160-foot gravel wall atop which is perched a restaurant. Other entertainments are an old beached barge, newer barges moored offshore, driftwood and dune lines and even a tiny lagoon marsh, and views to ships, and directly across to Ruston and its smelter stack and, farther out, Point Defiance.

The beach becomes industrial-filthy and ends in a marina. The unsigned road down from Marine View Drive to the marina parking lot gives access to this beach, which offers the odd combination of lonesome beachwalking in full view of the metropolis.

Past the marina the beachwalking is difficult but Marine View Drive is beside the water, with many turnouts, and the next 1 mile of shore cottages and shacks, derelict (or nearly) houseboats, is picturesque, as are log rafts, and gray and rusting Navy escort vessels.

The bluff continues on up the Puyallup River, indeed growing higher; right in the city is a wildland bluff strip more than 3 miles long and up to ½ mile wide, rising abruptly from sealevel to over 400 feet. But its paths were not surveyed for this volume.

The Trail leaves the bluffs for a final 3 miles on 11 Street East across waterways of the Puyallup River flat. In a nature-oriented book the scenes will be simply noted: crudely industrial, workaday-grimy, where the world makes its money so it can afford time off for beachwalking; rows of ships berthed along waterways; lumber yards and factories; a pulpmill belching clouds of steam. One is likely to feel, after closely studying this terminus of the Puyallup-Carbon-White Rivers, three of the major streams flowing from Rainier glaciers, that no similar use should be made of the outlet of another Rainier river, the Nisqually.

At long last the Puget Sound Trail enters Tacoma. To end? By no means. Tacoma has some of the best parts. But those and the way south are for another volume.

Bus: Duwamish Head-Alki Point, 37 and 15; Lincoln Park, 18 and 34; Seahurst Park, 136 to Ambaum and SW 144, walk a few blocks to park; Three Tree Point, 136 to Marine View Drive at SW 170, walk to point; Des Moines, 130 and 132; Saltwater State Park, 130 to Marine View Drive at S 240, walk 1 mile to park; Redondo Beach, 432 to Redondo Way, walk 1 mile to beach

Cormorant in Commencement Bay

Seattle's Waterfront Park

PUGET SOUND TRAIL — SEATTLE TO EVERETT

Most of the way north from Seattle the Puget Sound Trail has two lanes: the low-tide path on the beach; the high-tide path atop the handsome seawall of granite blocks. While lamenting the miles-long violation of natural beach one must score this point — the all-tides easy walking — for the railroad. And immediately score a second point for the way it has kept homes at a distance from the water, thus providing a quasi-public access lacking the NO TRES-PASSING problems so common on the Trail south from Seattle.

Mind that "quasi." Since those tracks were laid, people have been walking them; to describe them as a "trail" is to do no more than record an historical fact. But the roadbed and the beach it follows are private property. That trail is for trains. Feet are trespassers. Whatever walking is done on these or any other railroad tracks must be done humbly. And the walking must be done carefully, one eye over the shoulder for trains that are not making as much noise as the waves slapping the seawall.

Speaking historically again, the railroad never has been so naive as to think it could enforce private property rights all the way along Puget Sound, could wall off the people from the water. The walking of railroad tracks is a form of trespassing so long and so widely tolerated that it almost assumes a special legal status. However, at such times and places as great throngs of people assume they have an inalienable right to walk the tracks, and exercise that "right" in such manner as to interfere with passage of trains and to risk being squashed, the railroad necessarily gets tough. It will be noted that at many public parks the access to tracks is fenced off, skybridges perhaps provided from inland to beach. These are very bad places to walk the tracks, are precisely the spots where on a fine Sunday a trespasser may be arrested. Here or elsewhere on railways there is no safety in numbers; when a thousand people decide to march the tracks all at once, the railroad is going to call for a hundred or so police.

As characteristic of the Puget Sound Trail north as the railroad is the bluff, lifting an abrupt 200 to 400 feet above the shore — and constantly slumping down to the shore. Composed partly of concrete-like glacial till, partly of bedded sand and gravel and varved blue clay, it ranges from quite to ex-tremely unstable. Homes are built on top by people gambling the bluff edge will not, in their lifetimes, retreat to the point occupied by their houses. Sometimes homes even are built on terraces formed by chunks of the bluff slumping off the top, the hope then being the slump terrace will descend at a rate no faster than inches a year. Sometimes homes are built below the bluffs, the residents going to sleep on wet winter nights only after prayers. But mainly the bluff is given up as a lost cause, permitted to remain houseless. Extending nearly the full length of the Trail is thus a strip wilderness, houses pretty much out of sight at the top, the steep, wooded, vine-tangled slope harboring a thriving population of birds and small beasts, the water-side walker for hours at a time "away from it all" while right in the middle of it all, strolling along in the heart of Puget Sound City.

And deeply sliced into the bluffs are numerous creeks, some in slot can-yons, others in wide-bottomed, steep-walled valleys. From the shore wildland these short-to-long fingers of wildland poke into urbs and suburbs. Many (more than have been noted in the following route description) have trails inland; due to private property or lack of parking, they generally are not good accesses to the beach except for local residents, but for a hiker on the beach they provide a change of beauties, walking up a trail into a cool canyon of tangled greenery and splashing waterfalls.

So much for the land side of the Trail. What about the water side? Well, it's just your standard, routine, Puget Sound mix: waves on the beach, shorebirds on the sands and waterfowl swimming and gulls and crows above, the changing panorama across the waters to islands, Kitsap Peninsula, and Olympics, the parade of tugs and lografts and barges and freighters and ferries and fishing boats and sailboats, and memories of the water traffic that was, the old pilings, remnants of docks last used half-a-century ago, ghosts of the vanished mosquito fleet.

USGS maps: Seattle South, Seattle North, Shilshole Bay, Edmonds West, Edmonds East, Mukilteo, Everett

Mile 0-3: Pioneer Square-Alaskan Way-Waterfront Park-Myrtle Edwards Park-Elliott Bay Park-Smith Cove (Map - page 53)
Milepost 0 of the Puget Sound Trail belongs in Pioneer Square or Occidental Park or perhaps the King Street Railroad Station. The first 1½ miles down Yesler Way and north on Alaskan Way do not, however, make their primary appeal to students of nature and thus will be briefly noted here. The walking is secondary to the sightseeing: docks and berthed ships, curios and fish and chips, terminal for Bremerton and Winslow ferries, fireboats, the Waterfront Park viewpoint adjoining Seattle Aquarium (tidal basin, fish ladder, underwater viewing room, a cross-section of marine life indigenous to Puget Sound) at Pier 59, sidetrip up the hill to the Pike Place Market. Having thus gotten Seattle out of the way, one can proceed north with easy conscience.

At Broad Street, Alaskan Way ends and Myrtle Edwards Park begins. A large metered area extending to Bay Street permits parking long enough for a leisurely walk north to Smith Cove and back. The 1200-foot length of Myrtle Edwards Park (City of Seattle) is succeeded by 4000-foot-long Elliott Bay Park (Port of Seattle).

In the whole of its green-lawn 1¼ (walking distance) miles through the two parks, the path is close by the seawall; at low tide the beach can be walked instead. New-planted trees in time will make the lane a shady stroll. Train-watching (adjacent tracks are fenced off) is superb, and ferry-watching and general ship-watching. Also available for watching are ducks, gulls, crows, joggers, bicyclers (most of the way on a separate path), Elliott Bay, and the Olympics. The 200 tons of granite and concrete arranged in a sculpture have caused considerable remark. So too, notably among residents of Queen Anne Hill, has the huge grain terminal at Pier 86.

The path ends at Pier 89 on Smith Cove. A large parking lot on 16th West (¼ mile from Elliott Avenue and reached via West Galer Street) permits the walk to be done from this end.

Mile 3-7½: Magnolia Bluff-Discovery Park-West Point
To stay on the beach from Pier 89 across the Smith Cove Waterway a

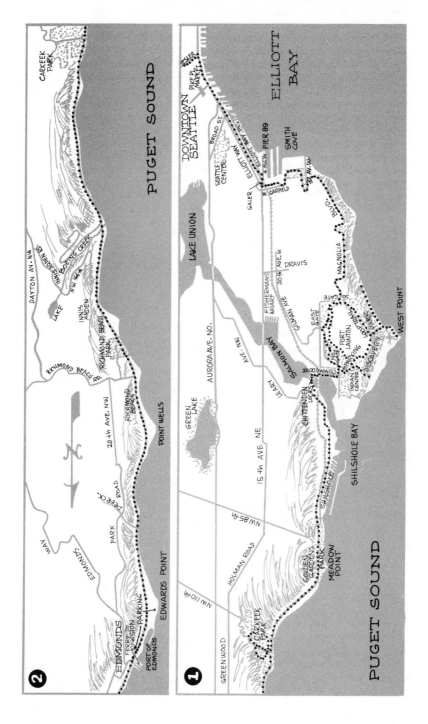

PUGET SOUND TRAIL—SEATTLE TO EVERETT

pedestrian needs a low tide and a lot of gall. The Port of Seattle has provided a public viewpoint by Pier 91 (access from 21 Avenue W off Thorndyke Avenue W; very limited parking) but walking from the viewpoint onto the beach is discouraged. Furthermore, the beach all the way around Magnolia Bluff is private property (for comment on that, see Puget Sound Trail — Seattle to Tacoma). At Smith Cove the Trail therefore splits in two: a low-tide route and a high-tide-and-legal route.

The legal and high-tide route detours from Pier 89 around the head of Smith Cove on the Garfield Street Bridge to Galer, then follows Magnolia Boulevard. Grand bluff-top views from Magnolia Park over Elliott Bay and Seattle. Where the boulevard swings north to the Magnolia Shopping Center it crosses a gulch, down which 32 Avenue descends to the beach. Parking here is very limited and the beach is private. But if a person happens to be on the beach and is cut off by incoming tides, 32 Avenue is an escape, ½ mile from Smith Cove and 3 miles from West Point. Meanwhile, back atop the bluff, the route follows Magnolia Boulevard (more stupendous views) to Emerson Street and the South Gate of Discovery Park, thence the Loop Trail (discussed below) to West Point.

The low-tide illegal-but-often-tolerated-trespassing route is only practically done from West Point walking back toward Seattle, but to maintain some semblance of order will be described as if headed toward Everett. (Of interest, this was the first scheduled walk taken by The Mountaineers, weeks after founding of the club; standing by the water looking out to the Olympics, one feels very close to 1907.)

Particularly in the first 2 miles from Smith Cove the major attraction is the "working bay" — the parade of ships and ferries and other boats to and from the downtown waterfront and the industrial Duwamish Waterways. Other views are to Four Mile Rock and across the mouth of Elliott Bay to Alki Point where it all began. Look up the vertical till bluff to the line of madronas (when that fellow gave the bluff the name he thought they were magnolias). Gamblers Row, where Perkins Lane follows slump terraces down the very face of the bluff and where residents so value the combination of nearness to city and distance of mood they are willing to risk losing homes in a slippery spell, intrigues the passerby who has no stake in the game. Old pilings at the bluff foot and litters of boards on the slope speak of gambles lost over the decades.

The way swings from westerly to northwesterly to northerly, Seattle and its towers lost around the corner, the view now over the water to Bainbridge Island and the Olympics. At low tide the beach is a broad tideflat, the walker at such distance from the bluff he is scarcely aware of houses tucked in the trees. A sign announces "End of Public Beach"; in the direction described, this is the start, the entry to Discovery Park. Now the bluff is a great wilderness of trees and bushes, outcrops at the base of blue clay continuing to be carved by waves, and up high, the famous sand cliffs.

Then comes West Point, the most splendid such feature on the entire Seattle-to-Everett route. On its tip stands the near-century-old West Point Lighthouse, destination of The Mountaineers in 1907, and on 80 acres that have the potential to be one of the best parts of Discovery Park is the Metro sewage-treatment plant. Metro is considering enlarging the plant but many citizens feel Metro, though a very Worthy Cause, can and should locate its

facilities elsewhere and that when the existing plant requires replacement, 30-40 years from now, a new site should be chosen and West Point returned to its pristine natural beauty.

Discovery Park (Map - page 53)

Made possible when a portion of Fort Lawton was declared surplus to military needs, Discovery Park has helped ease Seattle's shortage of park space. The intent is to maintain a dispersed-use nature-oriented park. This will not be easy, what with the habit Worthy Causes have of looking to parklands for places to roost.

The principal access to Discovery Park is the very large North Parking Area (and bus stop) located by the North Gate. A dependable way for strangers to get here is: from 15 Avenue NW turn west on Dravus, then north on 20th Avenue which becomes Gilman Avenue which becomes Government Way and leads to the East Gate. At the East Gate turn right and follow the winding road to the parking.

The Discovery Park beach ranks among the very best on the entire Puget Sound Trail from Tacoma to Everett; the wild (railroad-less) bluff and spectacular sand cliffs, the West Point Lighthouse thrust close to shipping lanes in cross-chopping waves, and the easy and guaranteed public access combine to give deserved popularity. Distance from the North Parking Area via the Loop Trail (see below) to the beach is 1 mile. From there it is ¼ mile past the Metro plant to the lighthouse, 3½ miles to Smith Cove.

Complete beach-tour round trip 9½ miles, allow 6 hours

The mandatory introduction to Discovery Park is the 2.8-mile Loop Trail, which connects to all park entrances and roughly circles the periphery. From the North Parking Area walk up the hill on any of several paths ¼ mile to intersect the Loop Trail. In the counterclockwise direction it soon passes a sidepath to the North Bluff, with views north out Puget Sound, then the service road-trail down to West Point (see above). At South Bluff, atop the great sand cliffs, are glorious Sound views; inland are old sand dunes dating from a drier climate and now arrested by vegetation. Proceeding up and down, passing old Army buildings, going through woods, the trail completes the loop.

Loop trip 3 miles, allow 2 hours
High point 300 feet, elevation gain 500 feet

Mile 7½-12: Kiwanis Ravine-Commodore Park-Chittenden Locks-Salmon Bay-Shilshole Bay-Golden Gardens Park-Meadow Point

The beach north of West Point is walkable at low tide but there is no way to get off the beach at Salmon Bay that doesn't risk a broken neck and/or arrest; this 1½ miles of the proper Trail route therefore must be done, if at all, from West Point, walking north and back.

The Trail thus must make its only inland detour. From West Point ascend the bluff to the Loop Trail. For the pure (future) route, unsurveyed for this book,

Fish climbing fish ladder at Chittenden Locks

walk to near the East Gate and there find a way down along Kiwanis Ravine, an undeveloped city park, to Chittenden Locks. For the surveyed (chicken) route, leave the Loop Trail on a path to the North Parking Area and at 1 mile from West Point exit from Discovery Park through the North Gate onto 40th Avenue. Turn right on Commodore to the railroad bridge over Salmon Bay and the start of Commodore Park; fine views of the Lake Washington Ship Canal. Turn off sidewalk onto the promenade path along the waterway banks, in 1 scant mile from the North Gate crossing the pedestrian walkway over Chittenden Locks.

Pause to examine the fish ladder (a new one, completed in 1976) which salmon and trout ascend on their way to spawning grounds in the Lake Washington basin. A below-ground viewing gallery gives the best close looks at big fish available outside a fish market. (After studying the fish you may wish to study fishing boats, another endangered species. For a sidetrip, walk east on Commodore 1 mile to the fleet based at Salmon Bay Terminal, "Fishermen's Wharf.")

Hiram M. Chittenden Locks ("Ballard Locks") are the key component of a navigation system dedicated in 1917. A channel was dredged from Puget Sound through Shilshole Bay to Salmon Bay, joining this body of water via the Fremont Cut to Lake Union, and that body via the Montlake Cut to Lake

Washington. The latter was lowered from the natural elevation above sealevel of 29-33 feet to the level of Lake Union, 21 feet, and Salmon Bay was raised by the dam at the locks. Lake Washington, which formerly emptied via the Black River to the Duwamish River, thence to Elliott Bay, now drains through the Lake Washington Ship Canal to Shilshole Bay. The Black River dried up. The Cedar River, which flowed into the Black and thus the Duwamish, was diverted up the old Black channel, reversing flow direction, into Lake Washington, which it thus furnishes a constant source of flushing water from the mountains, the uncelebrated other half of the clean-up-the-lake success story for which Metro is always given full credit. Awareness of all this fooling around with Mother Nature adds interest to watching ships and boats being lowered or raised through the locks. Footnote: the Ship Canal never made Lake Washington, as everyone imagined would happen, a great seaport.

Adjoining the locks are the 7 acres of the Carl English Botanical Gardens, displaying plants from lands all over the world.

At the Chittenden Locks begins a connection on streets to the Burke-Gilman Trail (which see). Onto it from the Puget Sound Trail turns the Sound-to-Mountains Trail (which see).

The Puget Sound Trail proceeds westward from the locks on the north shore of Salmon Bay. Staying close to the water on sidewalks and dirt paths, in 1 mile a walker leaves Salmon Bay for Shilshole Bay and its enormous jetty-protected moorage for hundreds (or is it thousands?) of pleasure boats. The Port of Seattle has decorated the way with Leif Ericson's statue, a monster 19th-century wrought-iron anchor, and other marine artifacts. Across the street is Gordo's, which makes the greatest peanut-butter milkshake available on any trip in this book.

The moorage at last yields to the 76 acres of Golden Gardens Park, with bathing beach and unobstructed Sound views. Meadow Point is the last point in Seattle retaining all elements of a complete beach: driftwood line, dune line, lagoon. It does not have a swimming pool (as does Colman) or a sewage plant (as does West). There was a plot to decorate it with an aquarium but saner heads squelched that dizzy idea.

Mile 12-14: North Beach-Carkeek Park

The railroad tracks having joined the route at Chittenden Locks, from Meadow Point on north to Everett they constitute the high-tide lane.

The bank above the tracks is not high and is quite solidly built-up through the Blue Ridge area and what used to be called North Beach.

Then the bluff suddenly rears up 200 feet from the water, tall and steep and unstable. From now on a common feature of the route is the sensor wire at the base of the bluff; when chunks of bluff slide over the tracks, as they do every winter, all winter, a light blinks on in a control room and trains are signalled to watch out.

Carkeek Park (Map - page 53)

Carkeek Park is mostly a second-growth wilderness, one of the two largest on the Trail; few traces remain of long-ago logging or even a once-thriving brickyard. The park features an excellent beach and in its spacious 192 acres an extensive network of trails being built by Seattle Parks and Scouts of the Viking District.

Beach at Carkeek Park

Drive from Greenwood Avenue, turning west on 110th Street to find the entrance roadway winding down Piper's Canyon. From the large water-view parking area a skybridge crosses the railroad tracks to the beach.

The major trail is that up Piper's Creek. Near the tracks by the creek find a path leading upstream to the Metro sewage-treatment plant (yes, this park also has a Worthy Cause), a small parking area off the entry road, and a sign, "Carkeek Trail." The way ascends the steepwalled canyon floor in lush mixed forest, passing a dozen basalt-boulder half-dams, apparently an old erosion-control scheme. Crossing and recrossing the sandy creek, the trail climbs the narrowing canyon, at last leaving it to ascend steeply to a small parking area at the street-end of 6 Avenue NW, which leads to a bus stop on NW 100 Place close to Holman Road NW. This trail is 1¼ miles in length.

For a loop return, find one of the several paths climbing into wildwoods south of the canyon and wander along the hillside out to a bluff 175 precipitous feet above the tracks and beach, giving fine views over the water and south to Meadow Point.

Richmond Beach Park

For a separate walk on the north side of the canyon, from the beach parking area climb the bluff edge to the high flat and follow the path along the rim in woods ⅓ mile to the unmarked park edge. For a loop return, take a path inland and descend to the picnic and parking area on a path where red rubble shows this to be the site of the brickyard.

For the wildest walk of all, on the latter path watch for a slippery track dropping to a skimpy trail contouring the tanglewood bluff halfway between rim and beach. Take care not to become part of the slide terrain; the mucky slopes are tricky.

Total park sampler loop trips 5 miles, allow 3 hours
High point 275 feet

Mile 14-18: Boeing Creek-Richmond Beach Park (Map - page 53)

From Carkeek Park northward the bluff wildland-and-wildlife-refuge is a near-constant presence. Beside the high-tide lane atop the seawall are alders and maples, flowers in season, frogs croaking in marshy ditches, creeks tumbling down little gorges. One scarcely believes houses are at blufftop, usually set back from the lip a goodly distance. And with winter wind blowing by the ears and winter surf pounding, one may not hear trains creeping up behind; to avoid being crushed or — nearly as bad — being impelled on a leap into outer space by a train horn blowing in your ear, keep looking over your shoulder. Unless, of course, it's low tide and you're down on the beach, enjoying that other and parallel wildland and wildlife refuge.

North 1 mile from Carkeek Park is a canyon in clay and sand; generations of local kids have worked away at eroding the deposit while trying to break their necks climbing the vertical walls.

At 2 miles from the park (and all this way no houses by the beach, presence of a city seeming impossible) is Highlands Point and the wide valley of Boeing Creek, named for the logger-aircraft manufacturer who kept this section of forest as a private retreat; not until World War II was the magnificent virgin Douglas fir of the "Boeing Tract" logged. The newspapers enjoyed the picturesqueness of 19th-century-style logging so near the city so late in history; only a few people mourned the loss of the equivalent of a dozen Seward Parks.

On the south side of Boeing Creek a private road ascends the wild creek, in big trees that weren't worth logging (snagtops and the like) to The Highlands residential park. On the north side a road-trail with greenbelt easement but gated on the upper, inland side to keep out vehicles, ascends ½ mile to Innis Arden Way at NW 166th (very limited shoulder parking). A footpath goes around the gate, permitting beach access. In the valley bottom at NW 166th is a wide flat through which the creek meanders; until a flood took out the dam, this was Hidden Lake, Boeing's private fishing pond. King County owns half the lakesite and is considering a plan to rebuild the dam.

North from Boeing Creek is more wild bluff. Approaching Richmond Beach, keep a sharp eye for a path up a gulch to Innis Arden; this private trail makes an interesting sidetrip ½ mile up to a road.

At 4 miles from Carkeek Park is a sand hill that formerly was the site of shipwrecking; wooden ships were stripped of metal fittings and then set afire, the clouds of black smoke attracting throngs from all over the north Seattle area. Here is Richmond Beach (King County) Park. A skybridge crosses the

Bonaparte's Gull dwarfed by a Western Gull

61

railroad tracks to the parking area in a great amphitheater that until a quarter-century ago was a gravel mine and another favorite spot for local kids to get bruises and contusions and minor fractures. From the top of the park, elevation 200 feet, the view across the Sound is superb.

To reach Richmond Beach Park, on Aurora Avenue at 185 Street turn west on the Richmond Beach Road and follow it down the steps of wave-cut bluffs, each representing a different former level of Puget Sound. When nearing the water, only one more bluff to go, turn left at a sign directing to the park.

Mile 18-22: Point Wells-Edwards Point-Edmonds Ferry Slip-Sunset Beach Park (Map - page 53)

From the park the Trail goes through the old community of Richmond Beach to Point Wells, which in a pristine condition was perhaps second in beauty only to West Point (in a pristine condition) but ages ago was preempted by Standard Oil for an oil tanker terminal, oil storage tanks, and asphalt refinery. Wild bluff resumes at the complex, at whose north end, nearly 2 miles from the park, is a tiny strip of natural beach, trees growing to the driftwood line.

The ravine of Deer Creek has a tempting (unsurveyed) trail inland. At the palatial bluff-top estates of Woodway Park begins one of the most spectacular slide areas of the route, the naked muck slopes in motion from an elevation of 220 feet down to the tracks, which often are blocked by chunks of former palatial estate. But except for the kempt-looking bluff rim giving away the existence of lawns up there, one would never suspect homes, here or anywhere from Point Wells to Edmonds.

This metropolis is entered, 3 miles from the park, at Edwards Point, site of another tanker terminal (Union), storage tanks, and small refinery. But a considerable portion of the natural beach at the point is undisturbed.

At Edwards Point begins a 1-mile breach in the bluffs; in the cavity is a broad marshy valley, a pioneers' landing that became Edmonds.

The large parking lot at the point is accessible via shoreline streets from the ferry dock to the north. At the public beach begins the Port of Edmonds, the long breakwater-protected yacht basin offering a display of boats comparable to that at Shilshole Bay. A public observation pier and a public (city) beach enliven the walk. The aroma from a fish-and-chips restaurant is calculated to drive a long-distance hiker insane.

The best thing about Edmonds is the ferry. For a lunch stop and an incomparable viewpoint, take the voyage to Kingston on the Kitsap Peninsula and back. At least pause to watch the ferry ease in to the slip, unload, and load.

Adjoining the dock on the north is Edmonds Underwater Park, sunken ships providing homes for marine life that scuba divers can look at but mustn't touch. Connecting to the underwater park is the abovewater Sunset Beach Park, located at historic Brackett's Landing.

To reach the park follow signs from I-5 to the Edmonds-Kingston Ferry and cross the ferry lane into the park, where cars may be parked for 4 hours maximum, enough for short walks. If using this as a base for a longer trip, park south of the ferry dock in the vast free lots of the Port of Edmonds.

Another feature to note here is the only Amtrak station between Seattle and Everett.

Mile 22-26½: Browns Bay-Meadowdale Beach Park (Map - page 65)

For many years one of the favorite stretches of the Puget Sound Trail has been from Edmonds to Meadowdale (and onward to Picnic Point). The overwater views become distinctly and dramatically different. The north-of-Seattle

Edmonds ferry and the Olympic Mountains

shore and Bainbridge Island fade south in haze, the vista now being across to the Kitsap Peninsula. But one sees out northwest between the peninsula and the white till cliffs of Whidbey Island to Admiralty Inlet, the route to the ocean. For the first time, and only briefly, there is a water horizon.

Immediately north of Edmonds there's no bluff and houses crowd the way. Then the wilderness wall rises again, cut by gulches and a sand canyon, offering a series of trails inland — doubtless to private property and thus not public accesses to the beach.

At about 3 miles the shore bends in to Browns Bay. In a lovely gulch is Lynnwood's sewage-treatment plant (the old story) and the first road access to the beach since Edmonds, via a sideroad off 76 Avenue W (see Meadowdale).

At 4 miles a structure juts out on the waterside of the tracks —Laebugten Fishing Wharf. On slumping hillsides above is the village of Meadowdale. To the north ½ mile is the fine broad sandy Meadowdale Beach at the mouth of Lunds Gulch.

Meadowdale Beach Park (Map - page 65)

The delta-point thrusting far out in the waves, views up and down the Sound virtually the full length of the Trail, the large creek gushing from wide Lunds Gulch and rippling over the beach, these are the features most famed in this undeveloped Snohomish County Park. But in addition, Lunds Gulch is one of the two largest chunks of wildland (Carkeek Park the other) on the shore between Seattle and Everett.

The village of Meadowdale is reached from Olympic View Drive (known from logging days of the 19th century as the Snake Trail, so sinuous is the route) via 76 Avenue W from an intersection signed "Laebugten Wharf." (Partway to the beach a sideroad drops left down a ravine to the Lynnwood sewage treatment plant — see above — and a public parking lot with beach access.)

Parking on Laebugten Wharf is strictly for customers. Parking elsewhere in Meadowdale, entirely on road shoulders, is extremely limited. The public is an obvious pain to residents, who barely have room on their ever-sliding hillside for houses and streets much less visitors. This therefore is not a place to go on weekends and summer evenings. What parking is planned for the park is not known at this (1977) writing; the access may have to be elsewhere than from the village, perhaps from up on the plateau east or north of Lunds Gulch.

At present, park with care wherever possible on a road shoulder, not blocking traffic or driveways. One route north the ½ mile to the gulch is the beach. Another is 75 Place W, barricaded at the edge of residences but as a foot trail continuing, the grade partly slid out, across the face of the bluff in woods, and descending to the valley bottom.

Meadowdale Country Club, it once was, a good long while ago. Nature is reclaiming foundations and charred timbers of the burned lodge, fields of what must have been a rather minute golf course, and valley roads.

To explore the wildland, walk upvalley on an old road that dwindles to trail. The creek flows over sandbars and little waterfalls. The valley walls, rising steeply to the plateau top at 450 feet, are massed alders, fern-hung maples, hemlocks growing from huge cedar stumps notched for the fallers'

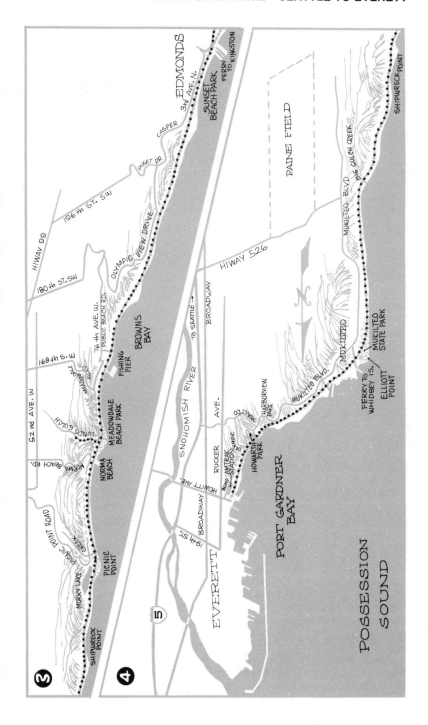

Great Blue Heron hunting near Picnic Point

springboards, and appropriate other vegetation. At 1 mile from the beach the trail, still ½ mile from the head of the gulch, comes to a Y, the two branches scrambling up mossy-lush, black-mucky slopes on either side of the gulch to suburbia. Downvalley from the Y several other paths similarly climb the walls. A trail system built at various levels of the gulch on both sides could have a total length of up to 10 miles.

Sample gulch round trip 3 miles, allow 1½ hours
High point 450 feet

Mile 26½-28: Norma Beach-Picnic Point Park (Map - page 65)
   Just around the corner, ½ mile north of Lunds Gulch, is another fishing wharf; this one at Norma Beach shows its half-century age, seeming about to sag to the sands. No access from the public road to the beach except for wharf customers.

A high sand cliff catches the eye, and a trail to the blufftop; there's another way there (see below). Then, on a slump terrace above the beach, appears a row of homes (see below).

Ghosts now crowd the beach — lines of old pilings, remnants of docks, visions of the vessels of the mosquito fleet that steamed up and down the water road until the 1920s. More ghosts — concrete foundations of beach cabins. Are those mandolins we hear in the summer twilight?

All this, 1 mile from Norma Beach, is none other than far-famed Picnic Point, a great sandy spit at the mouth of a superb valley, a lovely creek rushing across the beach.

Picnic Point Park (Map - page 65)

Candidate for honors as one of the best places on the whole Puget Sound Trail, Picnic Point does not have a sewage plant, swimming pool, or aquarium. But it almost had a refinery. When the oilers realized they'd better seek a more cooperative county to the north, they decided to turn a profit another way. Chevron Land Development Co. plans to build a city on the uplands and shore. Meanwhile it has leased (not sold) an itty-bitty piece to Snohomish County for a park which essentially is just a parking lot and an access to the beach.

But what a beach!

Take the Paine Field exit from I-5. Drive west to Highway 99 and turn south to the Mukilteo Road, Highway 525. Turn northwest (right) to the Beverly Park-Edmonds Road. Turn southwest (left) a short way to a yellow blinker. Turn northwest (right) on the Picnic Point Road and descend a forested, undeveloped, beautiful, wild, parkless gulch (passing the Alderwood Manor wastewater treatment plant, that the valley should not be a total loss) to the beach parking area.

There's no park to put a trail system in but there is a nice bluff walk from here. Maps still show Puget Sound Boulevard contouring the bluff face south to Norma Beach. But it doesn't make it all the way and hasn't since about 1960. Don't drive south of Picnic Point on what road remains; the residents on the slump terrace need every bit of the single-lane pavement. From the parking area walk ¾ mile along the row of houses (that are, seen from the geologist's vantage, riding the sliding hill down to the waves), to the road-end (no parking). Trail continues on the remnant grade (haunted by ghosts of Model Ts) across the bluff. The sand cliff admired from the beach (see above) is what finally discouraged the highway department; not a scrap of grade lingers here.

Here on the vanished section a hiker can sit in the woods, high above the beach, far below the blufftop, protected on every side from the 20th century. Gazing over the broad waters, one feels as remote from civilization as anywhere on the Puget Sound Trail.

It's not a large sanctuary — in ⅓ mile from drivable road is the edge of inhabited Norma Beach. But as one sits in the wild spot it grows in the direction of infinity.

Round trip 2½ miles, allow 1½ hours
High point 100 feet

Elliot Point Lighthouse at Mukilteo

Mile 28-33: Shipwrecking Point-Big Gulch-Mukilteo State Park-Elliot Point-Mukilteo Ferry Slip (Map - page 65)

The hiker who started the journey in Seattle now is aware of having come very far north. Indeed the route here leaves Puget Sound (in the limited, geographically-strict definition) for Possession Sound, across whose relatively narrow width is Whidbey Island. Still in view are the Olympics but now very close to the north, above Camano Island, is the white volcano of Baker. At hike's start the Bainbridge Island ferry shuttled back and forth from Seattle to Winslow. Then came the shuttling of the Edmonds-Kingston ferry, which now retreats southward in the distance as to the north becomes more prominent the green-and-white vessels ceaselessly voyaging from Mukilteo to Columbia Beach on Whidbey.

Just north of Picnic Point the way passes a murky lake dammed by the railroad fill; homes line the inland shore, leaders of flycasters festoon the telephone wires.

At 1 mile is "Shipwrecking Point," a sandspit once used for stripping and burning wooden ships; a carcass and some ribcages remain to be seen but not explored — on the privately-owned point is an inhabited house. Its access is just north, a footpath of steps cut in clay ascending the bluff to a waterfall (in hard rock, a rare exposure of non-glacial materials) and, atop the plateau, a path along the creek in wildwoods to Marine View Drive at 116 Street SW.

In ¼ mile more is a substantial ravine up which goes a trail. Homes of so-called Chenault Beach (which has no beach) then are seen atop the bluff.

In 1 mile more (2¼ miles from Picnic Point) is a point with a very wide beach at low tide, the mouth of the wild valley of Big Gulch. Not a park. In fact, it once was degraded to an open ditch down which ran raw sewage from Paine Field Air Force Base. Cleaned up and looking nice, it now harbors a Worthy Cause — the Olympus Terrace Sewage Treatment Plant. No public access. Thus lonesome country. The solitary plant operator frequently sights deer and bear and weasels and seals, eagles perched in favorite snags, fleets of thousands upon thousands of waterfowl swimming by.

North ½ mile is the first close house in a long while, in a creek valley on a flat beside the tracks; the road access is private. Shortly a public road descends a slump terrace to within 50 feet of the tracks, but is not recommended as a public beach access, having very little parking. An interesting portion of this community is built outside the railroad tracks on a bulkheaded invasion of the beach; the dozen cottages have walk-in trail access only; the residents tend not to buy new refrigerators very often.

After this ½ mile of scattered dwellings, in the final 1¾ miles mankind retreats from the beach, up to the top of the tall, wild bluff. The way features a tangled-green slot of a gorge, a great vertical cliff of white glacial till, another creek tumbling out of a gulch.

Rounding Elliot Point the railway swings inland and is fenced off through Mukilteo. The Trail thus follows the beach to small Mukilteo State Park. On the tip is Elliot Point Lighthouse, the first since West Point, a dandy. Adjacent is the ferry dock, suggesting a sidetrip over the water to Columbia Beach, a nice rest stop after the 5 miles from Picnic Point, before starting back.

Mukilteo is reached from I-5 via Highway 526-525.

Mile 33-38: Powder Mill Gulch-Merrill and Ring Creek-Harborview Park-Howarth Park-Pigeon Creeks No. 2 and 1—Weyerhaeuser Mill-Port Gardner Bay-Everett Amtrak Station (Map - page 65)

Gazing from Mukilteo to the industrial sprawl of Port Gardner Bay, the hiker may ask, "Who needs it?" But the wild bluff continues to guard the beach and the assemblage of wild ravines is arguably the best on the entire Puget Sound Trail.

The shore, previously trending north, bends sharply eastward at Elliot Point. The view thus is across Possession Sound past little Gedney Island to Saratoga Passage between Whidbey and Camano Islands and to Port Susan between the latter island and the mainland. No longer is there a parade of ships to and from the ocean and various ports of Puget Sound, but there is considerable traffic along Possession Sound to Everett.

Easterly for a scant 1 mile from the Mukilteo ferry dock the beach is blocked by another oil terminal and a series of storage tanks. A public road extends along the fence to a public parking area and beach at the far end, a good start for walking to Everett.

Passing a ravine and a trail-staircase up the bluff to a viewpoint, then the prettiest exposure of varved blue clay on the route, in 1 scant mile of continuous vertical cliff is the first of the exceptional wildland valleys, Powder Mill

Beach at Howarth Park

Gulch, with a large creek, a broad delta-point, and a path up the gulch an unsurveyed distance inland.

In ½ mile is a nameless but noble creek and in ¼ mile more is larger and superb Merrill and Ring Creek whose prominent delta-spit pushes far out in the waves and supports a driftwood line and dunes.

The bluff lowers and houses creep near in the next ¼ mile to a small creek and little Harborview (Everett) Park, located on Mukilteo Boulevard at Dover Street. An excellent view of the harbor. At the north edge, a deep green ravine.

In a scant ½ mile (3 miles from Mukilteo ferry dock) is Howarth Park, for which be praised and congratulated the Everett Park Department. The park is reached from Mukilteo Boulevard at Seahurst Avenue; parking is provided at the upper, blufftop level and, via Olympic Boulevard which descends to the floor of Pigeon Creek No. 2, at the beach level by the railroad tracks. Extending from Pigeon 2 south to a nameless ravine, the park has enough paths — on blufftop and in gulch depths and on sidehills, on wide-view lawns and in wildwoods — to permit 2 miles of walking with scarcely any repetition. Access to the beach is via a skybridge over the tracks. On the beach side a stairway winds around and down a wooden tower resembling a donjon keep but actually serving utilitarian needs for stairs and restrooms.

The final 2 miles of the Trail have a different appeal. Or to some tastes, perhaps none. Port Gardner Bay is entered and Everett Junction reached. Here is Pigeon Creek No. 1, which in another location surely would have been a park but here is a mucked-up truck road to the Port of Everett. From the

Foot trail in Howarth Park

Junction the tracks lie between surprisingly wild bluff and the mammoth Weyerhaeuser pulpmill complex. Then comes Port of Everett Pier 1 and the Amtrak Rail Passenger Station, at Bond Street off Hewitt Avenue. Plentiful parking.

A hiker might consider riding home. Two Amtrak passenger trains go daily in each direction, stations at Seattle, Edmonds, and Everett. Due to the awkward scheduling it is not practical (as of 1977) to take the trip both ways by rail on a single day. However, one probably can ride the bus from Seattle to Everett in time to catch the morning train south. But call beforehand to be sure.

Bus: Seattle waterfront, in walking distance of a bushel of routes; Magnolia Park, Metro 19, 24, and 33; Discovery Park, 19 to South Gate, 24 to East Gate, 33 to North Gate; Chittenden Locks, 17 and 30; Golden Gardens Park, 17, 30, and 48; Carkeek Park, 28 (to trail at upper end of Piper's Canyon); Richmond Beach, 305; Edmonds, Metro 316

January morning hike on the Tolt Pipeline Trail

OVERLAKE HIGHLANDS AND SAMMAMISH VALLEY

Urban and suburban and rural and wild, that's the 1970s mix in the overlake section of Puget Sound City. Close to home and largely bus-accessible, elevations topping out around 600 feet and thus open the year around, ranging from lakeshores to pastures to forests, it's an important walking province and a rich one. But less rich actually than potentially.

The survey for this book found few hikes of regional (as distinguished from local) significance on Mercer Island and the glacierized flats and bumps and bogs of the upland between Lakes Washington and Sammamish, and these mainly have been provided not by the municipalities but by King County and the State of Washington. The New Cities here pretty well blew their chances for spacious parks in the 1950s and 60s, when the land-planning was being done by speculators and their servants in government, taxpayers were concentrating on building schools and roads, and the suburban ideal in recreation was to buy $50,000 worth of toys and burn a barrel of gas a weekend dragging the portable kindergarten around the freeways. By the time the New Cities emerged from childhood into the present adolescence the land prices had rocketed out of sight. Heavily taxed and mortgaged, the citizens now seem to feel they can't afford big parks. (They apparently can't even afford sidewalks.) With maturity will come new values. However, what could have been done easily and cheaply at an earlier age will then cost the very devil.

Quite another story is the second major segment of this overlake province, the Sammamish valley. Not for future massive bond issues but right-now walking are the grand trail along the river and the magnificent county park at the north end of Lake Sammamish and the splendid state park at the south.

Still a third story is the broad highland between the Sammamish and Snoqualmie valleys, the area called Pine Lake-Beaver Lake Plateau in the south and Bear Creek Plateau in the north and East Sammamish Plateau in sum. And it's a story represented in this book solely by the Tolt Pipeline Trail. Sorry. Can't be helped. Presently the area, virtually all private property, is criss-crossed by hundreds of miles of paths on old logging-railroad grades and grownover woods roads; local residents, knowing where trespassing is tolerated, are temporarily, (as they await the impending doom) among the most blessed of Puget Sound pedestrians. But the routes cannot be advertised because they might then be posted. Moreover, not a one of these paths except the Tolt Pipeline can be guaranteed to be walkable next year or next month. To learn why, follow the real-estate pages in your newspaper: the East Sammamish Plateau is known as the "hottest spot" in King County; if developers have their way, here in the next dozen-odd years will be built a New Bellevue. And probably with no sidewalks.

USGS maps: Mercer Island, Bothell, Maltby, Kirkland, Redmond, Issaquah, Fall City

Lake Washington State Park (St. Edwards Seminary)

Far down the road toward total urbanization of the region there will survive on the shores of Lake Washington, right in the heart of Puget Sound City, a great big expanse of wild green.

Thanks to the benign posture of the property owner, the Archdiocese of Seattle, and the alert cooperation of a team of state and federal legislators and officials, St. Edwards Seminary has become a chief glory of the area's park system.

For a pedestrian the whipped cream on the blessing is that most of the 316 acres and 3000 feet of shore will remain as they are — wildwooded. Development will be concentrated on the plateau bench that forms the upper section of the park. The steep bluff dropping to the water, and all the shore except perhaps a swimming beach and fishing pier, will continue to be a magnificent second-growth wildland.

Acquisition having been completed only in October 1977, when this book was in press, the development plans and schedule are incomplete at this writing. Tentatively, the park will open for limited use possibly in mid-1978. Until the announcement is made, stay away. When the welcome mat is out, come running.

Drive Juanita Drive NE north from Kirkland or south from Kenmore to the park entrance (formerly the entry road to the seminaries) at NE 145. Turn west

Swimming after hiking, Luther Burbank County Park

to the parking area, the location undetermined at present (signs will guide you), elevation about 350 feet.

Over the decades the seminary students and local residents have beaten out with their feet a network of trails totalling perhaps a dozen or so miles in length. Some are quite posh. Others are half-overgrown, less used by humans than by deer and coyotes. And not to be ignored for strolling are the spacious lawns. All in all there's a lot of country to explore, enough to keep the feet busy for days. A newcomer logically will take an introductory tour, such as the one described below, then proceed to more complex investigations of the numerous paths spotted along the way.

From the parking area walk by roads and lawns to the main St. Edwards building. In front of it to the west, on the edge of the plateau, easily find the broad trail (an ancient road) entering the head of a prominent gully. Descend through maples, alders, dogwoods, madronas, firs, and cedars, contouring out of the gully, switchbacking down the steep bluff, entering another valley, one of three major gashes in the hillside, and at ¾ mile emerging on a grassy clearing at water's edge.

The obvious next thing to do is tour the trail that extends north and south the full length of the park shore, wending by the water on a flat terrace reaching a hundred feet out from the foot of the bluff, where the shoreline was before the lake was lowered. Cottonwoods and alders lean over the water. Window openings permit looks up and down the lake to Kenmore, Sand Point, sailboats, fleets of ducks. The entire park shore is used for mooring log rafts; surely this practice will be terminated and the beach freed to lapping waves.

The shore trail sprouts several major and several lesser paths leading up the bluff; the introductory tour ought to employ one of these for a looping return. An excellent path takes off at the north end of the park shore, paralleling a great ravine up to the plateau and the St. Edwards lawns. Another fine route starts up a few hundred steps south from where the main (old road) trail hits the water. Ascending the edge of a large ravine, it tops out on a narrow ridge crowned with a veritable cathedral of a fir forest, and at about 1 mile leaves trees for grass at the watertower near St. Thomas Seminary (which the Archdiocese is retaining). Roads and lawns lead northward (left) to the start.

Introductory loop trip 3 miles, allow 2 hours
High point 350 feet, elevation gain 350 feet
All year
Bus: Metro 240 to NE 153, at northeast corner of park; walk to entrance

Mercer Island Sampler (Map - page 77)

Mercer Island is one great forest ringed by bright waters. But the woods are practically all private and the lake is mostly fenced off. Nor can the roads be highly recommended for walking, despite the beauty of the scene, because a substantial portion of the residents are in perpetual training for the Grand Prix circuit. However, while thousands of private "parks" were being established several public ones, two city and one county, were set aside.

PIONEER PARK

Logged so long ago the firs now are quite big and very tall, Pioneer Park consists of three pieces, each a quarter-mile square, separated by streets but each block large enough to preserve an inner peace.

Drive Island Crest Way to SE 68 Street, turn west, and park in the small shopping center.

For an introductory loop, cross SE 68 into the Northwest Block and weave through on any combination of the maze of unmarked paths. Loop back to SE 68, cross Island Crest Way, and similarly weave-loop through the Southeast Block. Finally cross SE 68 to the Northeast Block and there, on Island Crest Way, find either entrance to the Nature Trail. Follow it across the island-crest plateau, along the rim of a deep green ravine containing a year-round stream, and return to Island Crest Way and the start.

Sample loop trip 2 miles, allow 1½ hours
High point 332 feet, no elevation gain
All year
Bus: Metro 202

ISLAND CREST PARK

The paths here are along a forested ravine deeply incised in the west side of the crest plateau.

Drive Island Crest Way to SE 58 Street. From the parking lot find the unmarked trailhead and descend to a large campfire circle from which radiate four trails. For an introduction, start on a path to the left, skidding down to a creek, then climbing to a ridge parallel to the ravine and descending. Near the lower park boundary slip down a steep trail into the ravine, clamber out on the far side, and ascend through big hemlocks and maples and firs back to the car.

Sample loop trip 1 mile, allow 1 hour
High point 325 feet, elevation gain 100 feet
Bus: Metro 202

LUTHER BURBANK COUNTY PARK
To finish off the island come out of deep woods into wide-view meadows beside the lake under the big sky. On the 77-acre grounds of a former school for delinquents are fields, marshes, trees, and 3000 feet of waterfront.

From the Mercer Island business district cross under I-90 onto 84 Avenue SE and from it at SE 24 Street enter the park.

To methodically "do" the park, walk a loop. From the parking lot by the headquarters building and tennis courts head north. Pass the amphitheater and a froggy cattail marsh to Calkins Point and views north over the water to Meydenbauer Bay and towers of the University District. Walk the meadow shore south, by clumps of willow and cottonwood, to views of the East Channel Bridge and the peaks of Cougar Mountain enclosing Coal Creek. Pass below the old school building, by the old brick power plant, walk out on docks where, in season, boats moor for picnicking. Follow the waterfront trail in willow-madrona-Indian-plum woods to the fishing pier, lawns by the swimming beach, and the marsh at the park boarder. Loop back inland through meadows, including an ascent of the Grassy Knoll.

Loop trip 1½ miles, allow 1 hour
High point 50 feet, elevation gain 50 feet
Bus: Metro 202, 210, 226, and 235

Mercer Slough-Kelsey Creek (Bellevue Bogs Trail) (Map - page 78)
West of Lake Washington is the necklace of parks called (in this book, if nowhere else) the Seattle Lakes Trail. On the east side is another necklace, not yet formally strung together on a connected route, that might be called the Bellevue Bogs Trail.

The "master stream" of the southern portion of the interlake highland is Kelsey Creek, in lower reaches called Mercer Slough. In a rural past a series of blueberry bogs and pastures, now the wet bottoms are invaded by freeways and such. Still, excellent bits and pieces have been preserved, mostly in Bellevue City Parks.

MERCER SLOUGH MOUTH
Surrealistic, that's what it is: the wide expanse of cattails and willow thickets a-rustle with flitting birds, the lakewater a-ripple with swimming birds, all

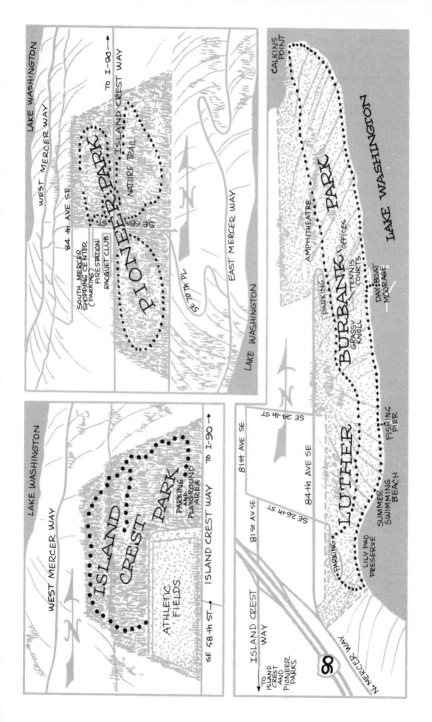

manner of wary critters skulking in the bushes — and inches away from this wildland, the concrete jungle of I-90. Indeed, this walk is possible by courtesy of the State Highway Department.

On Bellevue Way just north of I-90, where 113th goes west, a road unmarked save for a bicycle symbol goes east down to undeveloped Sweyolocken Park, which presently consists solely of a boatlaunching ramp (note ancient wood piling of an old, old bridge), a Metro pumping station, and a parking lot.

Walk the blacktop bicycle path on a graceful sky bridge over Mercer Slough, then a floating path through reeds beside and under I-90, in ½ mile reaching the far east side of the wide valley and 118 Avenue SE. Less than 1 mile south along this little old onetime-highway-become-backroad is Coal Creek (which see). And 1 mile north is Bellefields Nature Park (which see). Opportunities thus are excellent for creative combinations of walks.

Meanwhile, back on the west side of the valley, a footpath turns off the bike path and goes a short bit to the shore of Lake Washington and views over the

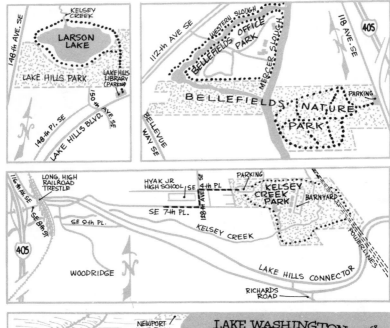

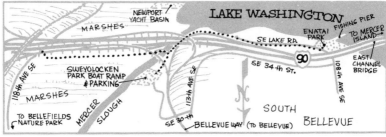

Canoeing at the mouth of Mercer Slough

water to the marina and homes of Newport Shores and to the west slopes of Cougar Mountain. The path leads to SE Lake Road, which in a scant ¼ mile reaches Enatai Bathing Beach Park, a dandy place to sit and watch ducks and sailboats and look over the East Channel to Mercer Island and Coal Creek.

**Complete round trip 2 miles, allow 1 hour
High point 25 feet, no elevation gain
All year
Bus: Metro 226 and 235**

BELLEFIELDS NATURE PARK

Something there is about a marsh that makes man want to fill it or drain it and turn it into "useful" land — a farm, freeway, or subdivision. Or maybe a golf course or baseball field. Siegfried K. Semrau, Bellevue Park Director, was among the earliest folk hereabouts to appreciate the intrinsic value of marshes. Thanks to his leadership, here is a beautifully useless soggy tanglewood.

Leave Highway 405 on Richards Road exit, drive west to 118 Avenue SE, and turn south 1 mile to the park sign and a small parking area. Spot the sign, "To the Trails," and go.

Hiking trail in Bellefields Office Park

Artfully arranged to make the 48 acres seem a dozen times larger, the 3 miles of trails weave through forest, over little creeks, beside Mercer Slough and its (often) hundreds of ducks and coots. Most of the trails are literally floating on a deep peat deposit. Brush from trail-clearing was placed as a base, over which was spread a layer of sandy loam from the hillside, then a layer of wood chips, also from the trail-clearing. The result is a unique springy surface. Names of the paths, signed at intersections, are evocative and entertaining as well as descriptive: Mud Lake Boulevard, Nightshade Avenue, Willow Grove, Skunk Cabbage Lane, Cottonwood Avenue, Cattail Way, Fireweed Lane, Gooseberry Avenue, Bee Trail, and so forth.

No map or guide is needed to savor this "living museum of natural history." Start on any trail, take any turns, keep going until it's time to go home. A good introduction is a perimeter loop, taking lefts at all junctions and thus circling the edge of the park. Then, on a second go-around, take all the right turns. Finally criss-cross to make sure you haven't missed anything.

Perimeter loop and embellishments 2 miles, allow 1½ hours
High point 50 feet, elevation gain 30 feet
Bus: Metro 240 to 128th, walk 1½ miles to park

BELLEFIELDS OFFICE PARK

The Nature Park is only a small (if the best) part of the Bellefields story. Across Mercer Slough from the trail system is another section of the city park, presently undeveloped. A plan has been put forth proposing acquisition of more of the marshland for an even grander nature park and a long marshland trail; to date, Bellevue voters have not approved the necessary bond issue.

On the west side of Mercer Slough adjoining the undeveloped section of the Nature Park is a 200-acre property that many people wanted preserved as open space and wildland marsh. Instead it has been developed as Bellefields Office Park. Let it be said, first, as a personal opinion, that this is an inappropriate use of a marsh. But let it be said, second, as a personal judgment, that the development has been done with some sensitivity. A second slough was dredged to complement Mercer, creating a 160-acre island. Office buildings generally are set back from the 2½ miles of slough front, surrounded by lawns and groves of trees. Parking lots are kept pretty well out of sight. Along the sloughs run paths with spots to fish, launch canoes (available for rental in summer), picnic, and watch birds — myriad ducks and coots and seagulls and crows, weird hybrid fowl with wild and domestic ancestors, and resident flocks of banties.

From 112 Avenue SE at SE 15 Street drive over the bridge crossing the dredged Western Slough. Park in any non-reserved space in any of the lots. Circle the island on pleasant-walking cinder paths. This is couth and kempt slough compared to that of the Nature Park but not bad, not bad at all. Unless you keep brooding about the lost wildland. But in a suburbia (now urbia?) that spends its money on expensive motorized toys and thus "can't afford" parks, a walker has to take what he can get.

Island loop 2 miles, allow 1½ hours
High point 50 feet, no elevation gain
Bus: Metro 226 to Bellevue Way, walk ¼ mile to the island entrance

KELSEY CREEK PARK

That the agricultural past of the Bellevue area be not utterly forgotten, and that children may know animals other than dogs and cats, this former farm has been revived, complete with barns and pastures, cows, pigs, horses, burros, goats, and sheep. Other attractions are the Fraser House, a cabin of squared-off logs built nearby in 1888 and moved here to be preserved, and an Oriental Garden to commemorate Bellevue's sister city, Yao, in Japan. There also are undeveloped natural areas, both valley marshes and hillside forests.

Leave Highway 405 on the Lake Hills Connector, turn north on SE 7 Place, then take 130 Place SE and finally SE 4 Place into the park.

For the maximum walk start near the entrance at the north parking lot. Walk south through the Oriental Garden, by the duck pond (quack quack), and over the meadows by a tributary of Kelsey Creek. South of the farmhouse and barns area, turn east on a path to a bridge over wide, marshy Kelsey Creek. Turn right and walk down the valley in wildwoods, then uphill to a powerline swath. North along the swath find a path skidding down in woods to the creek and bridge. On the west side turn north to the boundary with the golf course, ascend the hill to the animal corrals in a grove of firs, and drop down the far side to the parking lot.

Loop trip 3 miles, allow 1½ hours
High point 160 feet, minor elevation gain
Bus: Metro 252 to Lake Hills Boulevard, walk 1¼ mile to Lake Hills Connector and park

LARSEN LAKE

Much of Kelsey Creek has been condemned to underground storm sewers and most of its lake-marsh-wet-place headwaters have been filled and drained and covered with blacktop and houses. One source remains a lake, out in the middle of a working blueberry farm preserved as such in the Lake Hills Greenbelt, an island of peace amid storm and strife of highways all around.

Drive Lake Hills Boulevard to halfway between 148 and 156 Avenues NE and park at the Lake Hills Library. Find a path out into the marsh, thence to the shore, and circle the lake, the acres of berry bushes and the boggy ground keeping machines at a distance.

Loop trip 1½ miles, allow 1 hour
High point 275 feet, no elevation gain
Bus: Metro 252

Robinswood Park (Map - page 84)

A calendar-pretty, Christmas-card-idealized farm, centered on a small lake in a pasture vale ringed by forest, a most pleasing scene as viewed from a grassy slope, the neater for not being messed by animals. The Bellevue park retains and uses the farm buildings; for examples, the Main House is a community-center meeting place, the barn is a teen center. There's more walking to be done here than at first meets the eye, the unmarked, unsystematized maze of park paths leading to a pair of interesting sidetrips.

Drive 148 Avenue SE to the park entrance at SE 24 Street.

For an introductory loop that saves the centerpiece lake for last, walk south from the parking lot on a path near 148th. Enter a fir forest and hit an old, narrow blacktop road now closed to cars. Turn left (east) on it to houses at the park's east boundary. Here is the start of Sidetrip #1 (see below).

From this junction find a path left into park forest. Emerge from firs on the greensward beside the air-supported tennis domes above the lake. Admire the prospect from this eminence, then descend the meadow to weeping willows and cattails and circle the shore. A couple times. Complete the loop up to the parking lot and take Sidetrip #2 (see below).

Basic loop trip 1½ miles, allow 1 hour

Sidetrip #1: Airport and Phantom Lake

Continue east from the park on the old blacktop lane to 156 Avenue SE. On the far side a gravel road drops to the edge of Bellevue Airport and views up to the slopes of Cougar Mountain it harasses. On a fine Sunday, motorcycles razzing woods around the airstrip, their kin razzing around the sky, I-90 providing a background roar, here may be the noisiest spot this side of Seattle International Raceway or the Sea-Tac Airport.

For relief walk north on 156th a long ½ mile to the State Game Department public access to marshy shores of Phantom Lake, a droplet of quiet water ringed by lawns and woods and cattails.

Round trip from park edge 2 miles, allow 1½ hours

Old farm building in Robinswood Park

Sidetrip #2: Bellevue Community College and I-90 Vista

From the park cross 148th to the college campus. The school being young, the final landscaped form has not been achieved. Presently it consists of the academic complex, an intriguing system of covered walkways and courtyards, the gray concrete decorated in gaudy shades of sky-blue and flame-red, and a system of parking lots so enormous one gets the impression every student has two cars and wears them like skates. Currently one is reduced to walking roads, though the spacious campus, perched on a corner of the Eastgate Plateau with slopes falling off west and south, has the potential for a fine system of woodland paths. Above the playfields is a viewpoint out over Bellevue, Seattle, and the Olympics.

For a stunning sidetrip from the sidetrip, leave the southwest corner of campus on the sky bridge arching over the swath of I-90. Walk to the middle and look east to the Cascades, west to the Olympics. And up and down the 16 lanes of concrete from the Factoria Interchange to the Eastgate Interchange.

Round trip from park 2 miles, allow 1½ hours

Total Robinswood trips 5½ miles, allow 3½ hours
High point 425 feet, elevation gain 200 feet
All year
Bus: Metro 252

Weowna Park (Map - page 84)

A 1-mile-long, ¼-mile-wide strip of virgin forest here, of all places, in Bellevue? Yes! Astounding. A hiker accustomed to second-growth of the vicinity cannot but be staggered by the Douglas firs, up to 6 feet in diameter, and the equally fine cedars and hemlocks, and that special quality of dark green lushness that aside from tree size characterizes old-growth.

And the ravines! The creeks! Located on the brink of the Lake Hills Highland and the steep slope to Lake Sammamish, the park is deeply incised by streams. The outstanding one is Phantom Creek, the outlet of Phantom Lake just ¼ mile away. The creek enters the park in a 5-foot-deep trench hand-dug in glacial till decades ago to lower the lake and make more pasture. Shortly the creek plunges over a till cliff in a superb waterfall, flows in an impressive canyon, then waterfalls over another cliff, this of blue glacial clay.

That the virgin forest has been preserved seems due to the difficulty of logging the precipice in early days, then perhaps the nostalgia for deep woods felt by the owner, a logger himself, and then a subdivision scheme (don't try to figure out an Indian source for the name — it's "We own a park" — catch?), and finally a Forward Thrust purchase. There is no development, not even a sign announcing the park name, just signs saying "No Dumping. Cut No Trees. King County Parks." Things never will change much; plans are to keep it a wilderness park, little done except to systematize the trails.

Drive to 168 Avenue SE, which runs most of the length of the park on the upper (brink) side. Shoulder parking is very limited and must be done with care

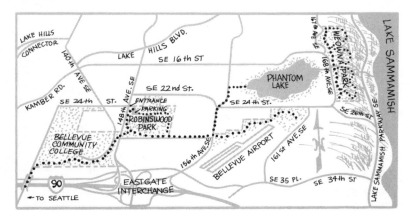

Douglas fir in Weowna Park

not to block traffic or clog bus stops. At the north end of the park, where SE 9 Street deadends at a gully, space is provided for a half-dozen cars to angle-park.

The informal trail system has been beaten out by local folks over the years. All along 168th paths take off, some dropping to private property at the park bottom (which doesn't extend to Lake Sammamish Parkway except at one point, this road therefore not being recommended as access), some side-hilling, high or low, up and down. It is not easily practical, without brushfighting, to do a systematic loop. The best plan is to take a path down from 168th, when it turns mean return to 168th, walk along the shoulder, and try another. Be sure not to miss Phantom Creek and its falls, reached by trails on both sides of the canyon. But be very careful to avoid the slippery brink, over which every now and then a child falls.

Introductory exploration 1-4 miles, allow 1-3 hours
High point 275 feet, variable elevation gain
All year
Bus: Metro 252 to SE 16th and 148th, walk 1 mile to park

Bridle Trails State Park (Map - page 86)

Smackdab in the midst of suburbia-urbia are 481.5 acres of second-growth Douglas fir and some big old-growth specimens too firescarred to interest the loggers, plus hemlock and cedar and the usual array of understory and groundcover. And honeycombing the forest are 28 miles of trails — 28 miles! As the ranger warns newcomers, "You can get lost in there." But not danger-ously. Just long enough for the fun of escaping the maze.

In south Kirkland or north Bellevue exit from Highway 405 onto the close-by and paralleling 116 Avenue NE. Between NE 40 and NE 60 Streets turn into the main park entrance and parking lot, elevation 400 feet.

Hikers should keep in mind that on all trails where horses are permitted, not just in this park, the animals have the right of way. The hiker should step off the path, act nonchalant, talk to the beast so it'll recognize the stranger as a human, and avoid sudden motions. Because of the park name, one may suppose hikers are not welcome and/or might be trampled by the cavalry. Neither is true. Despite the popularity with horsefolk the park is too large to get crowded; on an ordinary day a hiker won't meet many horses, particularly if he stays off the main trails that in winter are anyway churned to muck. Those

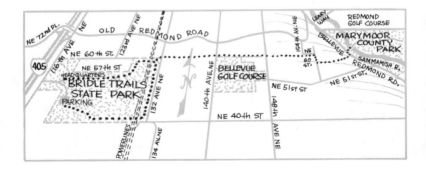

Horse trail in Bridle Trails State Park

pedestrians with persistent cases of equinophobia would do well to remember that the whole 28 miles are wheelfree.

To describe the complete 28 miles would require many pages — and be superfluous. There is little in the way of views out and the plateau has minor topographical variety; one place is much like another, one trail like another — wild and great. Getting confused is a distinct possibility but to stay lost long would require dedication; listening for the roar of Highway 405 gives a western baseline; the powerline swath down the center of the park provides north-south orientation. But since there are no signs at junctions, and myriad feeder trails enter from horse ranches, riding academies, and stables all around, even describing a basic introduction could get out of hand. One can only try.

For an introductory perimeter loop, start on the prominent wide trail taking off to the left from near the parking area entrance. At major trails take right turns, avoiding minor paths, and shortly reach the south boundary. Proceed easterly (shunning paths that enter the park), cross the powerline, reenter woods, and reach the east boundary, 132 Avenue NE. Turn left to the north boundary, NE 60, and turn left, west, jogging left to pass a large indentation of ranches. Return by the headquarter corrals to the parking lot.

That's the basic introduction — but not the best hike. To escape the churned major trails, to lose the sights and nearly the sounds of civilization, leave the perimeter, dive into the interior on the smaller paths. Get lost.

Perimeter loop 4 miles, allow 2½ hours
High point 566 feet, minor elevation gain
All year
Bus: Metro 251 to NE 70 and 116th, walk ¾ mile to park

Tolt Pipeline Trail (Map - page 89)

When the Seattle Water Department built the pipeline in 1963 from its new Tolt River Reservoir 30 miles to the city, it acquired for the purpose a strip of land some 100 feet wide. As an admirable demonstration of multiple use of such utility corridors (hundreds of miles of which traverse Puget Sound country), cooperation with King County Parks led to establishment of the first King County Forward Thrust trail. The route is 12 miles, up hill and down dale, from city's edge through suburbia to wildland, from Bothell to the Snoqualmie River valley.

The trail may be hiked straight through if return transportation can be arranged. Most hikers, of course, start at one end or somewhere in the middle and walk this way or that as far as inclination leads. Parking availability is a consideration. Some accesses have room for one or two cars, others for a half-dozen, others for none. On busy days the lot at the chosen start may be full up, forcing a switch to an alternate.

Blythe Park to Norway Hill, ½ mile, elevation gain 450 feet

The initial stretch of trail is not yet officially open. But notice must be taken of Blythe Park rising from the banks of the Sammamish River at an elevation of 25 feet up the lovely wooded hillside of Norway Hill. Here the Sound-to-Mountain Trail will come in, crossing the river from the (future) terminus of the Burke-Gilman Trail (which see).

From the center of old Bothell drive the bridge over the Sammamish River. Past the railroad tracks turn right to the park, which abuts the Wayne Golf Course.

Whether or not hiking the Tolt Pipeline, one easily can spend an hour or two poking along the riverbank and wandering paths on the hillside. One of these informally intersects the pipeline swath, where the official trail eventually will go.

Norway Hill to Highway 405, 1 mile, elevation gain 50 feet

To drive to the present official trail start, cross the Sammamish River from Bothell, and turn left. In ½ mile turn right on a road signed "Norway Hill." In ½ mile pass a road to the right, signed "Norway Hill"; this leads to 104th and the present official trail start, but at a point with poor parking. So continue ⅓ mile on 112th to the pipeline and parking for three-four cars.

Now, to back up and describe the route in sequence: From Blythe Park the (future) trail switchbacks ½ mile to the 480-foot top of Norway Hill and the official (present) trail start at 104th. Superb views down to the Sammamish, out Bothell Way and the valley to Kenmore, Lake Washington, and Olympics. From 104th the trail descends by houses, through woods a long ½ mile to 112th and parking. In ¼ mile more is the concrete jungle of Highway 405.

To cross the freeway, from the trail turn left up a farm road to a freeway access. Follow footpaths plainly marked on the pavement. Pass a Pool It Parking Lot (to get here to dump your car, take Exit 22 from 405 and cross the freeway on NE 160th to the lot on the west side). Beyond the freeway the route turns right to rejoin the pipeline, all this crossing business taking about ⅓ mile.

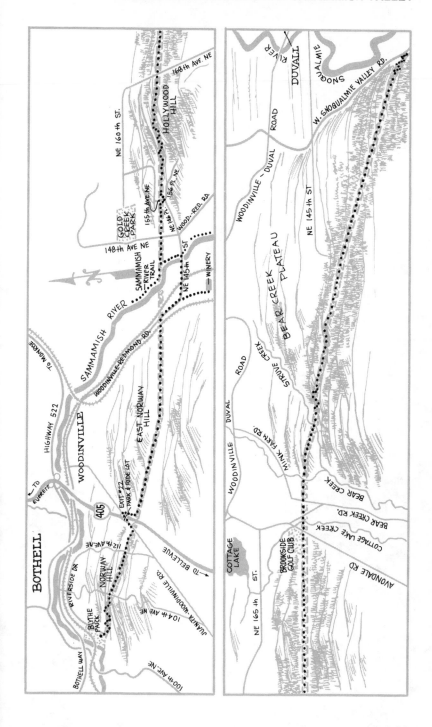

Highway 405 to Sammamish River, scant 2 miles, elevation gain 125 feet

Backyards. A good rest stop in tall firs of East Norway Hill County Park. Then more yards on right, wildwoods on left. Climb to cross busy 124th (some parking). A nursery marsh-field left, new houses right.

Ascend to 400-foot top of East Norway Hill. Fields. Acreage estates. Horses. Broad view east to Cascades. Descend to Sammamish valley. At bottom, cross railroad tracks to limited parking by Woodinville-Redmond Road.

The short stretch of trail to the Sammamish River is not officially open. And there's no bridge. So, to continue onward a detour is necessary.

Sammamish River to Bear Creek Valley, 4 miles, elevation gain 650 feet

Until a bridge is built, detour south to 145th. For compensation, at that point take a sidetrip into park-like grounds of Chateau Ste. Michelle Winery. Walk the trails. See the duck ponds. Have a sip of the juice.

Cross the river and turn north on the riverbank path (see Sammamish River Trail). Alternatively, if driving, go north on 148th to the swath and good parking. From the riverbank to 148th the trail is in undeveloped Sammamish Valley County Park; nice fields, marsh grasses, river, waterfowl. Total distance of this detour is 1 mile.

Ascend steeply from 148th to a 350-foot crest. Horse ranches. Nice woods. Views back down to the Sammamish and over to East Norway Hill.

Where the pipeline makes an air crossing of the deep gulch of 155th Avenue, find a path to the right down in woods. On the far side of the gulch climb steeply to a subtop hill at 350 feet. Big stable here. Horse estates.

Drop to a tangled ravine, then begin a steady uphill in big-fir forest. Pass a pleasant vale to left — pastures, barn, horses, sheep. Climb to the 545-foot summit of Hollywood Hill and a road, 168th Avenue NE; limited parking. Grand views west to downtown Seattle, Puget Sound, Olympics. Continue through pastures, cows, horses, old barns. Then into forest. At the east edge of the high plateau, views of Pilchuck, Haystack, Index, Phelps.

Descend in wildland to remote quiet. Continue on the flat, by pastures, marshes, to the green valley bottom of Bear Creek and Brookside Golf Course. Here at Avondale Road is good parking.

Note that all along this Hollywood Hill stretch are paths taking off this way and that. Many are not posted against trespassing. What marvels lie hidden in these woods?

Bear Creek Valley to Snoqualmie Valley, 4 miles, elevation gain 350 feet

Cross the splendid flat bottom of Bear Creek Valley, which actually has three creeks and tributaries, plus marshes, pastures, woods. In succession cross Avondale Road (parking), Cottage Lake Creek, Bear Creek Road (parking), Mink Farm Road (parking), Bear Creek, and Struve Creek. Passing houses secluded in woods, start upward in wildwoods, climbing to the summit of Bear Creek Plateau (Novelty Hill) at 525 feet.

Stay high nearly 2 miles, all in woods, mostly wild. Trails take off every which way over the plateau; not being posted, they may be open to exploration for miles.

Fog-filled Sammamish valley from the Tolt Pipeline Trail.
Mt. Phelps in distance

Views out to the Cascades, down to Snoqualmie pastures. Then the descent on a switchbacking service road to the West Snoqualmie Valley Road at 50 feet, close to the Snoqualmie River. Very cramped parking here.

To continue the Sound-to-Mountain Trail, turn south ½ mile, then east on Novelty Hill Road (NE 124th) 1 mile across the river and valley to join the Snoqualmie River Trail (which see) at Novelty.

One-way trip 11½ miles, allow 8 hours
High points 480, 400, 545, and 525 feet, elevation gain 1600 feet
All year
Bus: Metro 307 to Bothell, walk ½ mile to Blythe Park

Sammamish River Trail (Map - page 93)

Pastures and cornfields sprawling table-flat east and west to the wooded valley walls. The murky river floating ducks and coots. Small birds flitting in reeds, clouds of gulls circling, hawks on patrol high above. The path along the bank, far out in the quiet plain, distant from noisy roads. To a hiker accustomed to skulking in forests, an airy, wide-sky, liberated trail.

To be sure, the trail does not show us the old river — the river up which, before the lowering of Lake Washington, steamboats paddled to Lake Sammamish. Nor is it even the old "Sammamish Slough" that took half-a-dozen meandering miles to move water a mile downvalley, that was less a river than a maze of marshes, that on willow-snarled banks and in tangles of brush nourished a profusion of all manner of wild creatures; the Army Engineers answered the call of pork-barrel politicians and channelized and riprapped a wild river into a drainage ditch. No, it's not the old river, but even in degradation pretty darn good still. To see how good, walk the Green River valley on the Interurban Trail. Compare the industrialization there with the tranquil agriculture here. But don't celebrate prematurely: the sewers are installed here, too; Redmond from the south and Bothell from the north are eating away at the pastures. This is a frontline in the battle to save King County farmlands.

Surveyed in 1977 before it formally existed, the trail will here be described in the form planned upon completion in 1978.

The south end of the trail is Marymoor Park (which see). Walk out the Marymoor entrance road, over the bridge to the west side of the Sammamish River, and upstream to a new trail bridge recrossing the river to the east side at Redmond. (Until this bridge is built, cross the river on Highway 908, the main road into Redmond from the west, and find your way back to the bank.)

To avoid Redmond altogether, drive from town north on 164 Avenue NE, then west on NE 85 Street to the new Redmond City Hall, located beside the river. Plentiful parking. And from here on, all open and green. In King County Parks ownership northward to Woodinville is a 100-foot greenbelt strip, plus two larger bulges of parks. (Note: the west bank also is publicly owned most of the way to NE 145 Street.)

The Woodinville-Redmond Road, Highway 202, running the full length of the valley, on the east side north to 145th, then crossing to the west side, leads to accesses. NE 116th, crossing valley, river, and trail, is recommended; the large soccer-field-type county park here has a spacious parking lot. NE 124th also crosses but has little parking. NE 145th, present detour route of the Tolt

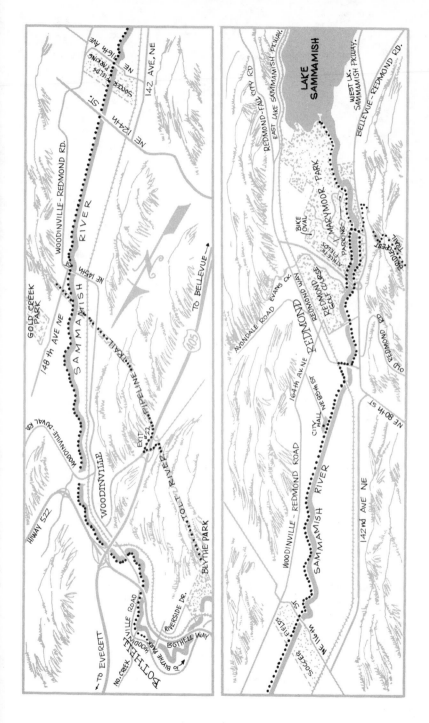

Marymoor Park

Pipeline Trail (which see) also is a poor place to park. But just north via 148th is the Tolt Pipeline Trail and an undeveloped county park with good parking not far from the river. It is also possible to park in Woodinville and walk to the river at the highway bridge in town.

From Woodinville to Bothell ownership or easement to the route is presently (1977) in process of acquisition by King County Parks and Bothell. A trail bridge already exists over Bear Creek. The way then proceeds along and under the forest of concrete pillars whose foliage is concrete ramps — the interchanges of Highways 405 and 522 and whatnot east of Bothell. The survey was halted in 1977 by the wide flood of North Creek beneath these constructions; however, a new bridge will solve the problem, permitting the route to continue a final mile into Bothell. A bridge will be built over the Sammamish River to take the trail to its end in Blythe Park.

When the Burke-Gilman, Tolt Pipeline, and Sammamish River Trails are all completed, Blythe Park will be quite the busy little hub. Note that among other possibilities will be a loop on the Sammamish River and Tolt Pipeline Trails.

One-way trip, Marymoor Park-Blythe Park, 13 miles
Various round trips 1-20 miles, allow minutes or a day
High point 35 feet, minor elevation gain
All year
Bus: Metro 307 to Bothell, walk highway 2 miles to Woodinville; Metro 251, 253, and 254 to Redmond

Marymoor Park (Map - page 93)

Largest of King County Parks, Marymoor occupies 485 acres of the flats at the north end of Lake Sammamish and along its outlet, the Sammamish River. In this spacious plain are soccer and baseball fields, children's play area, archery butts, model airplane airport, tennis courts, bicycle track, picnic tables, Pea Patch. In an open-air shelter is an exhibit of the archeological dig that established the fact of human residence on this spot 7000 years ago. An historical museum occupies the 28-room Clise (Marymoor) Mansion, headquarters of what began in 1904 as the Clise family hunting preserve, called Willowmoor, then was a dairy farm until purchased for a park in 1963. And there are lines of majestic poplars up to 4 feet in diameter, and groves of Douglas fir. A Dutch-like windmill. A river. A lake.

Just south of the center of Redmond, cross the bridge from West Lake Sammamish Parkway over the river to the park, elevation 36 feet.

What's to be done in the way of walking? By no means disdain simply striking off in the grass and roaming the fields. This book spends most of its time in forests. It's bracing to wander wide-open spaces under the big sky of pastures and lake.

The basic walk, of course, is downstream along the machine-free riverbank, first in fields and by the Pea Patch, then in willow thickets, finally in people-free marshes, a great big critter refuge. Mingle with ducks and coots, blackbirds and hawks. In pre-park days the walk would have ended in the frustration of impassable marshes; now, a wooden walkway leads through muck and reeds to a concrete viewing pier at the meeting of marsh and open lake, by the beginning of the Sammamish River, with views down the 9-mile-long lake to Tiger Mountain rising a tall 3000 feet above the south end.

Described separately, but best done as a walk from Marymoor Park, is the Bridlecrest Trail (which see).

Round trip to lake 2 miles, allow 1½ hours
High point 35 feet, no elevation gain
All year
Bus: Metro 251, 253, and 254 to West Lake Sammamish Parkway, walk ½ mile to park

Bridlecrest Trail (Map - page 86)

A gorgeous forest, seemingly virgin, of huge firs, including a snagtop some 7 feet in diameter, and big hemlocks and maples. That's the best part of a trail that connects Marymoor Park to Bridle Trails State Park. Most of the route is rather undistinguished and primarily of interest to horseriders and local walkers, but no hiker visiting Marymoor should miss the first stretch.

From Marymoor Park (which see) walk out the entrance road. By the river a "Bridlecrest" sign points north; this segment extends up the slough a bit, a pleasant walk but not the main show. For that, cross the river bridge, walk the riverbank trail south, cross Lake Sammamish Parkway to a "Bridlecrest" sign and enter the forest.

Ascend the steep hill in the marvelous trees. Down in the mossy bottom of the creek to the right, spot an ancient bridge, an old concrete water tank, nurselogs. The trail climbs above the splendid ravine to a ridge between two gullies, through a fine alder-maple jungle, to lawns of a Redmond city park at 156 Avenue NE. This is as far as most hikers will care to go. But the way west has attractions, particularly to a fan of horses, an admirer of horse ranches. There also are cows and views to the Cascades.

From the neighborhood park the trail jogs north a block, then turns west on the line of NE 60 Street, which except for a couple blocks at the start is not cut through, so the trail is a lane between fences, removed from vehicles except for crossings of 148th and 140th Avenues. Passing pastures, a posh apartment complex, greensward of a golf course, at 132nd Avenue the trail reaches the northeast corner of Bridle Trails State Park.

Round trip 4 miles, allow 2½ hours
High point 500 feet, elevation gain 450 feet
All year
Bus: Metro 251 to NE 70 and 116th, walk ¾ mile to Bridle Trails Park, thence to the trail; Metro 251, 253, and 254 to West Lake Sammamish Parkway, walk ¾ mile to trail

Lake Sammamish (Map - page 97)

Summer cottages of the remote past, when the lake was way out in the boondocks, grew to the splitlevels of commuting suburbia, except at north and south ends pretty well blocking off the public from this smaller but by no means inconsiderable (9 miles long) sibling of Lake Washington. However, as happened elsewhere in Puget Sound, the railroad very early on preempted some prime view property, still remains, and breaks through the myriad fences. Very much like the Burke-Gilman Trail along Lake Washington is this line along Lake Sammamish. If you can't quite get to the water, you can get close. For miles.

Leave I-90 on Exit 17, signed "East Sammamish Road," and drive East Lake Sammamish Parkway 2 miles north. Turn left to the parking area of the state park boat-launch area, elevation 25 feet.

Walk back out the entry road to the railroad tracks. (These are still in occasional use, so watch out.) No further route directions are required. Mostly paralleling the highway but at sufficient distance, with enough screening greenery, to feel safely removed from all that, and for substantial sections out of sight and sound of traffic, the line follows the shore, always near and often beside the water. (But all beaches are private, so stay off.) The foreground is sometimes of lakeside architecture and landscaping, sometimes of private parks with trees, lawns, and docks, sometimes of wild-tangled greenery. The background is the lake — sun-sparkling waves, sailboats, ducks, and forest shores beyond. Particularly on the walk south, when eyes are pointed that way, the panorama is a real whistler down the lake to the green Issaquah plain and up the wooded slopes of the Issaquah Alps — to the many ravines and peaks of Cougar, here seen at its best advantage, and Squak and Tiger, and on either side of Squak, the deep glacial valleys of Issaquah and Tibbetts Creeks.

North from the state park are other places to park the car without blocking traffic and to get to the tracks. Gaps between houses increase and more wild spots give close looks at shore and water. At 8 miles from the park are stubs of

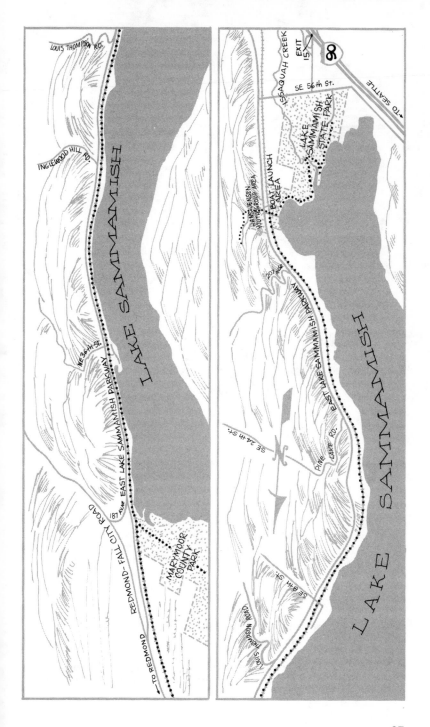

Footbridge across Issaquah Creek, Lake Sammamish State Park

old pilings reaching far out in the water; here at the north end of the lake begin the mile-wide marshes-pastures of Marymoor Park. Shoulder parking here, and paths (not surveyed) from highway over tracks into the willows. In another 1½ miles of woods and fields the tracks reach downtown Redmond.

Use of two cars or the hitchhiker's thumb permits a one-way walk. Except for the long-leggity, most hikers doubtless will do the complete round-trip route in two or more separate expeditions.

One-way trip from boat-launch to lakehead 8 miles, allow 5 hours
High point 50 feet, elevation gain 25 feet
All year
Bus: Metro 210 to Issaquah, walk railroad tracks 2 miles to boat-launch area; Metro 251, 253, and 254 to Redmond, walk tracks 1½ miles to lakehead

Lake Sammamish State Park (Map - page 97)

Not for a hot summer Sunday, when this is the most Coney Island-crowded of state parks, but for any quieter day, and a particular joy in lonesome winter, is the shoreline walk starting on lawns crowded with ducks and coots, proceeding into marsh. Frequently sailplanes are soaring, parachutists floating. All along are views up the lake and to the Issaquah Alps — Grand, Cougar, Squak, and Tiger — dramatically huge above the Issaquah plain. The topper is an unsuspected trail in a wildwood gorge to a secret waterfall.

Leave I-90 on Exit 15, drive a short bit north to SE 56 Street, and turn left to the park entrance. To maximize the walk, park at the first opportunity. Elevation, 25 feet.

Cross lawns through groves of cottonwood and weeping willow to the lake and follow the sandy shore east to the mouth of Issaquah Creek. Turn right upstream to the handsome footbridge and return downstream nearly to the mouth. Now manicured park yields to reeds and tall grass and willow tangles and masses of lilypads, and to soggy footing of a meager mucky path that may require getting the ankles wet. The cause is worthy. Soon the path improves and pavement is reached at the boat-launch area, some 1¾ miles by this devious route from the start. For a 3½-mile round trip, turn back.

For the second main feature, go on. Cross railroad tracks and East Lake Sammamish Parkway, jog right, and enter the least-known section of the park, the Hans Jensen Youth Group Area. Proceed through the campground field up the valley of Laughing Jacob's Creek to the edge of the woods. There, in a cool-shadowed cedar grove by babbling water, the trail splits.

For one tour, cross the little bridge and ascend a steep ¼ mile up the gorge wall on a rude path. On the rim are big firs and views some 200 vertical feet down to the fine frenzy of greenery along the creek.

For the other, don't cross the bridge, continue on the trail up the gorge into a pocket wilderness. In about ⅓ mile, ¾ mile from the highway, a blowout down a tributary has obliterated the trail under a heap of muck; gentlefolk may wish to conclude the tour here. Walkers willing to brave the tangle can step across the creek above the blowout, shortly recross, and in some ¼ mile on crude and rude and confusing traces of trail, be bewitched. There it is, the water splashing down moss-black sandstone slabs in a jackstraw of moss-green logs, Laughing Jacob's Falls.

Complete-tour round trip 6 miles, allow 4 hours
High point 350 feet, elevation gain 400 feet
All year
Bus: Metro 210 to Exit 15 (Highway 900) walk ½ mile to park

Issaquah and Lake Sammamish from West Tiger Mountain

ISSAQUAH ALPS

Remnant of an old range that stretched across the region now occupied by the Kitsap and Olympic Peninsulas to Cape Flattery, the Issaquah Alps are a geographical oddity, a finger of mountains reaching 20 miles out from the Cascade front and poking Puget Sound City right in the eye.

And the Issaquah Alps are a social opportunity, the steep topography and cruel climate having discouraged subdivision until quite recently, preserving a chance for spacious wildlike parks and long forest trails on the very outskirts of Puget Sound City, indeed virtually in the middle, compensation for the past generation's failures of foresight.

If not primeval wilderness it's prime second-growth wildland. And though the heights can be white anytime from October to May, the hiking season is the whole year. And the trails are minutes from the masses; many of the hikes described here begin at or near Metro bus stops.

Closest in is Cougar Mountain, lifting from the shores of Lake Washington to a highest peak of 1595 feet. Of the mountain's 22 square miles only several are suburbanized, the rest partly rural and mostly wildwoods. The three hikes in this chapter are a grossly inadequate survey — it's the old problem, private property; the trespassing of locals is tolerated but not that of the general public. And another old problem, speculation fever, is growing, money flooding in from as far away as Las Vegas and Arabia to get a piece of the action. In fact, as of 1977 the question is whether public awareness of Cougar will increase to a sufficient level soon enough to dictate limits to the developers.

Next east is Squak Mountain, 2000 feet high, so steep-sloped on east and west where tongues of the Puget Glacier pushed by in canyon channels that some scraps of virgin forest survive on andesite cliffs. Again, the private-property complication prevents proper description here of the trails. The one Squak walk in these pages is in the undeveloped state park — up to whose very boundary line the newest neighborhood of Issaquah is planned to snuggle.

The situation is different on Tiger Mountain, the 3004-foot monarch of the Issaquah Alps. Though the lower slopes are subject to development, 20-odd square miles are secure, managed as a tree farm in alternately-owned sections by the Weyerhaeuser Company and the state Department of Natural Resources, both of whom accept some degree of multiple-use, including recreation. Neither, however, is empowered by stockholders in the one case or state law on the other to let anything interfere with maximum production of cellulose; the second-growth wildland (and in some part virgin forest) is all scheduled for logging in years immediately ahead. Only the expressed concern of the public can convince the managers to preserve certain climactic ravines and ridges in logging-free blocks and strips. Nevertheless, tree-farming can be a good neighbor on Tiger and perfectly compatible with trail recreation.

The viper in the Eden is the ATV — the motorcycle, the jeep, the "fun truck," the yahoo. Though the "ATV park" recklessly proposed for Tiger by a public official has been scotched by local protest, the road-razzers and off-road gougers have not been ousted. Exploiting the neglect of government, the ATV has taken by force what the law would not grant. But the razzers cannot be allowed to prevail, nor will they, given some stout-hearted pedestrians who will fight for the rights they adore. There is room on Tiger for both wheel and foot recreation. But there is no room for noise sports. Nor, on a tree farm, is there room for activities that destroy vegetation and erode the soil. As of 1977 the principal managers are preparing a use plan for Tiger: let the public feet be heard; certainly the motorcycles are.

Completing the province are Grand Ridge and Mitchell Hill, mostly in private hands and thus merely glanced at here, and Taylor Mountain-Brew Hill, largely in the off-limits Cedar River Watershed.

The Raging River, that intriguing stream heading not in the real Cascades but entirely in the "Old Range," is the east boundary of the Issaquah Alps; on the far side of its valley rises Rattlesnake Mountain, the link between the Alps and the Cascade front.

USGS maps: Mercer Island, Issaquah, Maple Valley, Hobart, Fall City, North Bend

Coal Creek

East Channel (Map - page 105)

A green lane along the shores of Lake Washington, sort of an east-side version of the Burke-Gilman Trail, offering close-up studies of the dwellings of boat people, views over the East Channel to Mercer Island, and a sidetrip into the tanglewood marsh of an undeveloped park.

Drive Highway 405 to the Coal Creek Parkway interchange and exit west, toward Newport Shores, onto old Lake Washington Boulevard. Finding a spot to park the car is the problem; look for a wide-enough road shoulder on the boulevard between its crossing under the railroad and the entry to Newport Shores. Or somewhere near. Elevation, 30 feet.

Paths climb from the boulevard to the railroad tracks, which head south in woods that muffle the roar of the freeway. Note: This line is still used by trains; keep a sharp eye out. In ½ mile a miniature wilderness is passed — this is Bellevue's undeveloped Newcastle Beach Park, posted against entry to keep the rowdies out. Doughty explorers can pick a way through marshy woods to the beach.

Past the park the railway nearly touches the shore and stays there 2 miles, going through backyards of waterside homes, by docks and yachts and all, of the Pleasure Point and Hazelwood neighborhoods. Then swinging inland to cross the delta of May Creek, the way proceeds in 1½ miles by industrial concerns and more homes to Kennydale and Coleman Point, with views to the end of the lake at Renton, industries of the flat plain, and, South Point of Mercer Island having been passed, Seattle. Beyond Coleman Point the tracks soon enter Renton, best avoided.

Round trip 8 miles, allow 5 hours
High point 40 feet, no elevation gain
All year
Bus: Metro 210 and 240 to Coal Creek Parkway, walk under Highway 405
to railroad

Coal Creek (Map - page 105)

Cougar Mountain, once known as Newcastle Hills, could as well be called the Coal Creek Range, the half-dozen or so peaks being arranged in a rough horseshoe around the valley of the stream, which flows 6 miles from 1595-foot "Wilderness Peak," Cougar's highest, to Lake Washington. So near freeway roar and thickening clots of suburbia, down in the cool green depths of Coal Creek gorge, the steep walls and lush forest blocking out sights of civilization and soaking up the noise, making space for the babble of creek and chirping of birds, a hiker feels miles away in the main range of the Cascades.

Leave Highway 405 at the Coal Creek Parkway interchange and drive the "parkway" (this is what engineers call a freeway when they build it where no sort of road ought to be) southeasterly 1¼ miles. Where the parkway dips to cross from one side of the valley to the other on a fill, park. Elevation, 150 feet.

If not torn down (again) by vandals, an obscure sign announces this as Coal Creek County Park. Undeveloped. This is the best place to begin hiking the creek, doing it in two trips, downstream and up.

Downstream

Cross the parkway and drop down the fill to the west side (on your left) of the creek. Installation of a Metro sewer line (the best places to build sewers and freeways are in beautiful ravines, which otherwise are useless except for dumping garbage) tore up the bottom but the monster cottonwoods and maples are filling in. In a scant ½ mile the trail fords to the east bank; in high water you'll get your ankles wet. Shortly thereafter, due to a row of creekside houses downstream, a detour is necessary. Where the Seattle City Water East-Side Pipeline crosses the creek, turn right up the service road to the parkway and turn left. In about ⅓ mile leave the parkway, going left a few feet on 125 Avenue SE to a resumption of the trail downstream. Ford the creek (wet ankles again) and proceed to a fish stairway close by the interchange maze of Highway 405, 1¼ miles from the start.

For a complete knowledge of Coal Creek one must continue, though the rest of the route is road-walking. Taking your chances on the pedestrian walkways, cross under the freeway and railroad tracks (see East Channel) and follow cracked old concrete of what used to be Lake Washington Boulevard a few yards to the entrance of Newport Shores. Turn left and walk Newport Key to the outlet of Coal Creek, ¾ mile from the fish steps.

ISSAQUAH ALPS

Because no solace can be taken from the way high-born and noble Coal Creek slinks through backyards into Lake Washington like so much ditchwater, go south on Cascade Key to undeveloped (and closed to the public) Newcastle Beach (Bellevue) Park, a marshy jungle reminding that had not the county muffed the chance this riotous green would now be the condition of the entire Coal Creek delta — Lake Washington's grandest wildland preserve, a Bellefields Nature Park writ large.

Or, for views of the lake and Mercer Island, go north a bit to Newport Yacht Basin and the public boat launch, where the public, even lacking a boat, is permitted to get to the water, and you can't say that about many places around here.

Round trip 5 miles, allow 3 hours
High point 150 feet, elevation gain 150 feet
All year
Bus: Metro 210 and 240 to Coal Creek Parkway, within a short walk

Upstream

Here's the wild walk, the deep ravine of big alders, cottonwoods, maples, smaller hemlocks and cedars (and 8-foot stumps of long-ago-logged cedars), wiry vine maple and elderberry, devils club and skunk cabbage, swordfern and moss and flowers and outcrops of sandstone and coal. After an easy start (and an interruption by 1977 sewer construction) the trail deteriorates and walking is slow with many wet-ankle fords — or in season, wet-knee. Sidetrails are numerous, inviting extra explorations to points of "No Trespassing" turn-arounds. If staying on the "main" path is difficult, one hardly can get lost; the rule is, follow the creek, taking the line of least resistance, this involving repeated crossings and recrossings to dodge thorny tangles and occasional detours up the slopes.

Civilization, in the form of small farms and the Newcastle Brick Plant, largest on the West Coast, is just up the green walls, but unseen and scarcely heard. Its "new" gorge deep-notched in its "old" valley, Coal Creek is a world apart.

The refined hiker may call a halt after a mile or so, whenever the mud is too deep, the brambles too fierce, the path too faint. But at about 1½ miles (much farther as the boots go!) is the most spectacular section of the gorge, a veritable canyon, the creek slicing through sandstone walls in waterfalls, green walls rising a sheer 175 feet, and a tributary containing a mysterious iron-oozing spring from the collapsed Mary Tunnel, one of the earliest of the major Newcastle coal mines.

Upstream from here the ravine was the dumping ground of waste rock from the Newcastle mines, which operated in a big way through the 1920s and in a small way another 30-odd years. Ignited by spontaneous combustion, for decades the coal in the waste burned, converting the dump into cinders which are now being mined.

From the cinder mine there are two routes, down by the creek on a pathless bottom, and up on the sidehill along the remnant of the ancient Newcastle Road, predecessor of the modern one. At 2 miles from the start (near the entrance to the garbage dump which originally was intended to fill virtually the entire Coal Creek valley) the creek is thoroughly blocked by wastes and debris

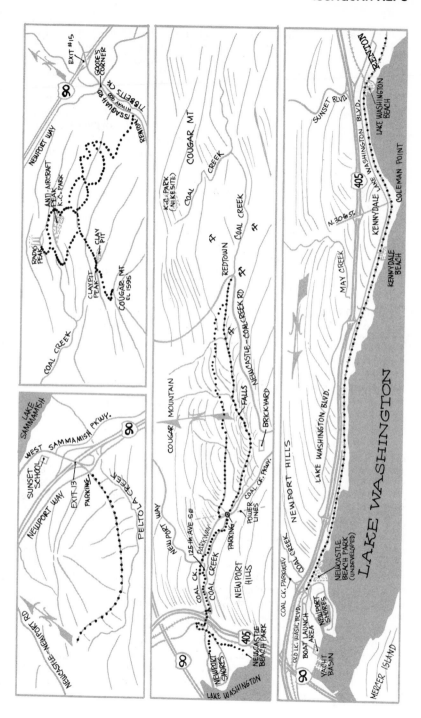

of the mines and by a tangle of Himalaya berries. Here the old road crosses the creek and no further progress upstream is practical. Turn around and — surprise! — look out the valley to towers of downtown Seattle. Incredible, after these wild 2 miles (and as many or more hours) that a city is so close.

(Just above here, at the big bend of Newcastle Road, was Red Town, the third and final site of Newcastle. Upper Coal Creek would be a happy hiking ground but is barred by "No Trespassing" signs and is so full of pitfalls — old mine shafts — as to be off limits. However, this final 2 miles of the valley to the summit ridge of the Cougar horseshoe has the potential to become the supreme super-park of the east side of Lake Washington. Through it a proposed King County trail would continue over the top and down to valleys and mountains beyond.)

Having battled upvalley a hiker may yearn for an easier return. If so, cross the creek and ascend to a gravel pit. In the maze of woods roads choose one headed downvalley. At the many Ys take the forks that seem logical. A few false starts can be expected; no harm done; backtrack and try again. Though motorcycle-infested, the route through mixed forest is pleasant on quiet days, crossing nice creeks, nearing the rim of the gorge, with interesting looks down the green wall. Continue to subdivision roads which lead to Coal Creek Parkway at a point ¼ mile downvalley from the start.

Loop trip 5 miles, allow 4 hours
High point 600 feet, elevation gain 500 feet
All year

Lakemont Gorge (Map - page 105)

Were Cougar Mountain to be inventoried for the most environmentally destructive locations for highways, the areas with the loveliest creeks in the lushest rain-forest-like canyons, the steepest slopes and most unstable rock-and-soil structures, the most potential to play havoc with downstream residences, at or near the top of the list would be the valley of "Peltola Creek," so called here for the coal-mining and farming family which has lived at its headwaters a half-century. Yet precisely here did King County, in order to gratify developers, propose to build Lakemont Boulevard. A preposterous plan — had construction been attempted, Nature would quickly have shown up the engineers as a pack of fools. Or worse. Yet construction would have been attempted in 1975 had not the Cougar Mountain Residents Association, assisted by indefatigable newsmen and certain enlightened public officials, made much ado about the scandal. However, developers consider the setback temporary; they feel that the city they are proposing to build in the headwater marshes will force construction of Lakemont. If so, the careers of some engineers may well be destroyed. But meanwhile, so will the creek and its wild-jungled gorge. Go see it now, hiking the public right-of-way.

Take Exit 13, signed "Newport Way," from I-90. Note the concrete stub from the interchange deadending in a little valley. Assuming Lakemont was a sure thing, the State Highway Department provided the county with this connector. Taking care not to block the obscure paved driveway to a hillside home, park here. But if the space is full (bicyclists use this for a staging area) cross under I-90 to parking areas near Sunset School. Elevation, 200 feet.

Lakemont Gorge Trail

Walk across the valley fill, become a sort of lawn, and on the west side find a rude footpath in the woods. In several hundred yards of mean, wheel-stopping, up-and-down, mucky brushy sidehill the path hits the end of the 1974 pilot road gouged by the cats. The gullied clay-slick track, narrow and already overgrowing, ascends the steep-sided gorge at some distance above the creek, in mossy-ferny maples and big cedars and firs, a dank green twilight. Continuing into small alders dating from the logging of a subdivision scheme that failed in the 1960s (the promoter left the state), at 1 mile the way tops out on the rim of a flat at 600 feet.

The walk can be extended another scant ½ mile or so along the pilot road through fine mixed forest, across the marshy area that would be paved and covered with houses, dooming the creek even if the highway were not built. Before private homes and pastures are reached, hikers must turn back. On the way will be noted a path to the creek, leading to a network of trespassing trails used by locals. In future a route ought to be formalized for the public, making legal the 3-mile hike from here to the summit area of Cougar Mountain.

If a hiker feels deprived of intimately knowing the creek itself, he can pick a skiddy way 100 very vertical feet down to the gorge-within-a-canyon where white waters tumble through a green chaos of mossy logs and devils club and salmonberry thickets.

Round trip 3 miles, allow 2 hours
High point 650 feet, elevation gain 450 feet
All year
Bus: Metro 210 to Exit 13, Newport Way

Cougar Mountain

Cougar Mountain — Anti-Aircraft Peak (Map - page 105)

Views east to Squak and Tiger and Grand and Si, plus Issaquah. Then views north over Lake Sammamish. Finally views west to Seattle and south to Rainier. A logging road, much of the year too mucky and rutted for most wheels, climbs the east slope of Cougar (through a proposed high-elevation city) to a summit of the mountain and an undeveloped King County park.

Leave I-90 on Exit 15, signed "Renton," and turn south to the intersection (historic Goode's Corner) with Newport Way. Continue straight on Highway 900, the valley of Tibbetts Creek, a long ½ mile. Just before a highway sign for a right turn, advising a speed of 35, spot a power pole with three white wraps. Do not park here; find a highway shoulder some distance off, out of everybody's way; be inconspicuous. Elevation, 150 feet.

The private road ascends in forest ½ mile, then turns sharp right, passing private drives, onto a broad flat at 500 feet. Here are pastures and orchards of a farm that was a Shangri-La for 40 years, until developers arrived to extend the road and "open up" Cougar. Resuming the climb, the road switchbacks into vast and ever-growing 1975-and-on clearcuts which are denuding the east slope, preparing it to become a suburb of Issaquah. In 2 miles from the highway at about 1200 feet, the angle of the slope lays back and the views east and northeast reach their maximum.

Avoiding logging sideroads, continue upward, less steeply, on the main developer's road ½ mile to near the 1450-foot top of "Anti-Aircraft Peak," where in World War II the gun batteries protected Issaquah and in Cold War I were located support facilities for the Nike missiles based a mile away. When officially open the park will give broad views over Cascades and lowlands.

Round trip 6 miles, allow 4 hours
High point 1450 feet, elevation gain 1300 feet
All year
Bus: Metro 210 to Highway 900, walk ½ mile to hike start

As for some other peaks of Cougar:
Near Anti-Aircraft Peak and equal in height is "Radio Peak," site of most of Seattle's FM radio station towers, the cluster visible for miles around. But the summit is inhabited so leave it alone.

At the 1200-foot point 2 miles from the highway, follow meandering logging roads southward to the broad plateau-saddle at 1220 feet which is the divide between drainage east to Tibbetts Creek and west to Coal Creek. Through here would pass the proposed trail from Coal Creek (which see). Close south across a stretch of pathless woods is the gaudy gash of the pit where Mutual Materials mines fire clay for its Newcastle Brick Plant. At the top of the colorful pit, a scene reminding of Southwestern "painted deserts" and with broad views to the Sammamish and Snoqualmie valleys and the Cascade front, is the wooded summit of 1525-foot "Claypit Peak." To the south ½ mile, on clay-prospecting gouges and then game trails, is the highest summit of Cougar, densely forested and utterly viewless "Wilderness Peak," 1595 feet.

Squak Mountain (Map - page 110)

The worst? Were a hiker to survey the whole of the Issaquah Alps, he might so describe the Squak of today, its network of old woods roads so harassed by four-wheelers and motorcycles that walking on weekends, or after school is out, is sheer madness — or will quickly lead there. The best? That's what it may well become when Squak Mountain State Park is developed, because in making the gift of nearly the entirety of Section 4, densely forested with big second-growth and considerable virgin timber, the Bullitt family specified there should be no machines whatsoever in the park. Nor even horses. And no trees cut, not even to open views. It's to be purely and totally a wilderness park. A walkers' park.

Due to this proviso the State Parks Commission cannot open the park until funds are obtained to purchase adjoining property for parking, restroom, and trailhead facilities. These are planned for the northeast corner, down in the valley of South Fork Issaquah Creek. From there a trail system will lead along the precipitous eastern scarp and through the intricate topography of creek ravines and spur ridges on the north slopes. That the 2000-foot summit of Squak and its thicket of microwave towers are outside the park (though on public property) is of small concern; the views from there are meager, as they are most everywhere on the mountain, which is notable not for vistas out to the horizon but vistas inward to luxuriant greenery.

From the four-way stop in downtown Issaquah, drive west on Sunset Way to Newport Way. Cross the latter onto Mountain Park Boulevard SW and follow its windings steeply up 1 scant mile to Mountainside Drive SW. Turn left to near the present upper limits of suburbia at Timbercrest and park on the road shoulder. Elevation, 600 feet.

Walk the woods road, the pigpen delight of sport-drivers, upward in nice forest, passing any number of sidetrails and sideroads. In absence of razzers, these routes richly repay exploration. Several on the right plunge down the western scarp to Tibbetts Creek (from where those knowing the way often make the ascent). Some on the left lead to the eastern scarp and paths dropping to Issaquah Creek. Among the attractions are the moonscape of a fire-clay pit (that previously was an open-pit coal mine), virgin forest on cliffy slopes, a building-stone quarry in andesite, mossy-bald cliffs.

The main road scarcely does more than touch park property until in a scant 2 miles it attains a first summit, 1800 feet, and a stone fireplace and concrete slab that are the last remnants of a summer home systematically stripped by thieves over the years. A short way beyond on the ridge crest is a Y. The right fork climbs steeply up outcropping andesite to a 1925-foot summit; the sole view is along the swath of a former powerline that dips to a saddle and rises to towers on the 2000-foot summit, ¼ mile distant. Since the trail along the swath quits prematurely, the left fork is the better way to the top. Follow it down to a T and go right, in ½ mile from the fireplace reaching the top.

Having gotten the summit out of the way, few hikers will bother with it again. Instead they will, after this introduction, return to explore old woods roads, logging-railroad grades on the east side, even some trails. But be sure to heed "No Trespassing" signs.

Round trip 5 miles, allow 4 hours
High point 2000 feet, elevation gain 1600 feet
February-December
Bus: Metro 210 to Issaquah, walk 1¼ miles to hike start

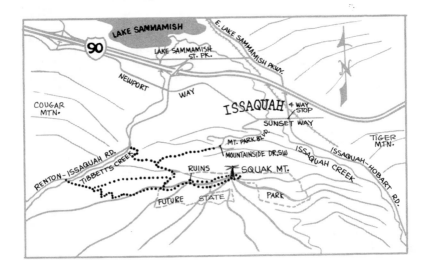

Communication towers on Squak Mountain

Issaquah Trail (Map - page 113)

An unofficial trail along an abandoned railway bed starts near the center of Issaquah and, making a switchback the locomotives needed to gain elevation, loops south through town, then north to the valley of East Fork Issaquah Creek, deadending where formerly a trestle crossed the highway to head east. The woodsy trail is pleasant in itself and is a good lead-in to hikes in the Issaquah Watershed and on Tiger Mountain.

Park on a street or in a shopping center, or get off a bus, in the middle of Issaquah, elevation 150 feet. The end of the active railroad line and start of the trail are on Bush Street just east of 1st Avenue SE.

Walk the trail south through woods and marsh and residences, with fine views of Squak, the 1976-77 clearcut on Tiger, and Issaquah Mountain (the local name for West Tiger 2). At the end of the loop the trail crosses 2nd Avenue SE and passes the high school football stadium. Here, 1 mile from Bush Street, is the turnoff to the Issaquah Watershed and trails to Tradition Lake and West Tiger (which see). The trail now gradually moves up onto the forested sidehill, with views out over the town to Cougar Mountain. The route seems to end abruptly above the swath of I-90. But it doesn't. To continue to Preston, see East Fork Issaquah Creek.

Round trip 4 miles, allow 3 hours
High point 200 feet, elevation gain 50 feet
All year
Bus: Metro 210 to Issaquah

Tradition Lake (Map - page 113)

In a grassy-marshy bowl at the northeast foot of West Tiger Mountain, fed by waters draining the steep forest slopes, is Tradition Lake. (Known to oldtimers as Snake Lake; early settlers reported encountering writhing coils of serpents.) Located mostly in the municipally-owned Issaquah Watershed, the lake is reached on powerline swaths with views out to peaks of the Issaquah Alps. Sidepaths dip into cool dark woods.

Walk the Issaquah Trail (which see). To save nearly 1 mile afoot, or 2 miles round trip, when school is not in session park along 2nd Avenue SE, where students at Issaquah High do. Where the trail passes stands of the football stadium, turn right, cross a pair of woods roads, and climb a few feet to a third one, gated, up on the slope. Turn right and ascend nice big-fir forest, by a view out Issaquah Creek framed by Squak and Tiger, to a marsh, creek, and at a scant 1 mile from 2nd Avenue, a broad powerline swath, 500 feet. On the far side is the route to West Tiger 3 (which see).

For the lake turn left on the swath. In a scant ½ mile pass a clearing on the left, the fields of an old farm being swallowed by forest. Walk in on a sideroad a few yards to Round Lake, a small half-marsh that dries up in summer. Back at the powerline, on the east side of that swath and the parallel natural gas pipeline swath note an obscure road entering the woods — this is the outlet of an alternate return (see below).

In a long ¼ mile from Round Lake is an intersection with a west-east powerline. Turn east on its swath ¼ mile to Tradition Lake, which rises and falls on marshy shores at an elevation of just under 500 feet. Ducks love it. And herons. Reeds harbor myriad birds and little critters. On the far side note a massive beaver lodge; don't approach it, leave it strictly alone, in order to encourage the beaver to hang around.

For the alternate return continue east a bit on the powerline to a woods road branching off right. Though it divides and redivides in a maze of lanes, a walker who stays moderately alert can't get lost. Take a sidetrip down a path along the inlet creek to the lakeshore. Look for apples (in season) on gnarled trees of another old farm. In about ½ mile emerge on the gas and electricity swaths at Round Lake.

Round trip from 2nd Avenue 4-5 miles, allow 3 hours
High point 500 feet, elevation gain 350 feet
All year
Bus: Metro 210 to Issaquah

West Tiger Mountain 3 — Many-Creek Valley Loop (Map - page 113)

An excursion not for the novice walker, who would be made unhappy by the crudeness of the route and does better to aim for the higher West Tiger 1 (which see) and 2 (Issaquah Mountain). The experienced navigator, however, is likely to share the opinion of most Tiger connoisseurs that this is the best of the three summits, for reasons stated below. And the loop return through Many-Creek Valley is a thing of beauty and a joy forever. Or at least until logged.

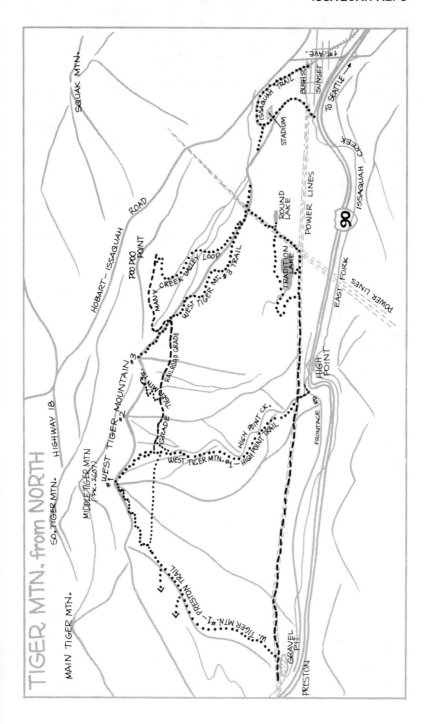

Round Lake

Walk the Issaquah Trail (which see) and then the service road to the powerline swath, elevation 500 feet, that leads to Tradition Lake (which see). Ascend across the swath on outcropping andesite slabs to a narrow road plunging into deep forest. (To the south 100 feet note another road, obscure at the start, angling into the forest; this is the loop return.)

The old road is too short to offer razzers much entertainment and thus is minimally molested. The way climbs steeply in excellent mixed forest with screened views down to Tradition Lake, at 1000 feet crossing a large creek and getting steeper. At 1350 feet, after a short flat stretch, the road ends. But trail does not start — the blazed and boot-beaten route has many logs to crawl over, slippery slopes of dirt to scramble up, and many spots for getting off the track and instantly lost.

At about 1600 feet is a magnificent stand of virgin forest, tall firs up to 2½ feet in diameter and a lavish understory of hemlocks, that gives the sense of being deep in the Cascades wilderness. (As of 1977; logging is planned in 1978 or so.) A surveyor's line trail is crossed; don't follow it and if descending this route beware of being led astray by it.

At 1900 feet, some 1 mile from the powerline, is an intersection with an old logging-railroad grade. The trail going right on the grade is the loop return (see below); the trail left continues across the north side of West Tiger, intersecting the High Point and Preston Trails (which see) and forming part of the Tiger Mountain Trail (which see).

At 2100 feet the way flattens briefly at a small ridge-crest saddle, climbs again to more virgin forest, firs now running 3½ feet, and finally to smaller trees, at last emerging in young shrubs and salal openings. If planning to descend this route, mark the spot carefully with biodegradable toilet paper. This point is just a few yards from the summit, 2522 feet, about 2½ miles from Second Avenue in Issaquah.

One reason connoisseurs favor Number 3 is it's virgin. Number 1 is cluttered by a mess of overcommunication towers and gouged by the service road. Number 2 (Issaquah Mountain, so named because it is the highest peak seen from the town) is a horrible example of wheel erosion, the slopes from Issaquah Gap to the summit churned bare of vegetation. At least as of early 1977, Number 3 has no towers and has not yet been invaded by machines — though they are at work pioneering a track down from Issaquah Mountain to West Gap.

A second virtue of Number 3 is it feels alpine. The thin soil not fully covering andesite slabs supports a skimpy crop. Burned naked by the fire of many decades ago that made this entire ridge of no interest to First Wave clearcutters and decorated it with striking snags, the summit displays only shrubby hemlocks and cedars and firs, which are stunted to pseudo-alpine appearance by cold storms and hot sun, by frost and drought. And in season, the blue of lupine and yellow of desert parsley add mountain-meadow-like color.

A third claim made for Number 3 is that it has the best view. Though lower than neighbor summits, it is the farthest west and seems to hang suspended in air over Issaquah, just a swandive from the broad blue waters of Lake Sammamish, near enough the pastures of Issaquah Creek to hear the horses whinny. (For other elements of the view, see Number 1.)

From Number 3 the route is very easy through scrub down to West Gap, up to Issaquah Mountain (Number 2), down to Issaquah Gap, and up to Number 1. For loop trips and on weekdays a hiker may wish to so proceed. On a fine Sunday, however, a person looking up to the side-by-side jeeps and fun trucks parked atop Number 2, listening to the motorcycles squirrel around its summit, is unlikely to hunger to bag that befouled peak.

There is, in any event, the rest of the loop to anticipate. Descend to the railroad-grade trail at about 1900 feet and turn south. Saunter lazily along, the only change in elevation to cross creeks whose bridges have rotted out decades ago; note the broken-back stringer logs and at one creek the intact stringers and other timbers. The trail contours into the wide bowl of "Many-Creek Valley," crossing tributaries of the two main streams, "Issaquah Gap Creek" and "West Tiger Creek." Forest of big firs is left behind, forests of mainly alder entered, bright and airy, with screened views out in winter.

Having swung around the valley to the ridge on the south side, and still at the same elevation, after roughly 2 miles on the grade enter a dense stand of small conifers. Here watch carefully for a 6-inch cedar with 2 vertical feet of its bark "blazed" off; note an obscure path descending right. (The railroad-grade trail continues a short bit to an end, from which a rude path drops to the Tiger West-Side Road — which see — reached in about ⅓ mile and very near its 1977 end at about 1700 feet. The planned extension of the road in 1978 or so and subsequent logging will have unknown effects on this entire loop trip.)

Night lights of Seattle from West Tiger Mountain

The path, quite plain after the start, descends the divide ridge between two drainages of Many-Creek Valley, at 1600 feet passing a stand of 3-foot firs — and one 6-foot monster. At 1300 feet the trail hits the end of an old road, now a trail, and turns north on the flat. Soon comes one of the chief glories of the whole Tiger Mountain Range: West Tiger Creek, then Issaquah Gap Creek, tumbling down deep dark ravines, flowing over gravel flats, amid big cedars, firs, and maples. From here the road-trail gently descends to the powerline swath, at some 2 miles from the railroad grade closing the loop.

For comparison, this loop descent through Many-Creek Valley is about 4 miles, compared to the 1-mile length of the ascent route.

Loop trip (from Second Avenue) 8 miles, allow 7 hours
High point 2522 feet, elevation gain 2400 feet
February-December
Bus: Metro 210 to Issaquah, walk 1 mile to football stadium

West Tiger Mountain 1 — High Point Trail (Map - page 113)

Unreal as an aerial photograph is the view from West Tiger. Virtually the entire territory of this book — and a lot more besides — is spread out like an enormous relief map, a supreme lesson in the geography of the Puget Sound region. Rainier and St. Helens south. Baker and Shuksan north. Olympics west. Glacier and Si east. And the Snoqualmie valley and Lake Sammamish and Lake Washington and saltwater from Tacoma to Everett. And towers of downtown Seattle and sprawl of Bellevue and streets and fields of Issaquah. And closer, the other summits of Tiger and the other peaks of the Issaquah Alps — Grand and Squak and Cougar. And hawks and sailplanes soaring.

As the shortest and easiest wheelfree route, the High Point Trail is the most popular way up West Tiger, requiring minimal navigation skills and posing no unusual threats to life or comfort.

Leave I-90 on Exit 20, signed "High Point Road." At the stop sign turn right. At the frontage road turn left and park on the shoulder, elevation 500 feet.

Walk the frontage road east, crossing "High Point Creek" on a bridge of the old highway, and in ¼ mile turn right, uphill, on a powerline service road entering the woods. In ¼ mile, at 700 feet, emerge onto the powerline swath. (West 1 mile on this swath is Tradition Lake, suggesting the possibility of loop trips. East an up-and-down 1¼ miles is the Preston Trail — which see — and thus another loop.)

Cross the swath and follow the road as it turns left. Instantly you are confronted by a sizeable, bushy, but undistinguished hemlock. To the right, unmarked and obscure, is a trail, which once into the woods becomes plain and easy, though defensively built to bar wheels. In ¼ mile the trail joins the cat road of the buried powerline cable ascending to the summit of West Tiger 1 and the way proceeds up the steep valley of High Point Creek in gorgeous mossy-ferny forest of firs up to 2 feet thick and assorted other trees and shrubs, with enough stepover logs and mucky tributaries to discourage wheels. At about 2 miles is a succession of junctions. They're obscure and of no concern to the hiker aiming directly for the summit, which lies straight up the powerline path, but offer interesting variations.

First, at about 1700 feet, the Tiger Mountain Trail (which see) diverges to the right, ascending by a campsite knoll to intersect an old railroad grade at 1930 feet.

Second, at about 1850 feet, just a few yards above the last mucky flat of a tributary, a meager unmarked path takes off to the left. Part of the way on a railroad grade, it contours 1 mile to the Preston Trail (which see), and not only suggests looping possibilities but in fact is a more pleasant, if a bit longer, way to the top of West Tiger 1.

Third, at 1930 feet is the railroad grade and an alternative feeder to the Tiger Mountain Trail.

From that last mucky flat the powerline swath turns up very steeply. There is now no question of wheeling and the walking isn't a cinch, especially in a foot or two of snow. But the struggle is eased by views down the aldery headwaters bowl of High Point Creek to I-90 and out to Grand Ridge and the Snoqualmie valley. In a mean final ¼ mile the scramble ends on the very summit, 2948 feet.

Here is the cluster of towers, monument to American's mania for electronic non-communication. And here too are the ATVs. But also, by moving around from one part of the mountain to another, are the views.

For a loop descent, see Preston Trail.

Round trip 4½ miles, allow 6 hours
High point 2948 feet, elevation gain 2500 feet
February-December
Bus: Metro 210 to High Point, or to Issaquah and walk 3½ miles to trail

Tiger Mountain Trail (Maps - page 113 and 121)

There are a number of trails on Tiger Mountain. Why call this one **the** Tiger Mountain Trail? Because it samples the ridges and valleys, shadowed forests and airy scrub, and around-the-horizons views, on a route going from East Fork Issaquah Creek over West Tiger across Many-Creek Valley to Fifteen-mile Creek to Middle Tiger and (when complete) Holder Creek. Along the way it either intersects or connects (or will) to nearly every other trail described in this book.

Some call it the Longwell-Hall Trail, or the Hazen High Trail, for the teachers and students who built (are building) the trail, sampling the good things Tiger has to offer, constructing a minimal tread that defends against marauding wheels. In fact, the tread is so minimal at places that the route can be easily lost and the trip presently is recommended for experienced wildland navigators only.

The first 2.1 miles, to 1930 feet, coincide with the High Point Trail (which see). On the old railroad grade the route turns right, crossing two small feeders of High Point Creek and at 2.4 miles, 1990 feet, reaching a slide area. On the far side the railroad-grade trail continues contouring about 1¼ miles to the West Tiger 3 trail (which see); the Tiger Mountain Trail begins switchbacking around and up the slopes of Issaquah Mountain (West Tiger 2), deep woods yielding to open fir scrub and views north and east. Staying on the obscure tread in the gravel and rock, and avoiding game trails, requires care. At 3.0 miles, 2570 feet, is a rock cairn on the ridge crest. Views west. Here the trail leaves the crest, contours in claustrophobic forest to the west side of Issaquah Mountain, at 3.3 miles, 2500 feet, reaching West Gap, where motorcycles racketing down from the nearby summit confuse the issue. Now there are views west and south.

Contouring wide-view slopes of Issaquah Mountain, the trail climbs to 2600 feet at 3.5 miles, then switchbacks down, contours, enters dark woods, leaves them to switchback down some more. At 4.2 miles, 2340 feet, is a crossing of West Tiger Creek. At 4.7 miles, 2250 feet, the trail goes through Fifteenmile Gap, in the dividing ridge between Many-Creek Valley and Fifteenmile Creek valley. A bit beyond is the intersection with the Hidden Forest Trail (which see).

As of early 1977 the trail continues a scant ½ mile to a deadend in splendid views on a snag-and-scrub slope above the Fifteenmile valley. But construction continues as the volunteers find time and by 1978 or so may reach Middle Tiger, perhaps 3 trail miles distant.

Round trip (to 1977 deadend) 10½ miles, allow 8 hours
High point 2600 feet, elevation gain 3000 feet
February-December
Bus: Metro 210 to High Point

West Tiger Mountain 1 — Preston Trail (Map - page 113)

A longer summit route than the High Point Trail, the Preston Trail has other complications that make it a less-good choice for inexperienced hikers. However, navigators canny at unsnarling devils club and dodging tricky sidetrails will find it a refreshingly different experience, a more gradual ascent, largely

Poo Poo Point from West Tiger Mountain

along the east containing ridge of High Point Creek valley, than the steep climb up the valley. The two trails combine beautifully for a splendid loop.

Walk the High Point Trail (which see) to the powerline swath, 700 feet. Turn left on the service road 1¼ up-and-down miles to a spot where a huge gravel pit is located down left from the swath.

Here are those "other complications" — namely, residences, and their yards whose privacy must not be invaded, and their fierce dogs who will tell you the same thing. The long-established trail through those yards cannot be used by the public, which must beat brush. As follows:

Turn right from the powerline on a service road. Where it joins a neighborhood road which goes uphill to houses, dive into the bushes, where other hikers also have done so, perhaps leaving bootprints and plastic ribbons you may spot. In several hundred yards up the slope intersect the good wide obvious trail, which in a short way goes left to a yard; do not do so, turn right, into the woods, and flounder uphill to find the trail, which henceforth is easy and legal.

Following various old roads that for generations have been trails only, the way climbs by cedars up to 4 feet in diameter and accompanying big hemlocks and firs that simulate (and perhaps are) virgin forest. Becoming pure trail, the route attains the broad crest of the ridge. A whole batch of paths branch off left; unsurveyed for this guide, they lead to the Preston community, some of whose houses are ¼ mile away. The unwary or unlucky could go astray here.

At about 2000 feet is a junction with a trail that contours right 1 mile to the High Point Trail (which see). Proceed upward in open alder forest; when the limbs are bare the views, somewhat screened, are broad out over the Snoqualmie to the Cascade front. Entering dense small-conifer forest, the trail switchbacks to the summit, 2948 feet, some 3 miles from the powerline swath, achieved at the east end of the summit ridge by some towers. Walk the service road the short way to the main mess of towers.

For a loop trip see High Point Trail.

Round trip (from High Point) 10 miles, allow 8 hours
High point 2948 feet, elevation gain 3000 feet
February-December
Bus: Metro 210 to High Point

Tiger West-Side Road (Map - page 121)

For many years the roads of Tiger Mountain were the principal hiking "trails," being shared amicably with polite four-wheel vehicles and the handful of motorcycles out to enjoy the scenery. Harassed now by the ATV crazies, the roads cannot be recommended for quiet summer Sunday strolls. There ain't no quiet summer Sundays on Tiger. But there are winter Tuesdays.

The West-Side Road, constructed by Weyerhaeuser and the state Department of Natural Resources in 1976, is a fine walk its entire length. And afoot it can be enjoyed, whereas in a car the width seems much too narrow to accommodate the logging trucks that will be rumbling along from now on as the west side of Tiger, wild-green these many years since the railroad loggers went away, is brought into Second Wave-clearcutting timber production. If the full length is too long a trip, drive partway and hike.

Another recreational value of the new road is that it intersects a series of trails formerly not accessible to the public due to the crossing of private land.

Drive Highway 18 north from the Issaquah-Hobart Road 3¼ miles, or south 4¼ miles from I-90, to the broad pass, 1350 feet, between Deep Creek flowing to the Raging River and Holder Creek flowing to become Issaquah Creek. In the large borrow pit now used for motorcycle squirreling and parking, two roads, side by side, take off into the woods. The left one is the West-Side Road.

The road ascends 1 scant mile to round a spur at 1600 feet, drops into the valley of Holder Creek and crosses the stream at 1450 feet, 1¾ miles from the highway. At 2¼ miles is another creek draining into little "Otter Lake"; here a sideroad goes left to South Tiger Mountain (which see). At 2½ miles, 1675 feet, the road tops out, at a quarry displaying columnar basalt, above the saddle in the ridge between South Tiger and Middle Tiger. It then descends, switchbacking, and at 1 mile from the columnar basalt, or 3½ miles from the highway, at 1225 feet, passes the first sizable creek since the basalt and, just beyond, the Mirrormont Trail up Middle Tiger (which see). The switchbacking descent continues, at 5 miles and 800 feet passing the trail to the Grand Canyon of Fifteenmile Creek (which see) and at 5¼ miles, 750 feet, crossing Fifteenmile Creek.

Now a climb commences, then a swing northward from the Fifteenmile valley, at 6¼ miles, 1325 feet, going over a flat and crossing three small creeks in quick succession. At this point leaving alder-dominated forest grown up since the railroad logging, the road enters virgin fir dating from various forest fires, the trees ranging from small to medium, mixed with blackened

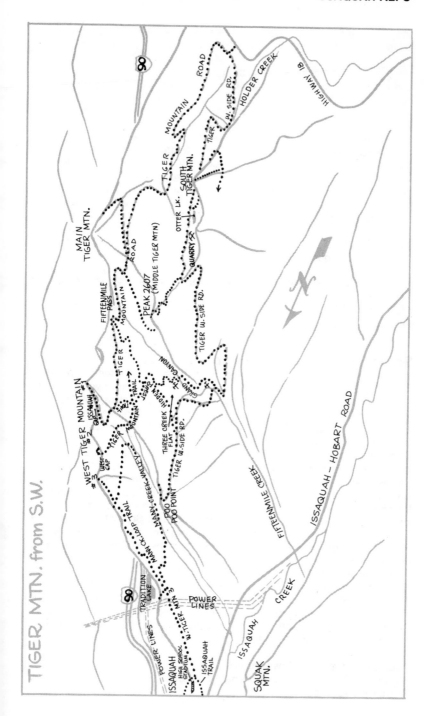

TIGER MTN. from S.W.

snags on a steep sidehill. The ascent is now steady and mostly steep. At 6½ miles, 1450 feet, the Hidden Forest Trail (which see) is crossed. At 7½ miles, 1825 feet, is the knoll from which in the winter of 1976-77 came the "poo! poo!" of loggers' whistle signals, bringing the sounds of tree-farming to downtown Issaquah; thus, Poo Poo Point. Descending into the southernmost drainage of Many-Creek Valley, the road ends (1977) at 8 miles, 1700 feet.

Plans are for the road to be extended in 1978 across Many-Creek Valley to the slopes of West Tiger Mountain, where it will then deadend. Spurs will lead to clearcuts as scheduled, here and the entire distance.

During periods of logging the road may be temporarily closed. So much the better for hikers, of course. Among trips that can be recommended, when the road can be driven (carefully!) to Fifteenmile Creek or near is Poo Poo Point. The creek and its deep cool valley are delicious, the progress through alder forests into virgin fir mixed with snags interests, and the view from the clearcut on Poo Poo Point ranks with any on Tiger, extending from Rainier to Baker, over adjacent Squak to Cougar, and to Enumclaw, Renton, Bellevue, and Seattle. But the special feature is the intimate look down on the pastures of Issaquah Creek and the buildings of Issaquah.

Round trip from Fifteenmile Creek to Poo Poo Point 4½ miles, allow 4 hours
High point 1825 feet, elevation gain 1100 feet
February-December

South Tiger Mountain (Map - page 121)

Lowest of Tiger's named summits, South Tiger is nevertheless a unique viewpoint, with close looks to the Hobart area, the Cedar River valley, a hatful of lakes (Wilderness, Pipe, Shadow, Meridian, Youngs, Desire, Kathleen, and more), and Renton and Enumclaw and Puget Sound. Moreover, the relatively modest elevation will make it an ascent favored by those wanting to walk for their views but not too far.

On the survey trip nothing was seen but the mossy vine maples and alders choking the fine wild lower valley of Holder Creek and the green-dark secret depths of second-growth covering South Tiger from toe to tip. But that will soon change because in early 1977 a new logging road was being extended from the West-Side Road. At this writing the sites of the first clearcuts are not known and thus the exact trip cannot be described. So, just go. Follow the logging action to the panoramas. And if you come too soon, enjoy the woods.

Drive the West-Side Road (which see) 2¼ miles to Otter Lake and park, elevation 1500 feet.

Tour the marshy pond and maybe spot the otter. Then follow the new sideroad, built along an old railroad grade, as it contours in superb forest down the valley of Holder Creek. Perhaps plunge the short bit through mossy jungle to the creek to see the water flow. Continue on the road to see where it goes. Or, along it 1 mile, take off up the hill and climb steep forest slopes ⅓ mile to the top of South Tiger, 2028 feet.

Round trip 3 miles, allow 2 hours
High point 2028 feet, elevation gain 500 feet
February-December

Issaquah from Poo Poo Point

Middle Tiger Mountain (Map - page 121)

Many a Tiger fan considers this to have the best view of any of the peaks. Though substantially lower than Main Tiger or West Tiger 1 (but a bit higher than West Tiger 3, the other leading candidate for best), the summit is not cluttered by tall second-growth. And the position on the ridge between Fifteenmile and Holder Creeks, and just about equidistant from Main Tiger and West Tiger and South Tiger, make it uniquely superb for studying the architecture of the Tiger "Range." As for the rest of the view, it's another version of the standard (smashing) Tiger Mountain textbook on the geography of Puget Sound.

Drive the West-Side Road (which see) 1 mile past the great quarry display of columnar basalt, or 3½ miles from the highway, to a deep-ravine creek at 1225 feet. Park here on the wide shoulder.

Beside the creek a dirt track ascends straight up out of the ravine to join good tread of the old Mirrormont Trail, built and maintained by horsefolk of that area, very decent for horses and hikers but with so many logs and mudholes and dirt scrambles as to bar wheels. Climbing steadily in mixed forest, then alder, at ¾ mile, 1800 feet, the trail reaches a Y. The right fork more or less contours some ¼ mile to the creek the trail started beside and has been paralleling. Go left. Instantly the trail emerges into small firs, bracken fern, and view windows. Vegetation grows steadily sparser, windows larger, until they

Otter Lake

connect and are mere windows no longer; at 1 mile from the Y is the summit, 2607 feet, half-naked and in season brilliant with alpine-like flowers.

Through the broad saddle northeast, Fifteenmile Pass, are the Cascades. Beyond Squak and Cougar northwest are Seattle and the Olympics. Osceola Mudflow, Tacoma Smelter, Green River Gorge, Blake Island, King County Cedar Hills Garbage Dump and Alcoholic Detoxification Center, Mt. McDonald TV repeater station, and a white horse that lives in May Valley — these are some of the sights enjoyed on a recent survey. Also seen were Rainier and Baker and Puget Sound and all that.

Round trip 3½ miles, allow 4 hours
High point 2607 feet, elevation gain 1400 feet
February-December

Immediately below the summit at 2440 feet is a deadend ½-mile spur road from the Tiger Mountain Road (which see). A motorcycle track connects summit and spur road, which can lead to all sorts of routes, looping and otherwise.

The Grand Canyon of Fifteenmile Creek (Map - page 121)

Rising in the broad saddle (Fifteenmile Pass) that breaks Main Tiger and West Tiger in two distinct masses, Fifteenmile (once called McCartney) Creek is the central watercourse of the mountain, the longest and largest completely in the "range". The most magnificent stretch of a valley beautiful its entire length is the "Grand Canyon," the 1-mile section where the stream tumbles in a series of cataracts between cliffs, some green with trees and shrubs, others gaudy browns and yellows and grays and blacks of sandstone and coal.

Drive the West-Side Road (which see) 5 miles to a large borrow pit just before the road drops to cross Fifteenmile Creek. Park here, elevation 800 feet.

Backtrack a few yards to an obscure woods road going through the forest and shortly emerging in an old field displaying concrete foundations and rusted machinery dating (presumably) from the coal mines. Rather infrequently bothered by sport-drivers, the road-trail ascends above the foaming creek, in ½ mile passing a half-open mine mouth (stay out!) and crossing the major tributary that heads on Middle Tiger. In ¼ mile more a stub goes left to the creek, giving access to Fifteenmile Falls. Here, at 925 feet, the creek splashes down a cleft in sandstones and shales, over great blocks of rock and chunks of coal, the water swirling in potholes, spraying the clambering explorer. The walls are banded in hues of carbon black, iron orange, and gray; oozy pools, if stirred, stink of rotten eggs. A stupendous spot.

Return to the main road-trail and continue to more falls and more mine mouths. At 1180 feet, 1 mile from the West-Side Road, the trail ends on the streambank. When the Tiger Mountain Mine was operating, early in the century, a bridge crossed to the far side. Getting there now to explore the mine and investigate cross-country routes can be easy or dangerous, depending on the season. For most walkers it's not worth the trouble. Best admire timbers of the fallen bridge and go back to spend more time at the falls.

Round trip 2 miles, allow 2 hours
High point 1180 feet, elevation gain 400 feet
All year

Purely for the experienced wilderness navigator and brush-buster is the following continuation of the route up Fifteenmile Creek to Fifteenmile Pass:

Cross Fifteenmile Creek to the mine and scramble steeply up the wooded slopes to escape the gorge at about 1550 feet. Proceed about ½ mile up a small ridge in easy-going alder forest and at about 1775 feet hit the Hidden Forest Trail (which see). Stay on it a short way, to about 1850 feet, keeping a keen eye out for meager tread going right, traversing and descending a bit and in several hundred feet joining an old railroad grade, apparently at its end. At a typically lazy elevation-gaining rate, the grade-trail ascends the Fifteenmile valley in open, airy, alder forest. At a Y of two grades take the left. (For a sidetrip, take the right ½ mile down to the creek.) At the intersection with the Tiger Mountain Trail (future) continue straight ahead. In 1½ miles from the Hidden Forest Trail is the Tiger Mountain Road, 2080 feet, just north of its crossing of Fifteenmile Creek where it flows from the broad saddle of Fifteenmile Pass.

For a loop return, turn left on the road to the Hidden Forest Trail (which see), descend it to the West-Side Road and thus to the start. Or turn right on the road to the Middle Tiger spur and from the summit of that peak descend the Mirrormont Trail (which see) to the West-Side Road.

Hidden Forest Trail (Map - page 121)

Residents of the Hidden Forest neighborhood often have a yen to walk or ride horses up in the woods of Tiger for the views or the berries, the flowers or the exercise. They long ago built and now maintain a trail (so defensive it has scared off the razzers) that can be walked to the first high views, safe from racket, or used as access to the Tiger Mountain Trail, Tiger Mountain Road, and Fifteenmile Creek (all of which see).

Travel the West-Side Road (which see) to Three Creek Flat at 6¼ miles, 1325 feet. Driving beyond here is not advised (as of 1977) due to narrow roadway on a steep sidehill; driving to here will not be everybody's cup of tea and must be done with care — consider doing the walk from Fifteenmile Creek crossing.

Walk the road from the flat, ascending ¼ mile to 1450 feet. Here, just on rounding the point of a small spur ridge, note ahead above obscuring alders the tips of a group of three snags. On the road cut spot an incipient path, marked at forest edge by a small cedar sloppily blazed.

Once in the woods the tread is plain, easy to follow, as it climbs through nice tall firs, then contours and ascends in alders. Lacking any view, but green-pleasant, crossing small creeks, the trail passes the sidetrail up the Fifteenmile valley at 1850 feet (see the Grand Canyon) and the intersection with the Tiger Mountain Trail (which see) at 2240 feet, 2 miles from the road.

Now, abruptly, in a final ¼ mile the trail emerges into scrub growth and views and almost immediately onto a promontory, 2360 feet, on the ridge dividing Fifteenmile and Many-Creek Valleys.

The view is superb, including the entirety of the Fifteenmile valley and the usual broad Tiger vista over lowlands west, and when the razzers are running a hiker may well be content and proceed no farther. However, if one so desires the summit of West Tiger 1 is 1 long mile away.

The connections this way and that for a variety of loops are obvious if you've been paying attention.

**Round trip from Three Creeks Flat to Tiger Mountain Road 4½ miles,
allow 4 hours**
High point 2360 feet, elevation gain 900 feet
February-December

Tiger Mountain Road (Map - page 121)

The main thoroughfare to the summits of Main Tiger and West Tiger can no more be recommended for walking on a fine Sunday than the Indianapolis Speedway on Memorial Day. When vehicles came for the scenery there was mutual tolerance between wheels and feet and they mixed quite well. However, until such time as law-enforcement arrives on the mountain the antics of the sport-drivers (who don't come for the scenery and might as well be razzing

Hidden Forest Trail

around inside the Kingdome) will put the road off-limits to walkers seeking to preserve their health, physical and mental.

On the other hand, since only by knowing the enemy can we fight him, it is suggested that every hiker go some summer Sunday to visit the Highway 18 "staging area," the old gravel pit that on good (bad) days is full up with rigs and is becoming as infamous as the Reiter Gravel Pit. See the squirreling. Climb high on the mountain and find that nowhere, on road or trails, are you free from the nagging snarl. Yes, every hiker should do that. Once.

Nevertheless, there still are times when this much-abused road is a glorious walk, part or all the way. A weekday morning. A winter day of snow not deep enough for snowmobiles but too deep for motorcycles; a hiker then must contend only with the four-wheel sports who love to chain up and churn up the white hills. The advantage of the road in snowtime is that it can be easily walkable when the trails are mean going and difficult to follow.

Mount Rainier from Tiger Mountain

Drive Highway 18 north from the Issaquah-Hobart Road 3¼ miles, or south 4¼ miles from I-90, to the broad pass, 1350 feet. From the large borrow pit two roads take off side by side. The right one is the Tiger Mountain Road.

The road ascends in second-growth, passing nice creeks, rounds a shoulder at 2050 feet and swings into the valley of Holder Creek. Views beginning, from the valley head it climbs to a Y at 2¾ miles, 2400 feet. For a shorter hike, park here, or at some convenient spot between here and the 2050-foot shoulder.

To reach the summit of Main Tiger turn right, sidehilling ½ mile across the peak's near-naked slopes to a T at 2650 feet. The right fork is the East-Side Road (which see). Go left, steeply up, a final ½ mile to the 3004-foot summit, Tiger's highest. Foundations remain of the lookout tower that until the mid-1960s provided an all-horizons view. A fringe of young trees now closes off much of the scenery. But the panorama is grand to Rainier and west over the lowlands. Much of the year the summit is easily reachable by family sedans — though when enough of them are doing so all at once the traffic jam on the single-lane cliff road is a nightmare. (Ultimately whatever government agency is running the recreation show here ought to provide a minibus shuttle from Highway 18 on Sunday.)

Round trip to Main Tiger 7 miles, allow 6 hours
High point 3004 feet, elevation gain 1700 feet
February-December

Now, back to the Y at 2400 feet. The left leads to West Tiger. In order not to throw away the trip, a hiker must park somewhere. And at some point nearer or farther the road can be expected to become impassable except to sports. The question is where to stop. Take your choice, depending on how much time you have for the walk. The longer the better: the unique attraction of this road as a hiking route, a quality that makes it competitive even with the honest-to-gosh trails up West Tiger, is the up-hill-and-down, in-valley-and-around-shoulder, on-top-of-the-world, views-this-way-and-that-way free-style rambling. Indeed, if the road were closed to wheels it indisputedly would be the champion West Tiger trail. Therefore, do not concede it to wheels. It's too good for 'em. But choose your time with care.

The road rises from the Y to 2540 feet, then drops, at 1 mile, 2340 feet, passing the sideroad left to Middle Tiger (which see). In 1 mile more the road crosses Fifteenmile Creek at 2060 feet — this is a favorite spot to park and a person is a fool to drive past here.

Now begins an ascent, and now the views are continuous and breathtaking, out the Fifteenmile valley to the lowlands west, then back through Fifteenmile Pass to the Cascades. In 1½ miles, at 2360 feet, the road crosses a saddle to Many-Creek Valley; here is a short stub road out on the ridge to the Hidden Forest Trail (which see). Rounding the head of Many-Creek Valley, in ¾ mile the road reaches 2560-foot Issaquah Gap.

To the left is the hideous scar made by ATV cowboys up the crest to the 2757-foot summit of Issaquah Mountain (West Tiger 2). To the right is the service road ½ mile up the ridge spine to the 2948-foot summit of West Tiger 1, formerly site of an airway beacon, now sprouting the towers of a society afflicted with a mania for overcommunication.

Round trip to West Tiger 1 from 2400-foot Y 9½ miles, allow 6 hours
High point 2948 feet, elevation gain 1600 feet
February-December

Tiger East-Side Road (Map - page 131)

The best-known to hikers and the least-known, that's the paradox of the Raging River slope of Tiger Mountain. Best-known because for many years only a handful of locals knew any other way to the summit than the service road from Preston. Least-known because with the gating of that road, and construction in the mid-1960s of the Tiger Mountain Road from Highway 18, and popularization of the trails previously described in this chapter, the hiking potential of the superb Raging slope, with its distinctive panoramas eastward and its series of delightful waterfalling creeks, has been neglected. Temporarily.

As is true of the others, the East-Side Road is a marvelous "trail" in its own right — if a hiker picks his day to minimize annoyance by razzers. Moreover, the perceptive pedestrian cannot fail to visualize the system of foot trails and horse trails that could be developed here, exploiting the maze of old logging-railroad grades, sampling the wide-view ridgecrests and the wild-arboretum ravines, tying in with existing trails to the summits and with a future Raging River Trail from Preston to Kerriston (which see).

Rattlesnake Mountain from East Tiger Mountain road

The East-Side Road has two entries from the bottom of the mountain. The north one (from Preston) is presently gated and impractical for use by the public; the south one thus will be described.

Drive Highway 18 about 1¼ miles east from the starts of the West-Side Tiger and Tiger Mountain Roads (which see), or south 3 miles from I-90. Spot an obvious narrow road, marked only with a "Stop" sign, taking off north, uphill, toward the powerline. Park near here, elevation 1100 feet.

Ascend to the powerline swath. (The swath itself is an entertaining short walk, upsy-downsy, open, airy, and scenic. It can easily be followed 1 long mile easterly, down over Deep Creek to the Raging River, or 1 long mile westerly to Highway 18.)

Turn right at the powerline and in ½ mile from the highway, at a fine view over the Raging valley to Rattlesnake, turn left into big second-growth. In 1 more mile, at 1282 feet, cross two delightful forks of "Trout Hatchery Creek" (which see). In another 1 mile, at 1421 feet, cross another beauty. In ½ mile, 1468 feet, is a 1975 clearcut offering the first views since the powerline — and magnificently, from Si north to Haystack and big peaks beyond. Here is the junction with the road from Preston.

(Crossing private property and gated, this road starts at an elevation of 600 feet in the pass between East Fork Issaquah Creek and the Raging River. Frontage roads off I-90, and residential subdivisions, may in future provide public access to the road at a point above the private property and gate; it thus

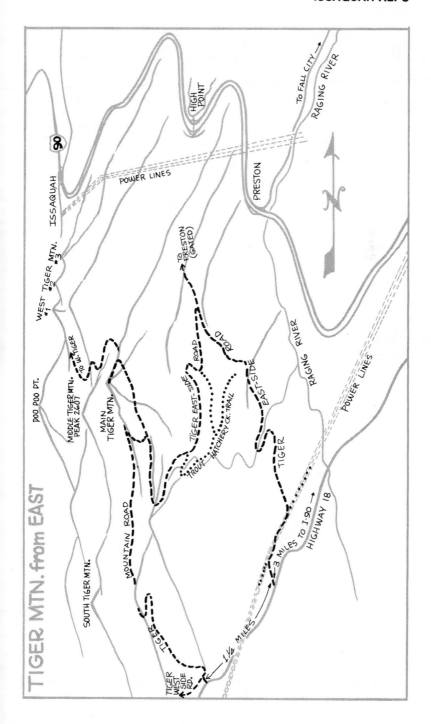

TIGER MTN. from EAST

ISSAQUAH

WEST TIGER MTN. *1 *2 *3

To W. TIGER

POO POO PT.

MIDDLE TIGER MTN. PEAK 2607

MAIN TIGER MTN.

SOUTH TIGER MTN.

MOUNTAIN ROAD

TIGER WEST SIDE RD.

HIGH POINT

POWER LINES

PRESTON

TO PRESTON (GATED)

TIGER EAST-SIDE ROAD

EAST-SIDE ROAD

TROUT HATCHERY CK. TRAIL

TIGER

RAGING RIVER

To FALL CITY

N

POWER LINES

HIGHWAY 18

3 MILES TO I-90

1½ MILES

must be kept on the "trail inventory." Climbing the lovely valley of Issaquah Creek, then entering a clearcut of 1974 with broad views down to Preston and I-90, and over the Raging valley to Rattlesnake, and far north, then ascending to cross two more fine creeks, in about 2½ miles the road comes to the junction at 1468 feet.)

From the junction the road switchbacks left and begins to climb seriously, recrossing the creeks. In 1½ miles from the junction, at 2000 feet, is the sideroad left to the Trout Hatchery Creek trip (which see). Now steeper (but with minimal views until more clearcuts open up the screen), in 1½ miles the road joins the Tiger Mountain Road (which see) at the 2640-foot saddle, proceeding from there the final ½ mile to the summit of Main Tiger.

Round trip 13 miles, allow 8 hours
High point 3004 feet, elevation gain 1900 feet
February-December
Bus: Metro 210 to Preston, walk through subdivision to intersect road above gate

Trout Hatchery Creek (Map - page 131)

Eventually there will be trails along the Raging River and up the slopes of Tiger Mountain from the stream to the summits. Providing a small glimpse of that future is this short sampler of the old logging railroad grades and the pretty creeks — this one named (here) for the one-time trout hatchery down by the river at the creek's mouth.

Drive the Tiger East-Side Road (which see) 4½ miles to 2000 feet. Note a small sideroad dropping left. Park on the shoulder.

Walk the sideroad, ignoring gully-trails dropping left (the soil-eroding tracks of the enduro-bikers who test their machines here), a scant ¼ mile to splendid big Trout Hatchery Creek tumbling over a rock outcrop amid boulders and huge timbers of a collapsed bridge. The old road crosses the creek and quickly ends. A wheelers' gouge contours a bit, then skids-slips straight down the steep forest to recross the creek at 1750 feet. Shortly beyond, ½ mile from the start, is the end of an old logging-railroad grade. A short bit along it is a Y; for the complete tour, walk both forks.

Start with the right. Alternately in deep shadows of big-tree fir forest and brightness of airy alder forest, the way enters "Silent Valley" — the north fork of Trout Hatchery Creek, whose north containing ridge surprisingly shuts out the roar of I-90, creating a quiet (not on Sunday, of course) nook in the headwaters marsh. In ¾ mile from the Y, at 1550 feet, the grade crosses a divide; turn back here rather than follow the razzer's gouges downhill to the East-Side Road.

Return to the Y and take the left fork, in more fine forest, ¾ mile to where it merges, at 1850 feet, with the East-Side Road, which can be walked (and very nice it is, too) back to the car for a loop.

Complete trip 3½ miles, allow 2 hours
High point 2000 feet, elevation gain 500 feet
February-December
Bus: Metro 210 to Preston, walk north branch of Tiger East-Side Road 4 miles to trail

Trout Hatchery Creek

Brew Hill (Map - page 135)

The site of a famous still in the era of railroad logging, shingle milling, and coal prospecting, when this now-wildland was dotted with settlements and stumpranches? More than likely. More than one. Now densely covered by second-growth, it's a lonesome hill, this east end of Taylor Mountain. But the wide-open powerline swath provides the definitive view of the upper Raging River valley and the full length of Rattlesnake. And much else. Moreover, though very near the infamous Highway 18 "staging area," most of the route is wheelfree.

Drive Highway 18 south 2¼ miles from I-90, or north 5¼ miles from the Issaquah-Hobart Road. Turn east on a narrow, unmarked, but obvious woods road. Drive (or if the mudholes freak out your car, walk) 1 long mile to a T and space for parking at the powerline swath, elevation 1100 feet.

Powerline over Brew Hill

The route ascends the service road right, entirely on the broad-view swath except for one switchback left into a clearcut and another right into pleasant woods. The grade is gentle at first, then steep — and just at the start of steepness an admirable creek has trenched a canyon, a perfect wheelstop, the rest of the way peaceful even on hell-roaring beer-can-tossing pistol-plinking Sunday (at least until the sporting engineers wrestle into place a bridge that sporting hikers do not instantly wrestle out of place).

Views expand out the Raging valley to I-90 and the Snoqualmie valley, from Rattlesnake to Si to Index to Pilchuck to Baker. The swath tops a ridge shoulder and continues to a splendid open promontory at 2440 feet, 2 miles, the recommended turnaround. Now the view extends beyond Rattlesnake up the Cedar River to Morse Lake, Washington, and the seldom-seen south side of McClellan's Butte, and over the Green River to McDonald and Boise Ridge and Rainier.

The service road proceeds a few yards to the fence bounding the KEEP OUT Seattle Cedar River Watershed. By easy offtrail walking through small firs and fields of bracken fern, avoiding the Verbotenland, a hiker can continue ¼ mile to the 2550-foot summit of Brew Hill — but to no purpose unless to bag the peak, since young forest blocks all views. Again shunning the watershed and its tempting but illegal road, one can stumble crosscountry along the flattish ridge crest 1 mile to the 2602-foot summit of Taylor. It's an interesting stroll in young forest; there's one grand view out over the Green River Gorge to Enumclaw, Tacoma, and Rainier.

Round trip 4 miles, allow 3 hours
High point 2440 feet, elevation gain 1400 feet
March-November

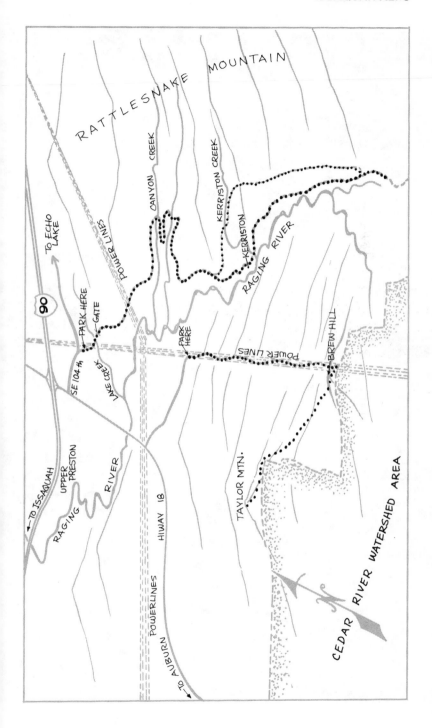

Raging River at Kerriston

Upper Raging River — Kerriston (Map - page 135)

No glaciers, no summer snowfields, no alpine lakes nourish the Raging River. It doesn't rise "in the mountains" at all but in the obscure foothill corner between Tiger, Taylor, and Rattlesnake Mountains. The lower valley, north of Highway 18, holds the settlements of Upper Preston, Preston, and where the river joins the Snoqualmie, Fall City. But despite Second Wave clearcutting the upper valley is mostly inhabited by ghosts — moldering artifacts of old logging railroads (the grades now obliterated by modern logging roads) and the old sawmill and coal-prospecting village of Kerriston.

Someday there surely will be a Raging River Trail from the mouth along the slopes of Tiger Mountain to Taylor and Rattlesnake. Now there are no trails whatsoever, merely high-speed logging roads traveled by trucks and by the motorcycles that sneak by the gate. But in proper season this can be a quiet and magical walk. What's proper? Winter. Because the route is nowhere significantly higher than at the start, if the snow there is not too deep for postholing (with enough members of the party to share the trail-breaking duty) the entire trip will be practical. On the survey day the ground was covered by half a foot of fluffy white, more steadily falling, and with animal-tracks book in hand the surveyor, though alone, never felt lonesome, not among fresh tracks of mice and rabbits, deer and bobcat, and Mysteries. And grouse and wrens flying, and chickadees and dippers. And a little shrew or something suddenly tunneling up out of the snow at his boots, taking fright, and diving into the fluff. And a coyote eyeing him from a hundred feet off, more surprised than spooked, and padding off in the woods. A great sort of day to visit Kerriston.

Exit from I-90 onto Highway 18. About ¼ mile from the cloverleaf turn left (east) on SE 104 Street. Where that road bends left to Echo Lake a logging road proceeds straight ahead. Park at this junction, elevation 900 feet.

Walk the high-speed logging road to a lovely marsh crossing of Lake Creek, passing a gate which is usually closed and even when open is never open to public vehicles. The valley is in process of being totally skinned; as of 1977 the walk is partly in woods, partly in the open, but the latter condition soon will prevail everywhere.

At ¾ mile enter an enormous clearcut and the broad swaths of two intersecting powerlines, elevation 1000 feet. Views begin of Tiger and Taylor across the valley of the Raging River. In 1½ miles more the road swings into the valley of Canyon Creek, soon crossed at 1300 feet. At 1396, ¾ mile from the entrance to Canyon's canyon, 3 miles from the hike start, road NB-R-1000 proceeds straight ahead. Turn right, downhill, on NB-R-1100.

Because new logging roads are yet to be built, the route from here can only be described as it was at the beginning of 1977. Keeping this in mind, an alert hiker ought to be able to avoid traps resulting from new construction.

Descending moderately in woods, at ¾ mile from the Y the way emerges in a recent clearcut extending down to the close-by Raging River. Ignore spurs climbing left and dropping right; contour upvalley another ¾ mile, under remnants of old railroad trestle, to a Y. The major left fork goes uphill; go right, straight ahead, on the smaller road (which, however, was flagged, as if for widening preparatory to clearcutting, so it may be bigger when you arrive).

Anyhow, you're close now. In a last scant ½ mile through woods on a river-bottom flat near the stream is the site of old Kerriston, 1186 feet, where "Kerriston Creek" enters the Raging River. (Modern maps incorrectly show

Kerriston up the creek at 1278 feet, where a couple tumbledown buildings remain; that was just a suburb of the metropolis.)

The U.S. Geological Survey map surveyed in 1910-11 shows a logging railroad (whose grade you've been walking), a sawmill, and 30 buildings on both sides of the Raging. Across the river on the side of Brew Hill were the coal prospects. More recently the site has been extensively used for elaborate camps whose structures are not entirely collapsed. For prowling artifacts a hiker really ought to come in another than snow time (or brush-lush spring-summer). Artifacts or not, and forest or not (one suspects those flags spell logging, very soon), the junction of Kerriston Creek and the Raging is a lovely place, the river coming around a bend to a delicious pool. Here, 5 miles from the gate, watch the snowflakes fall and the dippers flit and dip, and eat lunch, and look out for coyotes.

Round trip 10 miles, allow 6 hours
High point 1396 feet, elevation gain 700 feet
All year
Bus: Metro 210 to Preston, walk 3 miles to Highway 18

By simple navigation along old and new logging roads, the route can be extended another couple miles up the valley — which actually, up here, belongs not to the Raging but to a much larger river from the Puget Glacier. At the low divide to the Cedar River valley is the NO TRESPASSING Seattle watershed.

An alternate return can be made very simply in this wide-clearcut valley by taking this road and that up Kerriston Creek onto slopes of Rattlesnake and then downvalley on NB-R-1000 to the 1396-foot Y and so home.

East Fork Issaquah Creek (Map - page 141)

What? Deliberately set forth to walk the same little valley as is wallowed in by I-90? Surely this is insanity? Not at all. The screening trees and babbling creek have powers to dispel a grim fixation on concrete, which much of the route is a considerable distance off. And the pigs and ponies entertain, and the views over green plains to Tiger and Grand. And woods roads lead to miles and miles of forest explorations.

The abandoned railroad right-of-way from Issaquah to Preston has been purchased by the State Highway Department which is constructing a bicycle-foot trail that will then be maintained by King County Parks. The route can be walked from either end; by consultation of bus schedules it can be done as a one-way trip, returning via Metro 210.

To begin from the east, leave I-90 on Exit 22 (Fall City-Preston) and drive the short bit north to Preston County Park, elevation 500 feet. Walk by the community building and up a path to the abandoned railway grade and turn left.

To begin from the west, drive east in Issaquah on E Sunset Way and park before reaching 6th Avenue SE, elevation 150 feet. Walk east on Sunset until it starts rising to meet I-90. On the north shoulder of the road is a cement divider separating the highway from a narrow blacktop lane atop a rock wall above a home. Across Sunset, note a steep gravel path dropping from the Issaquah Trail. The blacktop yields to a wide trail crossing under I-90. Until the

East Fork Issaquah Creek trail passing under freeway

bridge is built over East Fork Issaquah Creek hikers must hop boulders or wade to a resumption of the trail, which switchbacks up the grassy slope to the railroad grade.

The trail turns right but a mandatory sidetrip is left, past an enormous glacial erratic and a short bit onward to the end of the grade, where the trestle used to cross the valley to the Issaquah Trail, plainly visible beyond. Climb the gravel cut high on the grassy hill and enjoy the view: down to I-90, the machine roar contrasting with quiet sailplanes serenely soaring and parachutists floating down. Spread out on the flat plain is Issaquah town and rising above are West Tiger 3, Issaquah Mountain (West Tiger 2), Squak, and Cougar — the Issaquah Alps.

Returned from the sidetrip, proceed east on the grade sliced in steep forest slopes of Grand Ridge. Watch for vestiges of old coal mines. Spot a woods road ascending the hill; incompletely surveyed for this volume, it leads to a

139

Grand Ridge trail

maze of lanes and also to the El Paso Natural Gas pipeline swath which goes on and on northward, to Canada probably, but also plummets back to the railroad grade, completing a nice looping sidetrip.

In a slot-narrow valley, the creek rushing-loud, the automobile torrent screened by fine big maples and firs and cedars, the way continues to an opening-out with views up ridges and valleys of West Tiger. Obliterated in places by highway construction, the grade will be restored or an alternate routing for the trail provided by the Highway Department. The path crosses the High Point Road (an alternate start-end if a shorter walk is wanted) and the valley widens. Pass views to Rattlesnake, Tiger, and Grand. Hobnob with bored cattle and friendly swine. The way enters the broad pass dividing East Fork Issaquah Creek from Raging River drainage, swings far out in a flat pastureland distant from the freeway, and at last enters Preston village and the county park.

Round trip 11 miles, allow 7 hours
High point 500 feet, elevation gain 300 feet
All year
Bus: Metro 210 to Issaquah and Preston

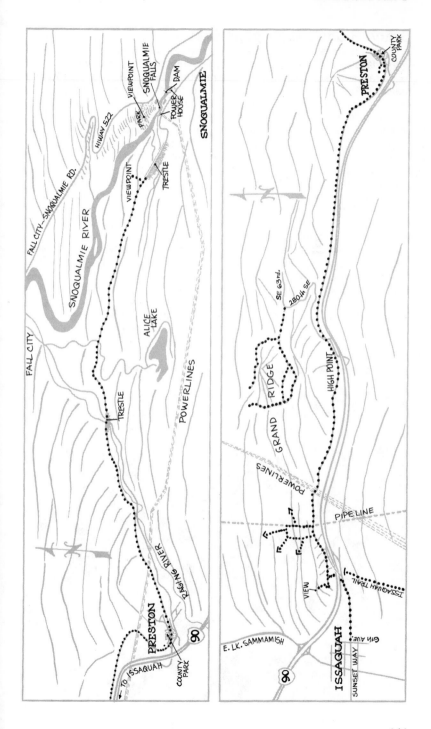

Grand Ridge (Map - page 141)

Cedars and firs and hemlocks so big one wonders they weren't logged in olden days — until one gapes at monster stumps of trees that were cut. An exuberant tangle of vine maple and salmonberry and devils club. Creeks and marshes. Tracks of — and maybe even meetings with — deer and bear. No real views out, but a fine inner experience of a superb second-growth wildland at lowland's edge, suburbia's edge. The same can be said of enormous acreages elsewhere in the Issaquah Alps and on the Pine Lake Plateau to the north; the difference is that here the land is publicly owned, partly by King County Parks, partly by King County Public Works, partly by the state, and thus is legally walkable without relying on tolerated trespassing.

Leave I-90 on Exit 20. Take the High Point Road under the freeway to the north side and proceed east, bending sharply north, steeply uphill, about 1 mile on 280 Drive SE. In ½ mile more, where the road turns sharply east and is signed SE 63, "Dead End," park on the wide shoulder by the street sign and a fence corner. Elevation, 880 feet.

Take the obvious unmarked horse trail (on public property) along the fence into the woods. Ascend a lush creek valley about ¼ mile to a Y. These are the two ends of a loop called the Hour Trail. (Because on horseback the loop takes 1 hour all the way around?)

Now for the caution. Despite a profusion of sidetrails this loop, emanating from the Black Nugget Stables, is easily navigated a considerable distance either way from the Y. However, at a certain point near the stables the Hour

Tracks of a horse and a very large bear share the Grand Ridge trail

Hemlock growing on an old stump

Trail not only enters private land but branches and rebranches into a maze, and for further confusion partly follows the access road to the stables. Signs erected at junctions by the stable folk would guide a hiker through — except that crucial signs are missing. An experienced navigator equipped with map and compass and having plenty of time can puzzle out the confusing section (presently, trespassing seems tolerated, but that can change overnight) to complete the loop and can also find fascinating sidetrails to old coal mines, to the surprising little valley of North Fork Issaquah Creek, to a powerline trail that goes on and on for miles with great views, and all manner of good things. A long rich day can be spent checking out paths here and there, in the course of events rather inevitably solving the puzzle of the "missing link." But an inexperienced hiker — or a careless one — can get thoroughly lost. The prudent course, therefore, unless a party has all day to mess around, is to take two out-and-back walks from the Y.

The left fork ascends a little valley to a ridge crest, dividing along the way into two branches which rejoin in a scant ½ mile. A descent having begun, at roughly 1¼ miles from the Y a hiker either will find the maze getting very confusing or will reach private homes. Whichever happens first, turn around.

The right fork also ascends, then crosses a pass to a valley dropping the other way, swings around a steep sidehill with screened views to the Snoqualmie valley, and in about 1 mile turns chaotic.

From one bewilderment to another on the missing link is only about ½ mile in a straight line — but in such country there ain't no such thing.

Round trip 5 miles, allow 3 hours
High point 1100 feet, elevation gain 600 feet
All year
Bus: Metro 210 to High Point, walk road 1½ miles to trail

Preston to Snoqualmie Falls (Map - page 141)

So near the roaring freeway and sprawling suburbs and yet so far from all that, on an abandoned railroad grade that slices through fine second-growth on the side of Mitchell Hill, following the Raging River, then crosses the valley, swings around a corner to a slope above the Snoqualmie valley, and proceeds upstream to the falls.

Leave I-90 on Exit 22 (Fall City-Preston) and drive the short bit north to Preston County Park, elevation 500 feet.

Walk by the community building and up a path to the railway grade and turn right. A few houses are passed and then the mood becomes totally woodsy-secluded. Now and then glimpse barns and houses down by the Raging River. Pass a fine wild creek with a path to the cool waterside, and a powerline swath with a path inviting a long exploration — to where? In 2 miles arrive at a spot where there used to be a trestle over the valley. If no footbridge has been erected to replace it, retreat a short bit to a woods road, drop to the Preston-Fall City Highway, walk north over the river, and climb the steep path back to the grade.

Now comes the best part. The line bends east, passing a window to the quarry of Raging River Mining Company, then leaves the Raging for the Snoqualmie. At the old Fall City Siding the way crosses the Lake Alice county road and goes into wilder and wilder woods, farther from road sounds. Tangled gorges are passed, and a powerline swath and horse path that could lead to miles of explorations on the Lake Alice highland, and views down to pastures and across to clearcuts of the Snoqualmie Tree Farm.

At 5 miles is a long high bridge over a deep gorge. Snoqualmie Falls is a scant mile distant but until the bridge is made safe for walking the trip must end here. But never mind — a short way before the bridge, on a fresh-logged scarp, is a satisfying lunch stop-turnaround with a view down to the valley bottom, over to the old Snoqualmie Pass Highway and the canyon of Tokul Creek, and to Snoqualmie Falls, Big Si towering in the background.

Round trip 10 miles, allow 6 hours
High point 500 feet, elevation gain 250 feet
All year
Bus: Metro 210 to Preston

Telephoto of Snoqualmie Falls

Green River in Flaming Geyser State Park

CEDAR AND GREEN RIVERS

Lumping together two fine rivers close to — partly in the middle of — Puget Sound City, mostly right on Metro bus lines, when some other streams in the FOOTSORE series rate two or four chapters each demands explanation. Simple: government has decreed the upper reaches are for drinking, deemed by Seattle and Tacoma (though not by Everett, whose Sultan River Watershed is open) to be incompatible with walking. This book will not contribute to fouling the precious bodily fluids of the cities. However, gracefully accepting the beheading of the two rivers makes them too short for a chapter apiece.

Take the Cedar. Some 15 or more miles of that stream would be featured here and highly valued for hikes on Taylor and Rattlesnake and Washington and peaks none of us ever heard of because we can't legally get near them. But the KEEP OUT fences leave only the dozen miles downstream to Renton and the outlet into Lake Washington, an area complicated by private property. On the government drawing boards are plans for an extensive system of trails. Bully. But for now the survey found only one hike to talk about in public.

Take the Green. The upper portion fenced off, the lower portion is flood-controlled, sewered, de-farmed, blacktopped, freewayed, industrialized. (When we can't afford high-energy California and Columbia Plateau vegetables we'll be sorry we covered up all that rich soil. Those who recall the former vast peaceful green of the Green, and the duck marsh that has become Southcenter, are sorry now. But that's progress, says the tax assessor.)

The Green nevertheless is very far from a total loss for feet, even now before plans are implemented for trails on undevelopable valley walls and in this gulch and that. The several segments of the river may here be separately examined.

The final stretch of the river into Elliott Bay is called the Duwamish, apparently because in olden days when it was formed by the confluence of Green and Black nobody wanted to slight one by calling it the tributary of the other. Now the Green changes to Duwamish north of Tukwila and the name is all that changes. However, the largely-industrialized lower valley has not been surveyed for this edition of a nature-oriented book. Maybe next time.

Upstream is the Big Valley, 2 miles and more wide — as any amateur geomorphologist can plainly see, much too wide for the Green River. What's going on here? Or what did? Some meddling by the Puget Glacier, no doubt. Note that Lake Washington, the Renton plain, the "Green River Valley" or "Kent Valley" south from Tukwila to Auburn, and the "White Valley" or "Stuck Valley" south from there to Sumner and beyond, are a single wide flat trough. The work of a single river, a big one? Or what? Walk the Interurban Trail through vanishing farms and growing industry and try to figure it out.

At Auburn, where the Big Valley continues south, the true and proper-sized Green Valley diverges sharply eastward and in no great distance reaches a supreme glory of low-elevation Puget Sound hiking, the Green River Gorge. When the master plan for that treasure is fulfilled a decade or so from now the area will require a trail guide to itself, and not a thin one.

Then comes the Cascade front and — for hikers — the end of the line. Comparable in lowland panoramas to those from such other mountain-edge viewpoints as Big Haystack, Tiger, and Boise, McDonald is the single trip in this chapter too high for an all-year season. (But the snowline-probing is good in early spring and during warm spells of winter when a green rain flushes away the white.) An "island mountain," McDonald is cut off by the Green River on the south, the Cedar on the north — and on the east, mysteriously, by Empty Valley. What's the story? Presumably a Big River, the combined waters issuing from the Cascades and bumping against the glacier, flowed here in its search southward for a clear way to saltwater. And obviously the ice also bulldozed through. Interesting.

And frustrating. Farther into this forbidden province of the Cascades the law-abiding hiker cannot go — not up the Cedar to its dam and reservoir, Chester Morse Lake, on the way passing sites of many an old logging-coal-mining hamlet, nor up the Green to its Howard Hanson Dam and reservoir which water Tacoma and permit industrialization of the Big Valley.

USGS maps: Renton, Maple Valley, Black Diamond, Cumberland, Eagle Gorge, Auburn, Des Moines, Poverty Bay

Cedar River (Map - page 151)

Despite the river's being crowded by highway and suburbs and all, the lower reaches of the Cedar valley remain attractive, the stream winding along a partly still pastoral green floor between forested valley walls where artifacts of coal mines linger.

The railroad, a living one, and a main line at that, so beware of high-speed trains, runs mostly beside the highway, but also much of the way beside the river, providing many easy opportunities to get down on the banks. The route can be walked in part — any part, from any of a number of points — or in whole. The bus can be employed to permit a one-way hike.

To do the whole route, drive the Renton-Maple Valley Road, Highway 169, to the village of Maple Valley, elevation 350 feet. Park where legal and convenient.

Paralleling the highway, the railroad tracks go north 1 mile to a bridge over the Cedar River. The highway also crosses and its bridge is the one walkers must use. Enjoy the river. frequently accessible for cool rests, and the pastures, the hillside relics of mining days. A second time the railroad and highway cross the river together. But the third time, at Maplewood Bridge at 9 miles, the railroad crosses and the highway doesn't; the railway bridge not being the sort of place pedestrians should dare, here the route must end.

Round trip 18 miles, allow 12 hours
High point 350 feet, elevation gain 250 feet
All year
Bus: Metro 161, weekdays only; Metro 42 or 107 to Renton, walk Highway 169 about 1 mile to rail bridge

Not surveyed for this book was the railroad on the final 1 mile into Renton, but this stretch, being cut into the bluff across the river from the highway, in fact appears the best part of the whole route and leads to trails up the hillside to

Cedar River near town of Maple Valley

good exploring country. A public trail from Renton is planned. (King County also has purchased land for a future trail extending several miles from Maplewood Bridge.)

Maple Valley to Black Diamond (Map - page 151)

A river, a lake, a marsh, and lots of second-growth woods. And an operating (as of early 1977) coal mine, a poignant memory of the past and glimpse of the future. All this on a low-key tour along the bed of the abandoned branchline railroad on the height of land between the Cedar and Green Rivers.

The tour is suggested as two hikes from Lake Wilderness. Take a short walk one way to the Cedar River, a longer one the other way to Black Diamond, or both.

Drive the Maple Valley-Black Diamond Road, Highway 169, south 1¼ miles from the Maple Valley bridge over the Cedar, turn right on Witte Road ¾ mile, then left and left again ½ mile to Lake Wilderness County Park, 475 feet.

From the parking lot walk north and east around the shore, through the University of Washington Continuing Education Center, and up woods to the rail grade on the wilder side of the non-wilderness lake, featuring a fine grove of large firs. This railroad grade currently is molested by little children on big noisy machines.

For Maple Valley turn left, in woods and then pastures, under and along highways and across the Seattle City Water pipeline. In 2½ miles is the gap where the railroad used to cross the Cedar River. The bridge now gone, transfer to the adjacent highway bridge to join the active railroad at Maple Valley junction. Along the way are views of McDonald and the many peaks of Tiger.

For Black Diamond turn right and, mostly in woodland, passing large marshes, briefly near the highway but usually some distance off, follow the grade 5 miles to the outskirts of Black Diamond and the end of the line. Along the way are looks out to McDonald and Rainier, looks in to creatures of wildwoods and wildmarshes. At the end is the big show: heaps of old cinders from the spontaneous combustion of waste rock, now being quarried for road ballast, running tracks, and building blocks; heaps of coal freshly dug; antique machinery, patched up for the recent reopening, on weekdays busy washing and sorting the black diamonds precisely as was done here 50 and 80 years ago. Fascinating. But don't get in the way.

Round trips 5½ and 10 miles, allow 3 and 6 hours
High point 600 feet, negligible elevation gain
All year
Bus: Metro 161 to Maple Valley, weekdays only

Puget Power Interurban Trail (Map - page 153)

Accentuate the positive. This is a grand stroll for railroad buffs, closely paralleling busy-working lines. And little wild pockets amazingly survive — drainage-ditch creeks a-swimming with ducks, bits of unfilled marsh with blackbirds a-nesting, pastures of as-yet-unsubdivided pastures with cows a-grazing. And views are long up, down, and across the Big Valley, from one forested bluff to the other.

Eliminate the negative. Forget if you can, as the energy crisis deepens, that until killed by the Pacific Highway in the late 1920s, for a quarter-century the Seattle-Tacoma Interurban Railway offered quick and convenient transit. Forget if you can, as a shortage of food (cheap food, anyway) impends even in fat America, that until killed by flood control, sewers, and the real-estate combine of speculators, tax assessor, other government officials, and energy-intensive irrigated agribusiness in California and elsewhere, the dairies and truck gardens on the rich black soil of the Big Valley richly fed Puget Sound City. Forget it.

The old interurban right-of-way, owned by Puget Power and used for power-transmission lines, is now — through granting of permission by the company — a public trail. The city of Kent opened 6½ miles in 1972 and King County is opening another 8½ miles in 1977-78, completing a route from Tukwila on the north to the Pierce County line. Extensions are contemplated north and south.

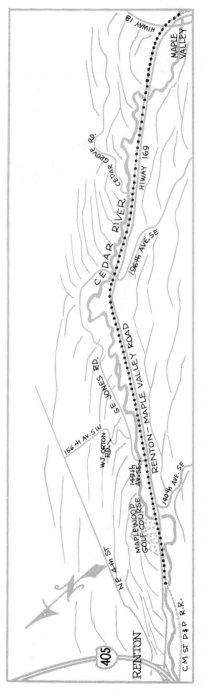

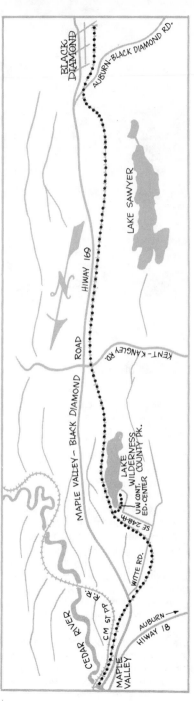

Townsite of Orillia

Unlike locals, who can walk or bicycle from home, outsiders have a parking problem — unless they come by bus. For that reason, though there are many possible starting points for many different trips, a sample introductory trip is suggested which goes south from Orillia and returns. (When the full length of the trail is open, and parking places devised and identified, easy use will be possible of the entire route.)

From Highway 405 at Tukwila, exit to the West Valley Road, then exit from that to the quaint little old hamlet of Orillia on S 180 Street (formerly a train station was a major reason for its existence) and park, elevation 50 feet. At the east town edge find the sign, "Interurban Trail Park. Open Daylight Hours. Bicycles Horses Hiking." Here, 1½ miles from the north end of the trail at Tukwila, begins the Kent-maintained segment.

Closely paralleling the Chicago-Milwaukee and Union Pacific and Burlington-Northern tracks, the trail proceeds south, now in heavy industry, now in surviving fields. At 3¾ miles (from Tukwila) the way crosses 212 Street (parking possible) and at 5½ miles, just after crossing under Highway 167, is James Street, site of a future Metro Park and Ride Lot that will provide good access. At 6½ miles is Meeker Street, in Kent; the downtown section east a block has handy parking and buses. At just short of 7 miles it is necessary to jog east to cross the Green River on a highway bridge (the interurban bridge long gone), then west to resume the trail. Parking is possible here. This is suggested as the turnaround for the sample introduction; enjoy the Green River, which has been nearby but unseen the whole way south.

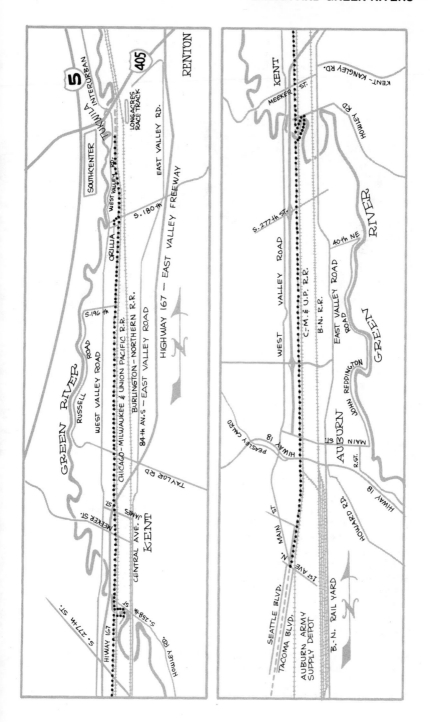

Farm alongside the Interurban Trail

At 277 Street, 8 miles, the Kent stretch of trail ends; parking is chancy here, though hikers can park at a distance with ease and walk the street to intersect trail. At 10 miles is Auburn's NW 15 Street, a crossing under freeways, and after a quiet rural stretch, increased industry. At 11 miles is the center of Auburn, with plentiful parking plus bus service. Having all the way to here followed a perfect north-south line, now the route turns southwest, passing Algona at 13 miles, Pacific at 14, and at 15 miles leaving the Big Valley and swinging west into the valley of Jovita Creek, ending (for now) at the county line.

Note: Hikers are advised not to do the section south of Pacific until King County formally and publicly announces opening of the trail, perhaps in 1978.

Sample round trip (Orillia-Green River) 11 miles, allow 7 hours
High point 50 feet, no elevation gain
All year
Bus: Metro 150 to Kent

Mill Creek Canyon (Map - page 155)

A green gash in the valley wall of the Green River, creek and forest preserved in a Kent city park the full length of the canyon from its beginning as a mere gulch in the upland down to its debouchment on the broad floodplain of the Big Valley.

From Central Avenue on the east side of Kent turn east on Smith Street (Highway 516, the Kent-Kangley Road) to a stoplight. Turn south a few feet on East Titus Street (confusingly signed "Jason Avenue" at the light) to the parking area of 100-acre Mill Creek park, elevation 50 feet.

Walk past the vehicle-barring gate to a fish pond. From here a trail leads up each side of the creek. The one on the right (south) presently doesn't extend to the canyon head, though trail-building by volunteer youth groups continues. For an introductory tour, take the north-side trail.

Now down by the creek, deep in shadowed depths, now slicing the steep sidehill, now high on the rim, the path proceeds up a valley in forest of fine big cottonwoods and other hardwoods, then mixed forest with cedars, hemlocks, firs, and a rich understory and groundcover. Street noises fade. Glimpses of houses on the rim diminish. Feeder trails join from surrounding neighborhoods, side-trails drop to creekside sitting spots, the main trail splits and unites, in a scant 2 miles ending at a paved road on the rim. However, by taking a side-trail down to the creek and up to the opposite rim, the trip can be extended a bit to a field (and private property) where Mill Creek is no longer in a wide wild canyon but a narrow gulch fouled with farmers' garbage.

Round trip 4 miles, allow 3 hours
High point 350 feet, elevation gain 300 feet
All year
Bus: Metro 150 to Kent, walk to park

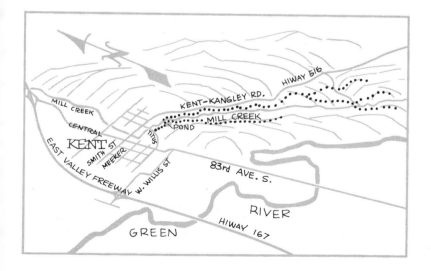

Steelhead fishing in Green River

Green Valley Mouth (Map - page 157)

The Green River flows in the Big Valley, which is called the Green River Valley. But it's not. The true Green Valley starts at the exit of the Green River Gorge in Flaming Geyser State Park and extends some 7 air miles (more as the water flows) downstream, in all this distance having a cozy floodplain barely ½ mile wide at most. Only then does the river leave its appropriately-sized homey valley to wander pathetically out into alien vastness of the Big Valley. A riverside walk samples the transition zone.

Drive east from Auburn on Highway 18 and just before its bridge over the Green River exit onto the Black Diamond Road. Shortly, just before this road's bridge over the river, turn right on the Green Valley Road (signed "Flaming Geyser") and immediately pull off left on the fishermen's riverside parking area, elevation 75 feet.

Walk downstream under the Black Diamond road bridge, the railroad bridge, the Highway 18 bridge, passing the mouth of Big Soos Creek, and proceed on a broad dike-road. To the left is park-like pasture, to the right the river, across it the willow-cottonwood wilds of the Green River College forest (which see). Swallows flit, ducks quack, hawks circle, and pterodactyl-like herons implausibly lift off from gravel bars and ponderously flop to treetops. Except in high water a hiker can leave the dike and walk gravel-sand bars. The dike road swings left and fades out in woodland paths between a murky pond and the river. At 1 mile from the start a path reaches railroad tracks. Along

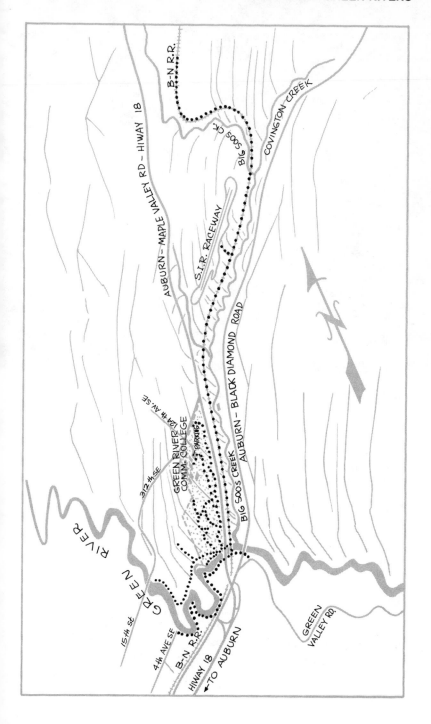

Hiking trails on the Green River College campus

them to the right a short bit another road leads right to another dike. More pastures and river and birds. Now, as the Green River is entering the Big Valley, snuggling the foot of the bluff for comfort, the hike ends, blocked by homes on the bank at 2 miles from the start.

Round trip 4 miles, allow 2½ hours
High point 75 feet, no elevation gain
All year
Bus: Metro 150 to Auburn, walk Main Street 1 long mile east to find the endpoint of the hike

Green River College Forest (Map - page 157)

On the high promontory whose bluffs fall west to the Big Valley, south to the Green Valley, and east to Big Soos valley lie the Green River College campus and its contiguous forest, used in an instructional program that encompasses the planting and tending and harvesting of trees and the building and maintenance of trails. Totalling 4 miles in length, the trails sample big-tree wildlands on the plateau, forests on the steep bluffs, tanglewoods of birdland sloughs along the Green River.

In various conditions of repair from plush to overgrown, the trails offer a range of experiences from leisurely strolls to sweating, face-scratched, shin-bruised, boot-soaked adventures. While crashing around in the brush it's hard to believe the campus and forest cover only some 300 acres. The trails are unsigned, no problem when spending a full day poking about to see where every path goes but causing indecision pangs when time for the exploration is limited. The following route is reasonably easy to stay on and samples the varied terrains and ecosystems.

Drive Highway 18 east from Auburn and shortly after crossing the Green River turn left and follow signs to the main campus entrance, elevation 425 feet. Buy a 25¢ all-day parking permit at a vending machine and park in any unreserved space. Find one of the many locator maps placed around campus and with its help navigate to the Veterans' Office. Across the street from it and a bit south, spot an unmarked trail into the forest. (There are four other trailheads on the campus edge and if you're lucky enough to get lost you may return on any of them.)

Walk over a bridge and by a pond .07 mile to a junction and turn right, continuing in superb big-tree forest, ignoring a sidetrail right at .23 mile, descending from the plateau to a bench, entering a 1976 clearcut and plantation, these obscuring a junction at .11 mile with a sidetrail right — the return trail of the route described here. Beyond the clearcut the way drops in lush forest .23 mile to the Green River. The path upstream leads to Big Soos Creek (which see). Turn downstream. A path on the bank attracts, but deadends at a slough; backtrack to a more inland route deep in cottonwood-willow floodplain woods. In .41 mile is an obscure junction beside a slough; note aluminum bits on an alder and a middling-large cedar a few feet along the uphill trail to the right, the route of the return.

But first make a sidetrip downstream, out of the college trail system, onto an old road with more forest, many ways to riverside, gravel bars, duck-watching spots, and ending at a public streetend in about 1¼ miles. As a sidetrip off the sidetrip, partway along take an old road-trail that climbs ½ mile to the top of the bluff and a broad view out to Auburn and the Big Valley.

Returning from this 3½-mile round-trip sidetrip, at Obscure Junction go uphill on perhaps the most spectacularly lovely part of the trail system. The way ascends steeply in stupendous forest to the crest of a spur ridge between two tanglewood gulfs, then completes the climb (.37 mile from the river) to a junction on the bluff rim. Turn right on the flat, then angle across the sidehill, dropping to a ravine and creek crossing, climbing to the clearcut, and in .40 mile rejoining the trail of the trip start. Return .41 mile to the Veterans' Office.

Or say the hell with it. You may not be able to follow these directions anyhow if new trail-clearing or logging confuse the issue. The best idea is to devote a whole day and plan to get lost.

Suggested round trip 5¾ miles (college forest loop 2¼ miles, off-campus sidetrip 3½ miles), allow 4 hours
High point 425 feet, elevation gain 800 feet
All year
Bus: Metro 153 to campus (weekdays only); 150 to Auburn, walk Main, M, and 8 Streets 1½ miles to Green River bridge, on far side walk the bank road to campus

Big Soos Creek (Map - page 157)

The Three Bears came in assorted sizes. So do these three valleys that also live together: the rather-too-broad-for-comfort Big Valley, the spacious but not overpowering Green Valley, and the petite (despite the name) Big Soos valley, partly miniaturized pastures, partly cool-shadowy wildwoods through which babbles the creek.

Farther upstream, north of Lake Meridian, King County owns and is holding for future recreational development 6 miles of Big Soos; farming continues there for the interim and barbed wire makes walking messy. But never mind, the best part of the valley, the Big Soos Gorge, is the route of a railroad that hobos and locals have walked since the tracks were laid.

Park as for Green Valley Mouth (which see), elevation 75 feet. Walk downstream to the railroad bridge over the Green River. (Alternatively, especially if coming by bus, approach from Green River College, which see.) Most of the way paralleled by a walker-horse path, the tracks pass cows in pastures, fish in a hatchery, and soon swing away from Highway 18 into quiet forest. Note: This is a mainline railway so keep a sharp lookout for speeding trains.

A deep, nameless tributary valley is crossed on fill. Then, out of sight but on Sundays not out of sound, is passed the Seattle International Raceway. Farms are left behind for a remote-feeling wildland. At a scant 3 miles the tracks cross Big Soos at its junction with Covington Creek, along whose valley is a woods road. A path to the creek gives a look at the handsome old fern-draped masonry arch of the Soos culvert; they don't build 'em like that anymore. Subsequent paths give further access to gravel bars and rapids.

At 4 miles the tracks return to farms, the gorge dwindles to a mere gully, and Jenkins Creek, larger than Big Soos, enters. A sand-cliff swallows' apartment house is the last sight to see before turning around. From here the tracks leave Soos for Jenkins Creek and proceed to points east in less interesting country.

Round trip 8 miles, allow 5 hours
High point 300 feet, elevation gain 225 feet
All year
Bus: see Green River College, Green River Mouth for two approaches

Green River Gorge

For some 6 air miles, or 12 stream miles, the Green River flows in a narrow canyon whose walls rise as much as 300 feet, always steep and often vertical or overhanging. Its meanders are intrenched in solid rock, slicing through some 9000 feet of tilted strata of shale and sandstone, with interbedded coal seams and imbedded fossil imprints of shells and vegetation. From the mid-1960s proposal by Wolf Bauer for "a unique natural showcase of free-flowing wild river and primeval canyon" came the plan for a Green River Gorge Conservation Area now being implemented by the Washington State Parks and Recreation Commission. The long-range intent is to acquire, as funds become available, properties and/or easements the full length of the Gorge; as of early 1977, some 1500 acres are in public ownership.

Part of the grand plan is a trail from one end to the other, sometimes at river level, sometimes on the walls, sometimes on the rim. By following old woods roads and fishermen's paths and busting a certain amount of brush a deter-

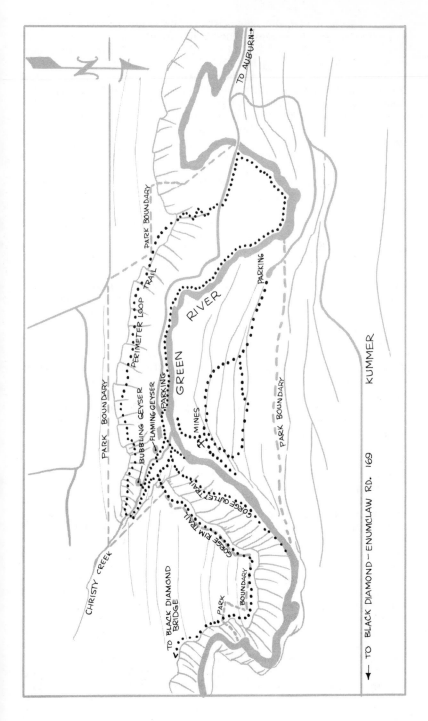

mined hiker can manage the entire distance now — but shouldn't. Aside from the remaining private property, much of the area is honeycombed with old coal-mine air shafts camouflaged by bushes; off-trail travel can be dangerous.

In late summer and early fall, when Tacoma is drinking so much of the Green there is only enough water left in the river to float the fish, much longer hikes can be taken than are described here. Indeed, since the river can then sometimes be easily forded at some points, by getting wet feet (and perhaps knees) a water-level route conceivably could be walked the full 12 miles.

The trips herein are the merest introduction to glories of the Gorge. They are, first off, limited to those possible during the high-water season of (roughly) winter and spring. Second, only described are hikes in the official trail systems or on undeveloped but safe routes open to the public. By no means are all the secrets of the region revealed; any wily fisherman-trespasser would consider this the most meager of primers.

New land acquisitions are being made virtually every biennium. The trail system is constantly being extended. Some descriptions thus will be obsolete in a year or two. But you can get the general idea.

FLAMING GEYSER RECREATION AREA (MAP - PAGE 161)

At the downstream end of the gorge, where the bluffs, though still high and steep, retreat from the river, which thereafter flows over a floodplain ½ mile wide, is the site of an old resort now a state park with a full-fledged (new) trail system.

East of Auburn, just before Highway 18 crosses the Green River, exit onto Auburn-Black Diamond Road and from that almost immediately exit right onto Green Valley Road, signed "Flaming Geyser." Drive 7 miles east to a Y and go right to the bridge over the river to the park. (Or, drive the Black Diamond-Enumclaw Road 1 mile south of Black Diamond to the Boondocks, turn west at the "Flaming Geyser" sign, and drive a scant 3 miles past Kummer to the bridge.) Parking is available at the park gates but the hikes are described here from a start at the far end of the park, 1¼ miles from the gate, elevation 225 feet.

Perimeter Loop, Hillside Trail and Riverbank Trail

Walk upriver from the picnic area parking lot past a series of concrete fish ponds. At the fence corner turn right up Christy Creek. Pass a pool bubbling with gas, the flow from a pipe ignited (sometimes) to form a flame 6-12 inches high. In 1911 a test hole probing coal seams was drilled 1403 feet down. At 900-1000 feet were showings of methane gas. In early days of the former private resort the "Geyser" was flaming many feet in the air; now it's pretty well pooped out.

Continue over a bridge and up the creek in mossy-ferny maple woods, the trail dividing and uniting, passing a bridge and stub trail to the gray mud of Bubbling Geyser. Up a short set of stairs and then again upstream, the main trail recrosses the creek and ascends the bluff and begins a long upsy-downsy contour along the sidehill in a green tangle of maple and cedar and alder and moss lichen and moss. Views (screened) down to the river. Sidepaths offer secluded nooks for lunch or rest or small adventures suitable for small folk. The way at length drops to the floodplain and road, the trail now a mowed strip (or strips) in pasture grass. Cross the road and walk out in the field to the park

Bubbling Geyser, Flaming Geyser State Park

entry bridge. Turn right and follow the riverbank upstream to the picnic area, by sandy beaches, through patches of woods, meeting ducks and water ouzels, gulls and herons, and kayakers landing after voyages down the gorge.

Loop trip 3 miles, allow 2 hours
High point 425 feet, elevation gain 200 feet
All year

Gorge Outlet

Beginning as before, past the fence corner cross Christy Creek to a Y. Go straight on the right fork (the left quickly ends at the river) and then left (the right goes to the rim) up the old road-now-trail, climbing 100 feet above the river, contouring the sidehill, then dropping to a sandy flat in fine woods. The width of the floodplain dwindles to zero, the walls crowd the river, and as the trail enters the very gorge it ends. Admire the 100-foot cliff of stratified rock, the river cutting the base. In low water a hiker can round the corner and proceed into the gorge.

Round trip 1½ miles, allow 1 hour
High point 325 feet, elevation gain 200 feet

CEDAR AND GREEN RIVERS

Gorge Rim

Beginning as before, at the Y just past Christy Creek go straight on the right fork, then immediately right again on a lesser road-trail which ascends to touch the Christy Creek trail and then veers left, climbing to the bluff top at 525 feet.

The inexperienced hiker should turn back here (or not start up at all). Canny navigators can proceed upvalley on woods roads along and near the gorge rim, consulting the map often, guessing right at the myriad junctions, backtracking when the guesses are wrong. This is all second-growth forest, lacking the lushness of the gorge depths, which can, however, be looked down into from a number of vantage points. Moreover, by persistent snooping one can find at least two paths slippery-sliding down into the wild gorge, visiting spots otherwise known only to kayakers.

One short stretch of (presently) private property must be crossed; if it is posted "No Trespassing," hikers must turn back. Otherwise, in 3 easy-walking (if sometimes bewildered) miles the roads connect with the route to the river from the Black Diamond Bridge (which see).

Round trip 6 miles, allow 4 hours (or more for getting lost)
High point 525 feet, elevation gain 500 feet, not counting sidetrips down
to river

Across the River and Into the Trees

Half the park is across the river, where trails are only now being developed from old mining and logging roads. If wild nature is a major attraction of the gorge area, so are memories of a long human past — mysterious ancient water pipes, collapsed buildings, roads dating from different eras, grades of logging railroads, and the like. Including old homesteads reverting to nature, as here.

To reach this part of the park, recross the river on the entry road, turn right, and in a scant ½ mile up the hill toward Kummer turn right off the Green Valley Road onto SE 345 Street. Descend to parking area on the valley floor, elevation 200 feet.

Pass the barn and keep left, crossing the green floodplain at the foot of the bluff. In ¼ mile pass a road-trail up the hillside; this is the exit of the loop trail noted below. At ½ mile are an old orchard and remnants of farm buildings and paths going every which way. Take the one that goes straight ahead and downhill into woods. In a short bit is a Y. The right fork goes ¼ mile through forest to the river; a trail is planned downstream along the bank 1 mile, looping back to the parking area. The left fork goes a similar short way past a sagging structure and interesting coal-mine garbage to the river; a trail is planned upstream to the outlet of the gorge.

For the complete tour (as of early 1977), return to the many-fork junction in the orchard and take the path uphill, bending leftward and sidehilling downvalley, then dropping steeply to the entry road, reached ¼ mile from the parking area.

Complete (1977) tour 4 miles, allow 3 hours
High point 400 feet, elevation gain 200 feet

Green River Gorge below Black Diamond bridge

BLACK DIAMOND BRIDGE (MAP - PAGE 167)

The view of the gorge the best-known to the most people is that from the Black Diamond (or Kummer) Bridge. Though not officially developed, long-used walking routes exist. WARNING: Caving-in mine shafts make this one of the most dangerous areas of the gorge. The route is described here because it is much used. But it shouldn't be at present — wait until the site is officially opened and a safe trail identified.

(Note: South from the bridge is a Department of Natural Resources campground signed "Green River Gorge Camp and Picnic Area." This is a splendid forest with a dandy ¾-mile nature trail but has no connection to the gorge.)

Drive the Black Diamond-Enumclaw Road, Highway 169, south from Black Diamond 2½ miles to the bridge. Cross and start uphill and in ½ mile spot an unmarked woods road to the right. Drive it a long ¼ mile to a Y and park, elevation 557 feet.

Walk the right fork, by a locked gate, ¼ mile to the edge of a vast, growing-over gravel mine. By a concrete foundation, turn right on a grassy road into the woods. Soon pass greenery-swallowed relics of a coal mine at the end of a powerline. After a vista down to the river and upstream to the bridge, descend steeply to the river level and a Y. The left goes downstream a bit to end at a pile of fallen-down timbers of a mine structure. The right proceeds upstream on a lovely alder-cedar flat, becoming a rude fishermen's water-side route. Nearly ½ mile up the river, close to the bridge, is the high-water end of walking; at low water the route can be extended on and on along gravel bars.

Round trip 2 miles, allow 1½ hours
High point 557 feet, elevation gain 300 feet
All year

Driving by, one almost always sees cars parked on the shoulder north of the bridge. This is because a protected sidewalk on the bridge offers thrilling views of the vasty deeps. And also because a path from the bridge dives to the river, where it goes downstream about ½ mile and upstream to the foot of an impressive sandstone cliff. And in low water much farther, of course.

HANGING GARDENS (CEDAR GROVE POINT) (MAP - PAGE 167)

This block of public land extends along nearly 3 miles of the river on the north side, half that on the south. One short south-side walk is suggested to sample this large, presently-undeveloped area.

Drive Highway 169 south from the Black Diamond Bridge 1½ miles and turn east on the Enumclaw-Franklin Road. Curving north, at 2¼ miles, just past a big old borrowpit, note a meager road crossing, the left segment blocked by a deep ditch, a feeble defense against razzers. Park here, elevation 680 feet.

Walk the road into the woods, shortly reaching the chainlink fence of the Black Diamond Watershed. Follow the fence to where it turns right; at a Y there, take the right fork down into lush mixed forest. The road soon yields to a trail plummeting down the bluff, following the crest of a finger ridge around which the river makes a sharp intrenched-meander bend. The point is distinguished by a noble grove of big cedar trees. It also features a sandy beach at the tip directly across from the Hanging Gardens, a vertical wall from which jut ledges sprouting shrubby trees and (in season) gaudy splashes of flowers — a phenomenon not unusual in the gorge but rather especially nice here.

Round trip 1½ miles, allow 1 hour
High point 680 feet, elevation gain 250 feet
All year

GREEN RIVER GORGE RESORT (MAP - PAGE 167)

Adjoining the public Hanging Gardens area is the private Green River Gorge Resort, operated for more than half a century, offering picnicking, car-camping, walk-in camping beside the river, and trails. A fee (as of 1977, $1.00) is charged for entrance to the trails, which are strictly "at your own risk" and no place for little kids to dash around unattended. The fee is modest considering the way the operators are busily extending the old trails, once of no length worth mentioning, upstream and downstream. Here, in the quintessential gorge of close-together sandstone walls, caves and clefts, buttresses

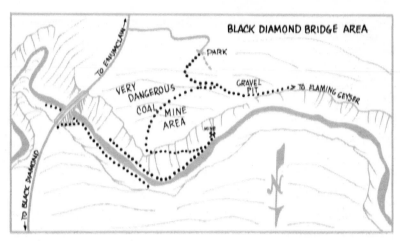

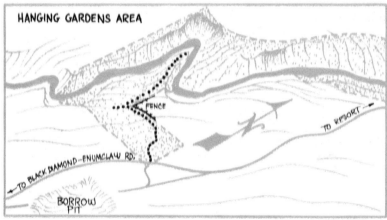

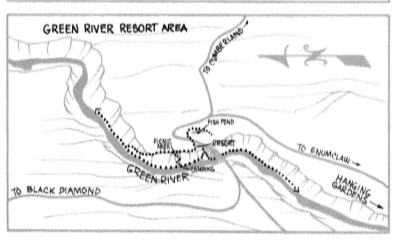

and potholes, green pools and green wall-hangings, is the quintessential gorge trail, under and over waterfalls, close under and spookily over cliffs, into dark, green, dank corners.

From Highway 169 in Black Diamond turn east on the road signed "Green River Gorge" and drive 4 miles to the site of the old town of Franklin and the Franklin Bridge. (Alternatively, from Highway 169 at 1½ miles south of the Black Diamond Bridge take the Enumclaw-Franklin Road 4 miles to the bridge.) Park near the inn, elevation 580 feet.

Built in 1914, the bridge is signed "one legal load limit at a time," which adds interest to walking out for the gasper view down. For a similarly vertiginous perspective, enter the trout-fishing area, find the Upper Campground Trail, and walk it uphill a short bit to a perilous-feeling overlook.

After dropping the trail fee in a box provided at the inn, descend the trail to a Y. To begin with the downstream route, turn left down a staircase-path over the brink of a waterfall to the river. There's too much to see to go fast and that's good; speed kills. Passing through dark clefts between huge mossy-green boulders, over slippery slabs by churning green pools, under fern-and-moss cliffs where in season hikers can get a free shower from a waterfall, the trail presently ends in about ½ mile — but is being extended; in low water no trail is needed to continue.

To go upstream from the Y, turn right, in ¼ mile descending a staircase to walk-in camps on a forest flat by the river. This is a loop trail — but only at low water because at high water a stretch of several hundred feet requires knee-deep wading. At seasons when the trail so enters deep water, turn back to the camp area and take a straight-up path to the gorge rim, reached in a picnic area. From the upstream end of this area find the other end of the loop trail and descend spectacularly on staircases to the river and a T. The left fork goes downstream (the loop way) to a high-water end at a wonderful great cave. The right fork, a delight every step, is being steadily extended upstream.

Complete round-trip all trails (early 1977) 3 miles, allow 4 hours
High point 580 feet, elevation gain 500 feet
All year

JELLUM SITE (BIG BOULDERS AND CINNABAR MINE) (MAP - PAGE 171)

Two undeveloped park areas are called the "Jellum Site." One is a magnificent spot for the special gorge sport of creeping through cracks between huge mossy boulders. The other is notable for relics of the ancient cinnabar (mercury) mine.

From the junction just uphill and east from Green River Gorge Resort, drive east on Green River Gorge Road ½ mile. At the top of a rise spot a woods road left barred by a white gate. Park here, 789 feet.

Walk the road (in private property but on a public easement) over a plateau in nice fir forest to a Y in a scant 1 mile.

For the bouldery place, go right a short bit to the bluff rim, down which the road sidehills to a broad bench, in ½ mile from the Y ending in a fir-grove camp, once the site of some complicated activity (mine-related?). From the bench a trail goes over the brink, instantly splitting in two pieces, left and right, the two ends of a loop demanding to be hiked in its entirety. It is, however, the

Deer track on trail

left fork that leads directly to The Place, featuring one enormous boulder that has atop it 18-inch hemlocks whose roots reach 25 feet down the rock to find nutritious earth. Not so much a trail as a clambering route, the way proceeds downstream, dodging through clefts, passing under a great overhang sheltering a ramshackle cabin, crossing sandy beaches, to a high-water end ½ mile from Camp Flat.

Round trip 4 miles, allow 3 hours
High point 789 feet, elevation gain 200 feet
All year

For the mine, go left at the Y to an old shack on a jutting point, then follow the switchbacking road-trail down to mine garbage and timbers. From here a path drops to the mine mouth (collapsed) and the waste rock sloping to the river. Mine artifacts and cinnabar ore are interesting, and the bouldery river, and the forest, displaying one 8-foot cedar.

Round trip from the Y 1 mile, allow 1 hour

PALMER (GORGE INLET) (MAP - PAGE 171)

Tentatively scheduled for early development, rendering everything said here obsolete, is the large park area downstream from the old coal-mining hamlet of Palmer located just where the Green River exits from the Cascade front and enters the gorge.

From the junction east of Green River Gorge Resort, drive the Green River Gorge Road 2 miles to Cumberland, turn north on the Enumclaw-Cumberland-Kanaskat Road a bit more than 2 miles to just short of the outskirts of Palmer. (If you come to houses you've gone too far.) Note a muddy road left over abandoned railroad tracks into the woods. Just across the paved

Youth-on-age

road is a sign, "MH H 170-88." Whatever that means. Park here, elevation 880 feet. (Towering above this area is Mt. McDonald, which see for an alternate driving approach: where the road to the McDonald hike goes straight ahead, make the sharp right turn to the bridge over the railroad tracks, reaching Kanaskat and the Green River bridge in 1 mile, proceeding on through Palmer 1 mile to the parking place.)

With development impending, lengthy description seems of small value. However, three interim accesses to the river may be suggested.

Walk the mucky road into the woods. Shortly it is joined by a road from the right. Just here note another road, blocked by heaps of dirt and stumps, going right. This road soon hits the bluff rim and drops to a cedar-grove riverside flat. Turn right a short way to a rock point by a big backwater across from the tip of a meander. This is the non-gorge Green River, close by houses of Palmer.

For a second walk, at the junction of the two roads continue to a clearcut a scant ½ mile from the railroad tracks. Here is a Y. The right fork goes to the rim, drops to the bluff-bottom flat, to a Y. The right leads to a maze of ways to the

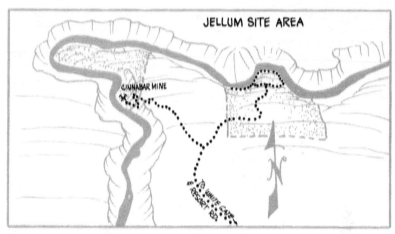

JELLUM SITE AREA

CINNABAR MINE

TO WHITE RIVER & RESORT RD

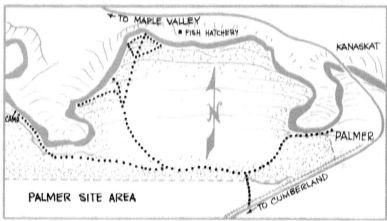

TO MAPLE VALLEY

FISH HATCHERY

KANASKAT

CAMP

PALMER

PALMER SITE AREA

TO CUMBERLAND

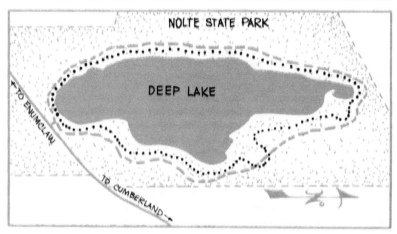

NOLTE STATE PARK

DEEP LAKE

TO ENUMCLAW

TO CUMBERLAND

river in the vicinity of the fish hatchery across the river. The left leads to a meander bend where — on this side anyway — gorge-like walls begin.

For a third walk, at the clearcut Y go left ½ mile to the road-end. A rude foot-only (nice if the razzers have got you mumbling) path plummets to a forest bench, then plummets again to the river. For all the plummeting on this side, on the far side the bluff is still low; not for another ½ mile does true two-sided gorge commence. The trail goes downstream on a bench in super-grand virgin forest — cedars up to 6 feet, firs and hemlocks nearly as broad. In a scant ½ mile terrace and trail end at a lovely camp.

Complete three-walk round trip 5 miles, allow 3 hours
High point 880 feet, elevation gain 600 feet
All year

NOLTE STATE PARK (DEEP LAKE) (MAP - PAGE 171)

Not in the gorge but nearby is 39-acre Deep Lake, owned by the Nolte family since 1883, operated as a private resort since 1913, and on her death in the late 1960s willed to the public by Minnie Nolte. Because during olden-day logging only the cream (the huge cedars) was skimmed, the forest of Douglas firs up to 6 feet in diameter feels virgin, giving a pristine quality to the quiet (no motorboats allowed) waters they ring.

From Cumberland (see the Palmer hike above) drive south 1 mile to the park, elevation 770 feet.

The trail loops 1 mile around the lake, through the big firs, plus 5-foot cedars and 3-foot cottonwoods, crosses the inlet, Deep Creek, passing a number of paths to the shore.

Loop and sidetrips 1½ miles, allow 1 hour
High point 770 feet, no elevation gain
All year

Mount McDonald (Map - page 175)

A supreme vantage for studying the geography of Puget Sound country. From the Cascade front between the Forbidden Valleys of the Cedar and Green Rivers, look across the upland sliced by the Green River Gorge to the Osceola Mudflow and The Mountain from which it gushed 5000 years ago. Look to the peninsula thrust of the Issaquah Alps touching shores of Lake Washington. See Seattle and the Olympics and smoke plumes rising from the pall customarily hiding Tacoma.

Drive Highway 169 south from Maple Valley 3 miles and turn east on SE 272 Street, signed "Ravensdale." In 2 miles is Georgetown, a grocery store, and a junction with the Hobart-Landsburg Road (an alternate access from I-90 via Issaquah). Continue straight east 1 mile to a Y and turn right on a road signed "Kanaskat." Proceed 3 miles, passing Lake Retreat and a Bonneville switching station (with a view of McDonald) to a dangerous Y. The right fork rises to a bridge over railroad tracks. Go left (straight) and in ¾ mile, at a deadend

Waterfall dropping into Green River at Green River Gorge resort   173

driveway signed "SE Courtney," park on the highway shoulder, taking care not to block access to driveway or mailboxes. Elevation, 874 feet.

Walk up Courtney Street through the passel of barking dogs to the railroad tracks. Turn left on a woods road to a gate, rarely open but bypassed by an outlaw track that lets four-wheelers as well as the motorcycles illegally razz.

The road climbs steadily in mixed forest, lesser spurs going off left and right. In ½ mile a window opens to pastures below and out to the Olympics and Rainier. At 1 mile is a waterfall-creek. As the road twists and turns around the mountain, the forest changes to young conifers, mostly hemlocks, and views commence over treetops and through them. At 3 miles, 2828 feet, is a Y where both forks are major. Go right, climbing. The views on this trip are cafeteria-like — something of this here, a bit of that there, never everything all at once. In this stretch are the best views north, down to the Cedar River and out to Taylor and Tiger and Squak and Cougar, as well as to Rattlesnake and Si, Baker and Index and Three Fingers.

In a final 1 mile, with a couple more switchbacks, the road reaches an open plateau atop McDonald Point, elevation 3280 feet. Here, formerly the site of a fire lookout, is a great monster of a TV repeater powered by a noisy diesel generator. Avoid the fumes and enjoy the grand view off the edge of the scarp. Then, for a variation, follow a sketchy road ¼ mile through small silver firs and western hemlocks to a 3301-foot point. See huge Rainier and distant St. Helens and nearby Grass. See the Enumclaw plain and silvery meanders of the Green River and hear the trains blow, boys, hear the trains blow.

Round trip 8 miles, allow 7 hours
High point 3301 feet, elevation gain 2400 feet
February-December

From Junction 2828, the left (straight ahead) fork goes on and on. The 3570-foot summit of McDonald ought to be accessible with some 6 more round-trip miles.

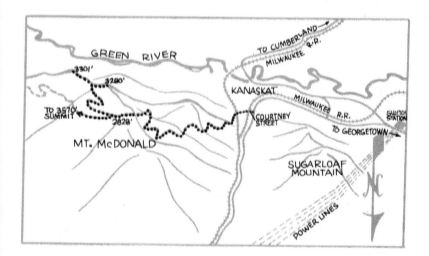

Mount Rainier from McDonald Point

Looking down the Clearwater valley from below Noble Naked Knob

WHITE RIVER

Something scary here. Arriving on the lower White utterly ignorant of the region, a perceptive visitor quickly — and nervously — would note the difference between this river and those to the north. The black sands, the black and red boulders. That's lava rock. There's a volcano upstream. And the murky water, the wide gravel bed with an interweaving of channels old and new. That's rock milk and channel-braiding. There's a glacier upstream. A dangerous combination, a glacier and a volcano.

Indeed. Tell it to the Indians who were peacefully going about their business 5000 years ago when the steam bomb exploded 30 miles away on The Mountain, melting thousands of tons of snow and ice, sending down the valley to Puget Sound a roaring slurry of muck, perhaps 2.5 billion cubic yards of it. The Osceola Mudflow. Leaving in the lowlands a deposit up to 70 feet thick. A once-in-a-dozen-eons rarity? No. Rainier has spewed countless such "lahars;" just 600 years ago the Electron Mudflow rumbled down the Puyallup to saltwater. Come the next big show and real estate in Enumclaw, Buckley, Kent, Auburn, Sumner, and Puyallup — all of whose sites were buried by the Osceola — won't be worth a nickel.

If man has performed no single so dramatic a stunt of river manipulation, he's puttered for decades, tinkering this way and that with the White. Long ago the farmers, weary of the river's habit periodically swapping outlets, sometimes flowing north in the Big Valley to join the Green and empty into Seattle's Elliott Bay, sometimes south in the Big Valley to the Puyallup and Tacoma's Commencement Bay, called in the engineers to build dikes to fix it in a southward course. At the point of diversion, where it exits from the narrower (true) White Valley into the Big Valley, the river changes name, golly knows why, to the Stuck.

After a disastrous flood of the 1930s wreaked havoc in the Big Valley and demonstrated the shortcomings of Commencement Bay for industrial development, the Mud Mountain Dam was built above Enumclaw; the river is no longer permitted to flood and on occasion is reservoirized upstream from the dam, whose fate in the next Osceola is a subject of amused speculation by neo-Luddites.

Last, Puget Power devised a scheme to put the White to work, at Buckley diverting water through a flume to a reservoir, Lake Tapps, thence into turbines at Deiringer and a return to the White (Stuck) in the Big Valley. As a consequence, when everybody is cooking supper and taking a shower and watching TV and making aluminum all at once the White-Stuck between Buckley and Deiringer dwindles to the minimum legally required for the comfort and convenience of fish.

The White thus is a tame and useful river — until the next Osceola. But it doesn't feel tame. None of these tinkerings diminish its excitement for the hiker. Especially the one who keeps an ear cocked, alert for dull distant booms up that-a-way.

The lowest segment of the province, the Stuck River in the Big Valley, was but cursorily surveyed for this book. Miles and miles of gravel-mining and boxes in a row were disheartening. Yet the dikes, open all winter, close to the city, are popular with locals and ought not to be ignored.

The detailed survey began at Pacific, on the edge of the Big Valley at the mouth of the White Valley — and discovered a wonder. Here at virtual sealevel, hikable all year, on Metro buslines in southern neighborhoods of Puget Sound City, is wildness. For 15-odd miles upstream the plain above the river canyon is thoroughly civilized; down in the canyon, on alluvial terraces and gravel bars beneath steep bluffs, are river and woods and solitude, a finger of wilderness thrusting far out from The Mountain to the city.

Where the White debouches from the mountain front to its canyon sliced in the Osceola plain there ought to be established a Cascade Gateway Recreation Area, centered at Enumclaw, to serve the masses of Puget Sound City living an hour and less away. (Other such Cascade Gateway Recreation Areas, centered at North Bend and Mount Index, are suggested in FOOT-SORE 2.) As the northernmost of Rainier's great rivers the White is the shortest route for the most people to the national park. But many a hiker would be pleased not to contribute to the overcrowding and boot-battering of the park, would be happy to take exercise much nearer home, at elevations from under 1000 feet, open all year, to high views at 3000 feet, open (with some snowline-probing) nearly all year. Buses currently do not usefully serve trailheads but development of the Recreation Area could correct that.

Though partly on state lands and partly on those of the U.S. Army Corps of Engineers, and farther up the valley in national forest, a major portion of the Recreation Area would be on the White River Tree Farm of Weyerhaeuser Company. On the north side of the valley is a continuous ridge which as it moves east is successively called Boise Ridge, Grass Mountain, Huckleberry Mountain, and Dalles Ridge. On the south side are outer buttresses of Rainier and the tributary valleys of the Clearwater, West Fork White, and Huckleberry Creek. In this intensively-farmed country, plantations ranging in date from the 1930s to a few minutes ago, the clearcutting proceeding now to elevations above 4000 feet, are hundreds of miles of superb, little-driven footroads. Down low, hikable except in dead of winter, are green tunnels in tall second-growth forests. Higher are excellent snowline-probers in younger trees. Highest are top-of-the-world freshly-scalped ridges with views from here to forever, always dominated by the immense white heap.

Farther up the valley, deeper in the mountain icebox and thus with a shorter season, are virgin forests. Prefaced at the mountain front on Corps of Engineers land above Mud Mountain Dam, in Federation Forest State Park and the Greenwater River are truly religious experiences for fans of the hamadryads.

Finally, though the book was not meant to go that far (the drive from many parts of Puget Sound City being closer to 2 hours than 1), and bus service is lacking (that'll change), and elevations are getting high (2400 feet minimum), it was found impossible to chop off the survey short of Camp Sheppard, hub of a stupendous Scout-constructed trail system. Only the lowest paths are sampled here; the highest lead to the Cascade Crest Trail and the Wonderland Trail. A great way to conclude a book.

USGS maps: Lake Tapps, Auburn, Sumner, Buckley, Enumclaw, Cumberland, Greenwater, Lester

For a free copy of a map of the company's road system on the White River Tree Farm, write Weyerhaeuser Company, Box W, Snoqualmie, WA 98065.

White-Stuck River (Map - page 181)

Here, where the White River begins to be called by some (not all) the Stuck, it also changes in other ways, emerging from the comparatively narrow valley appropriate to a mountain river onto broad flats of the Big Valley, flowing from its wild-seeming braided channels into a bed channelized by dikes and extensively mined for gravel.

White River

Two walks can be made through this White-Stuck transition zone. On the south side of the river is a much-driven gravel dike-road, garbage-scabby but easy; some measure of peace can be obtained by (1) choosing a quiet winter weekday morning, and/or (2) as much as possible, leaving the dike to walk on gravel bars at water's edge. On the north side of the river is the Sunday walk, cleaner, machine noise from the far side masked by river babbling, and past the first stretch perfectly wheelfree, but before long more a scramble than a walk.

From Auburn drive south on Auburn Way towards Buckley. Exit onto R Street and continue about 1 mile to the bridge over the Stuck-White. For the south-side hike, turn right just beyond the bridge on Stuck River Drive (gravel) and park, elevation 100 feet.

Walk the dike-road along the river, by riprap of columnar basalt, or drop to the black-sand and volcanic-rock bars. This is above the limit of gravel mining and the stream takes on the normal appearance of a glacial river at low water. (Most of the river most of the time is diverted through Lake Tapps for power production by Puget Power; in 1976, one sunny day when the river was abruptly "turned on" without notice, two children were drowned; watch out for unannounced "walls of water.") Soon the Big Valley is left, portal bluffs passed, the true White Valley entered. Ducks swim, fish jump, kingfishers dive. How far to go? The dike-road was surveyed 3 miles on a weekday afternoon and found good. Then school let out and the motorcycles arrived.

For the north-side hike don't cross the R Street bridge; just before it, turn right on 37 Way SE and in ¼ mile park by the river on the dead-end stub of 36 Street SE.

Walk the cable-barred dike-road upstream, passing the state game farm. Try to figure out where the White used to turn north up the Big Valley to join the Green River. In ¼ mile reach the bluff and enter the true White Valley. In another ¼ mile the dike ends and so do the wheels and the fun begins. From here upstream the way is strictly for pedestrians — on river bars, along the toe of the wildwood bluff, and where it is vertical cliffs of clay, gravel, and till, perhaps up to the knees in the river. Some problems may not be soluble by conservative hikers — or in high water by any sane hikers. How far to go? The way was surveyed a dozen miles upstream (see White River Bottom) — some of it doubtless too strenuous for most tastes. About 1-2 miles probably are sufficient entertainment for a Sunday afternoon.

Round trip 2-6 miles, allow 1-4 hours
High point 200 feet, elevation gain 100 feet
All year
Bus: Metro 150 south from Auburn on R Street to 29 Street, walk 8 blocks to the bridge

White River Bottom (Map - page 181)

One would never guess, driving through farms of the Osceola Mudflow plain, that a stone's throw distant, down the 125-250-foot bluffs at the edge of the plain is a river bottom where the human presence is virtually unfelt. Old and very old woods roads wander this way and that, and fishermen's paths seek riverbanks, and gypos cut alder and river-rafted cedar logs, and here and there are small pastures and glimpses of houses on the brink of the bluff. But most of the time, down there in the broad bottom up to 1 mile wide, amid braided, shifting channels, marshy sloughs, tanglewoods, and beaver ponds, one could imagine the year to be 1850 — or 1650.

The major problem is getting down to the river through the belt of residential land along the rim of the bluff. One access, open as of 1977, is from Highway 164, the Auburn-Enumclaw Road. On it, at a junction 4 miles west of Enumclaw, turn south on 196 Avenue SE to the bluff edge, where the road bends east and is signed SE 456 Way. In a scant 2 miles from Highway 164 spot a heap of garbage and two creosoted poles once supporting a cable blocking a narrow, mucky road. Don't park exactly here (elevation 640 feet); disguise your intention by parking on a shoulder a long ways off; as soon as cars start ganging up the "No Trespassing" sign will follow and some other tolerated access to the river will have to be sought.

Follow the road down the bluff. At the bottom is a Y; the left fork, upstream, was not surveyed for this book. The right fork proceeds downstream, goes out to the river, yielding there to trail and leaving the wheels behind.

The route beyond here cannot be described usefully; the maze of paths would only be made the more confusing and the river keeps changing all the time so that gravel bars are now dry, now underwater. However, even an

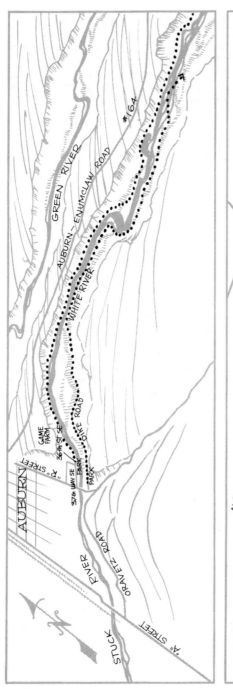

181

inexperienced hiker can find machine-free solitude by carefully picking a way on woods roads, paths, and gravel, now near the bluff, now near the river, now far from both. A fine encounter with the river comes in 1 long mile from the start. In another 4 or so miles (not streamflow or crowfly but footplod) the river cuts the base of a gravel-clay bluff, possible to skirt at low water but one of many logical turnabouts for a hike. The survey continued downstream to the White-Stuck River (which see) but though constantly rewarding encountered problems with brush and barbed wire.

Round trip 2-10 miles, allow 2-8 hours
High point 640 feet, elevation gain 400 feet
All year

Mount Pete (Map - page 182)

What accounts for the "Enumclaw Blobs," the miniature mountains pimpling the pastured plain? Hearts of hard basalt explain their steepness; the Osceola Mudflow provided the surrounding flatness. What accounts for the survival on the biggest of the blobs, Mount Pete (more officially known as Pinnacle Peak), of a grand stand of virgin forest? Who knows? The hiker must be amazed to find this noble bit of wildland arboretum so near the farms and so near a great huge lumber mill. Will it survive? Well, if not, the view will be improved.

Drive Highway 410 to the eastern outskirts of Enumclaw and at the Enumclaw Park swimming pool turn south on 284 Avenue SE. Follow it 1½ miles and turn west (right) on SE 472. In ½ mile, at a sharp bend right, park on the shoulder by the obvious trailhead, elevation 770 feet.

The often-slippery trail is very steep but wide and well-beaten; motorcycle infestation, however, is minor. Beginning in lush undergrowth of a moist,

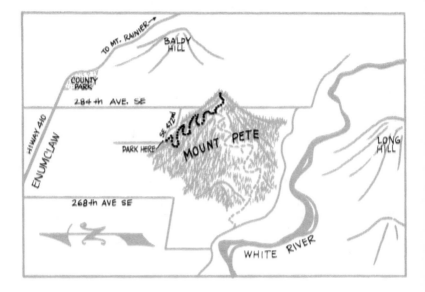

Columnar basalt near top of Mount Pete

mixed, second-growth forest with at least four varieties of ferns and lots of frogs, the way quickly ascends to startling big Douglas firs, up to 4 feet thick, plus a full assortment of other good green things suitable for a virgin forest. In ¾ mile the path joins the old road built to serve the lookout tower, removed in the mid-1960s. Little-driven even by sports and now narrowing to a trail, in ¼ mile the road, passing the finest of many displays of columnar basalt, curves around to an end close under the summit, 1801 feet.

With the tower gone and the trees a-growing, the panorama ain't the 360-degree circle of yore but is a still splendid 200 degrees. Only small windows offer looks at beautiful downtown Enumclaw and other points west but on the east side are vistas that, pieced together, extend from the Issaquah Alps to McDonald, Boise Ridge, Grass — and Rainier, with the Clearwater River valley and Three Sisters prominent. And a voyeur's view down to cows and chickens at the foot of the peak. In mind's eye one can see the Osceola Mudflow surging down the broad White River valley, dividing to sweep around both sides of Baldy and Pete and perhaps overwhelming camps of innocent Indians. (Is the racial memory responsible for the name, "Enumclaw," which means "place of the evil spirits"?)

Round trip 2 miles, allow 3 hours
High point 1801 feet, elevation gain 1030 feet
All year

Second Lake (Map - page 184)

A pleasant stroll along an abandoned "motor nature trail" on a hillock above the Weyerhaeuser Upper Mill, then through fields and forests to a quiet little lake in a secluded forest nook.

Drive Highway 410 east from Enumclaw County Park 1 long mile and turn left at the sign, "Weyerhaeuser White River Timberlands." In several hundred feet, where the main mill entrance is straight ahead, switchback left on a gravel road signed "Shipping Department, Truck Loading." Proceed straight, passing sideroads right, to a gate and beyond a short bit to a small gravel pit ½ mile from the highway. Park here, elevation 1120 feet.

Walk the narrow motor nature trail, switchbacking sharp right from the gravel pit and winding up the knoll, passing signs identifying tree species, to the 1280-foot summit, and descending to a T. The right leads to the mill; go left in fields, by a marsh, to woods, and shortly to Second Lake. Paths drop to the peat shore, the lilypads and skunk cabbage, of the small lake set in an outlet-lacking bowl at 1100 feet, ringed by low forested ridges.

Some ¾ mile north of Second Lake is Third Lake, actually a marsh.

The road proceeding straight ahead from the gravel pit is narrow and mucky, a fine footroad. It goes down and up, past a nameless inhabited lake and uninhabited marshes, some 2 miles to Newaukum Creek. Good walking when the sport drivers aren't around.

Round trip to Second Lake 3 miles, allow 2 hours
High point 1280 feet, elevation gain 400 feet
All year

Boise Ridge (Map - page 187)

Atop the abrupt scarp of Boise Ridge are airplane-wing looks down to Enumclaw and farms around, with naught but the murk from Tacoma to block views over the plain to Puget Sound and the Olympics.

Drive to Cumberland by any of several routes. One simple way is to drive Highway 169 to 4 miles south of Black Diamond and turn east on the Enumclaw-Franklin Road, following it under various names to Cumberland,

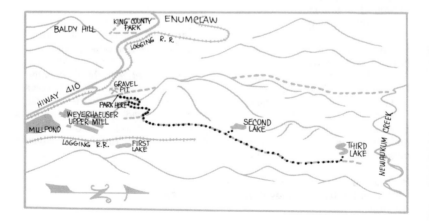

View from Boise Ridge

there intersecting the Enumclaw-Cumberland-Kanaskat Road. On the latter road at the north edge of Cumberland turn east on SE Kuzak Road. Twisting and turning through the fascinating glacier-complicated drainages of Deep and Coal Creeks, the road goes 2¼ miles to a T with the big wide Green River Mainline. Turn right on this major log-haul road (to the Weyerhaeuser mill) and proceed south 5 miles to road 5307. Turn left and drive ¼ mile to a gate and park. Do not drive on — weekends the gate is closed so you can't and weekdays log trucks are barreling out in a steady stream. Elevation, 1550 feet.

With the leisurely elevation-gaining rate of the 1902 logging railroad whose grade it follows, the broad road runs south through a young plantation, passing a sideroad left, into second-growth on the steep scarp, marked with basalt walls. Views to Enumclaw and the Weyerhaeuser mill at about 1 mile are left behind as the road swings around the south end of Boise Ridge into the valley of Boise Creek. At 1850 feet, 1½ miles, is a decision. The main road straight ahead is the long but self-evident way to the summit. The sideroad left, 5307-2, is much shorter but not recommended for inexperienced wilderness navigators. Both are splendid walks.

The long way: Continue sidehilling up Boise Creek, crossing two tributaries and passing sideroads down to the valley bottom, emerging into the vast clearcut that is being extended to encompass the whole of Boise Ridge and, across the valley, Grass Mountain's West Peak. In wide views of naked hills and of Rainier out the valley, the way climbs steeply beyond the end of the old railroad, attaining the ridge crest at 2950 feet, 3 miles from Decision Junction.

Look down to basalt-hearted hillocks dotting the green plain of the Osceola Mudflow, to houses and barns, cars and cows, and into the dimness where lies Tacoma, the Invisible City.

The 3080-foot summit of Boise Ridge, ½ mile south, was still forested and viewless in early 1977 but that will change and the hike should then proceed onward. Which it can now, if it's trees you like. A new logging road continues south, contouring at 2950 feet to a dead-end on the scarp edge ¼ mile past the summit. Here, if a loop trip is desired, can be found the trail of the short way.

The short way: Ascend road 5307-2 to a creek crossing at 2200 feet, ½ mile. Now, look sharp. At the next bend some 500 feet up the road (and about the same short of its 1977 end) watch on the cutbank left for a stump with a rusty cable wrapped around. By it, follow a meager cat road up the bank and the short bit to the forest edge. Spot a 12-inch fir with two large weathered blazes. Step into the woods (trust me) and soon discern unmistakable tread of an old old trail, unmaintained and virtually unused but quite good and still easy for an experienced pathfinder to follow. The trail goes straight up the fall-line of the slope on a 1902 log skidway. Attaining a subsidiary ridge at about 2600 feet, it goes near the crest, entering virgin forest, contouring to a saddle in the main ridge at 2870 feet. Here the route turns right, following blazes made in 1977 along the scarp edge to a natural (not made by logging) viewpoint at 2930 feet. A litter of shakes and rotting logs remains of a Boy Scout shelter, 1½ miles from Decision Junction. A few yards beyond is the dead-end road mentioned above, with the summit ¼ mile away.

As logging proceeds this trail will be progressively snipped off bit by bit but any remainder will be found by proceeding directly uphill from road 5307-2. The roads that replace the trail will continue to be the short way to the summit.

Long round trip 9 miles, allow 6 hours
Short round trip 6 miles, allow 4 hours
High point (both) 2950, elevation gain 1400 feet
April-November

Grass Mountain — West Peak (Map - page 187)

Little lower than the Main Peak (which see), the West Peak of Grass Mountain is far enough removed to be a whole different thing. It shares Rainier, of course, the monster heap of snow across the White River valley. With this it combines a broad panorama of the Puget Sound lowlands which commence just a couple miles away beyond the abrupt Cascade scarp.

Drive to Cumberland and the Green River Mainline (see Boise Ridge). Turn right on the Mainline a short bit to cross Coal Creek. Just beyond, turn left on road 5400, the gate usually open. Steeply ascend the good but narrow road above South Fork Coal Creek, switchbacking, avoiding lesser sideroads.

The question is, where to stop driving and start walking? The sports (fortunately in small numbers) go clear to the summit, but they of course get neither healthful exercise nor the full flavor of the scenery and beer. Two versions of the trip are suggested, one long, one short. For the long of it, park in a ridgecrest saddle at 2550 feet, 3 miles from the Mainline.

The route is partly in fresh clearcuts, partly in plantations of various dates back to the 1960s, and partly (less all the time) in cool virgin forest with nice creeks. A short way from the saddle is a Y; go right, uphill, in a clearcut with

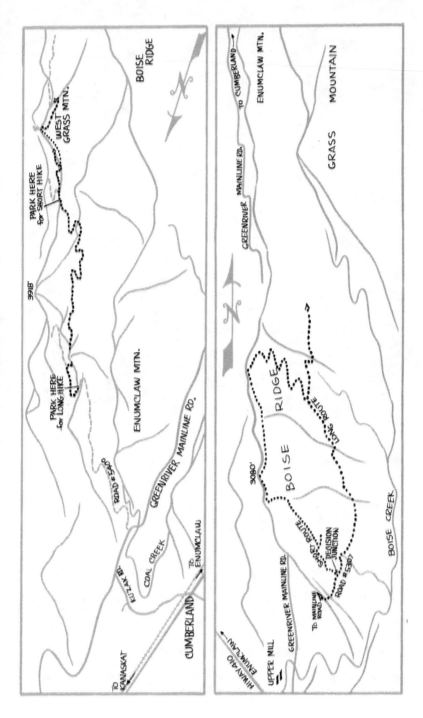

White River Trail

views across the East Fork Coal Creek to the northernmost peak of Grass, 3521 feet. At a 2800-foot saddle the road crosses over to the South Fork Coal Creek side of the mountain and traverses slopes of Peak 3921, whose scalping is only just well-started (when complete it also will be a good view-point destination). As lesser roads go left and right stay straight.

At 3200 feet, just past a big view west to Enumclaw Mountain and Boise Ridge and out to Enumclaw, a shoulder of a divide spur is crossed from Coal Creek to Boise Creek drainage. Passing more sideroads, the main road now descends moderately to a long wide saddle in the main crest of Grass, bottoming at 3050 feet, 3½ miles from Saddle 2550. Charley Creek is below to the left, Boise Creek to the right, and straight ahead rises the West Peak in all its naked glory topped by an enormous thingamajig. For the short hike, park here.

Go directly across the saddle, avoiding sideroads left and right, to the foot of Grass and a Y; go right. In a few yards a sideroad switchbacks right; go straight. Dodging deadend spurs, switchback to a 3550-foot saddle in a spur ridge, the view now extending to the Main Peak.

From this saddle the service road to the summit thingamajig takes a round-about route. Instead turn right up lesser roads and cat tracks that ascend the crest to the summit, a tad under 4000 feet, at 1½ miles from Saddle 3050.

Goggle at the Enormous Thingamajig; it appears to be the Bell System relay to Mars. Then look down Scatter Creek to the White River and across to the White-Clearwater-Prairie-Carbon sector of Rainier. And, of course, The Mountain. Look along the bald ridge to the Main Peak of Grass and north down Charley Creek to the Green River and out to McDonald Mountain and Cascades as distant as Baker. And look west past Boise Ridge to Enumclaw and farms and cities and smog and saltwater and Olympics.

Round trip 3 or 10 miles, allow 3 or 7 hours
High point 4000 feet, elevation gain 1000 or 1900 feet
May-November

White River Trail (Map - page 191)

The finest long low-elevation forest walk so near Puget Sound City? The new White River Trail above Mud Mountain Dam surely is a candidate for the title. Thanks to a 1976 project by the U.S. Army Corps of Engineers, the 5½ miles of valley upstream from the dam to the Clearwater River no longer are just a sometime (in flood-control season only) reservoir but a veritable park, the trail (for feet only, no wheels allowed) wandering along the canyon rim through green-lit depths of old forest, bits of which appear virgin.

Drive Highway 410 east from Enumclaw to the sign announcing Mud Mountain Dam and turn right on the entry road 2 miles to the family recreation area and parking lot, elevation 1300 feet.

Before or after the main hike, visit the Upper Vista and take the ⅓-mile trail down through big firs to the Lower Vista for looks at the dam, begun in 1939, completed in 1947, rising 425 feet above bedrock, one of the world's highest earth-core-and-rockfill dams. Built to control floods, the dam has a reservoir that, when filled, is a lake 5½ miles long and covering 1200 acres. But the upper portions of the reservoir area are normally not filled and most of most years there is no reservoir at all; except for a stretch above the dam the White River usually appears wild and free.

Beside the parking lot find the trail, starting from the "Dog Exercise Area" and signed "Scatter Creek Trail Under Construction." The way begins by paralleling the entry road on an old unused road which intersects a gated service road dropping to the river at 950 feet. A few feet past the gate on the river side the trail takes off left into the woods.

Note: As of 1977 this is not a finished trail. The Corps is developing a hiking network as funds and manpower are available. The tread has been roughed out nearly to Scatter Creek but at a number of points the trail joins (temporarily) a mucky old woods road. And the elk that have enthusiastically adopted the Corps trail as their own have unhelpfully supplied all sorts of sidetrails to destinations sought by elk but not necessarily man. Therefore, since no markers now exist, pay attention to where you come from so that on the return you can get back there. And please don't gripe about the sometimes poor tread. Instead, bless the Corps folk for supplying any tread at all. When they have the money, they'll make it smoother. But hardly can make it better — it's perfectly magnificent now.

Generally staying on the high alluvial terrace near the rim, the trail swings out on promontories for views down the gravel cliff to the braided White River, swings into green bays of lush ravines. There are forests of mixed alder-maple, and forests of big tall fir and hemlock and cedar and spruce. A second gated service road, leading down to a debris-burning site by the river, offers a second easy access to streamside gravel bars. For a way the trail is close to Weyerhaeuser's private log-haul road. But most of the time a hiker feels so far from machines he halfway expects to meet a wagon train descending from Naches Pass.

At about 4 miles the trail presently ends high on the steep slope above Scatter Creek. But elk trails can be followed down to a spot beside the creek, and near the river, that is so remote from sight or sounds of roads, and so thoroughly impossible for motorcycles to reach, that walking the bars of black volcanic sand one might well imagine the year to be 1776 — or 1066.

The Corps plans to let Scatter Creek be the trail end, leaving the upper couple miles of the reservoir "park" for independent wandering-around explo-rations on the wide gravel bottom, in the alder-willow forests, and for backpac-kers' campsites.

Ultimately the Corps plans another trail on the other side of the river, with access via the dam. Check the bulletin board at the parking lot; there may be more trail when you arrive than is described here.

Round trip to Scatter Creek 8 miles, allow 5 hours
High point 1360 feet, elevation gain 400 feet
All year

Mount Philip (Map - page 193)

A little trail but not to be belittled, ideal as it is for short walks and short-legged walkers. A sizeable reward for a small effort: a rock garden on a surprising cliff, views down to braided channels of the White River (at the upper end of the Army Engineers' White River "Park"), the tributary valley of the Clearwater, and footings of Rainier — though The Mountain itself is hidden.

Drive Highway 410 east 3 miles from the turnoff to Mud Mountain Dam. On the right (perhaps marked by a picnic table) spot a narrow road leaving the highway and paralleling it a few feet distant. In ½ mile is room to park a couple cars; if a couple are already there, continue several hundred feet to a rejoining of the highway and park on the shoulder. At the parking place is (maybe) a sign, "Hiking Trail to Vista Point ½ Mile Weyerhaeuser Company." Elevation, 1400 feet.

Passing big old stumps in an alder bottom, in a short bit the path reaches a Y; go right, as suggested by a post with an arrow. The trail switchbacks up through choked second-growth dating from the logging in 1931, breaking out in the open atop the cliff, a dandy spot for a picnic.

The company forester who built the trail for public pleasure named this little peak for John Philip Weyerhaeuser, former president of the firm.

Round trip 1 mile, allow 1 hour
High point 1700 feet, elevation gain 300 feet
February-December

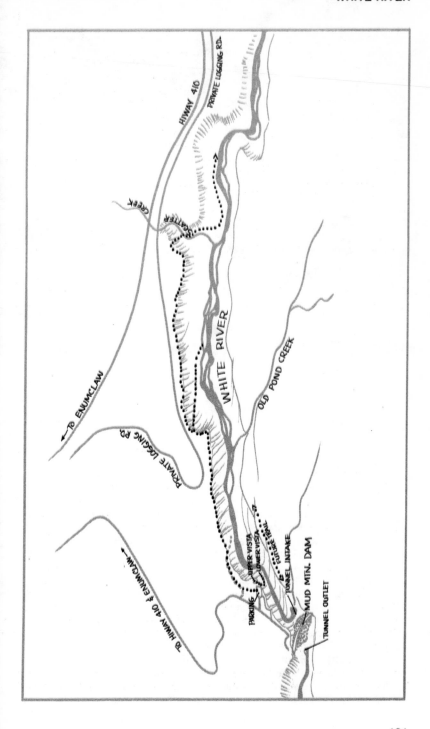

White River from Mount Philip

Stink Lake (Map - page 193)

A moody walk, much of the way claustrophobic in dense young forest; the views out, when they come, jar the hiker's reverie, which judging from the low beer-can count would ordinarily not be disturbed by razzers. Do it as a loop, saving the best for last.

Drive Highway 410 east 3½ miles from the turnoff to Mud Mountain Dam. On the left (north) side of the highway spot a woods road making a reverse turn downvalley. Park here, elevation 1450 feet.

Walk the woods road, narrow but solid-bottomed and thus occasionally driven by alder-loggers, gradually veering from the highway, passing an old railroad trestle whose stringers serve as out-in-the-middle-of-the-air nurse-logs for hemlocks. In ½ mile hit a more-used road from the west; turn right (east) on it, ascending upvalley. Pass obviously lesser spurs and in another 1¼ miles, after a switchback left, come to a Y; turn right on the little-used less-good road which drops to a mudhole, then ascends to cross a leftward-flowing headwater branch of Scatter Creek. The way is now up, in ¼ mile hitting another poor road; turn right. A bit later, at a Y, again go right, soon crossing a rightward-flowing creek and now, on the flat, following an old railroad grade northeasterly. In 1 mile from the Y, 3 miles from the highway, the "goal" is attained. Sort of. The road passes first a marshy pond littered with debris of beaver logging and then a window out to debris of human logging. By poking around in the woods one can get near — but not to — shores of the "lake," really a collection of marshy potholes in a little basin, 2300 feet. The

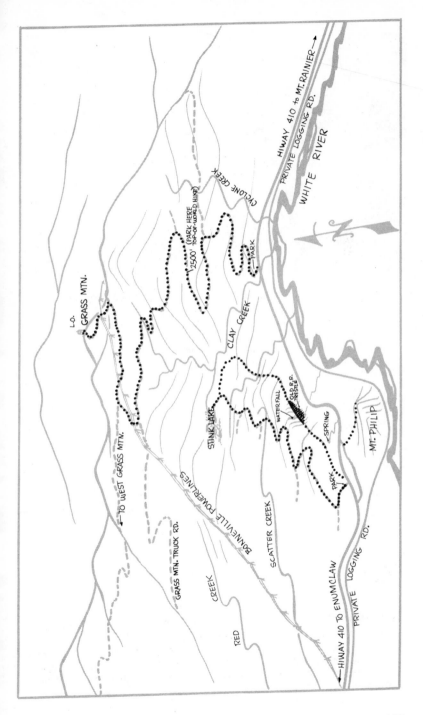

Looking up the Clearwater valley from below Noble Naked Knob

stink apparently is from gasses of decomposing vegetation — nostrils occasionally catch a whiff of rotten eggs.

Now for the fun return. Back at the beaver pond spot a boot-beaten path downhill, marked with red ribbons and paper arrows stapled to trees. The way descends near the Stink Lake headwater of Clay Creek, then trends away from it, drops off a scarp into the creek valley, sidehills on an old roadbed, and at ¾ mile from the beaver pond hits a logging-railroad grade abandoned in 1950 — one of the last such lines to operate in the state. Turning right (west) on the grade, the trail passes close by a Second Wave clearcut of the early 1970s; go out on it for clear views of big white Rainier and the White River valley. The grade-trail passes under an imposing vertical lava cliff, then a waterfall showering off an overhang and then (the best part for history buffs) a nearly-intact and splendid trestle bypassing the wall. Gradually the trail turns into an old road, mainly used by gypos during midnight logging but also by visitors to famed Goodwater Spring, reputed by locals to have the best flavor in the country. The path returns to the highway a few yards from the parking place.

Loop trip 6 miles, allow 4 hours
High point 2300 feet, elevation gain 850 feet
March-November

Clearwater Vista: Jensen Point (Map - page 195)

A long walk through a green tunnel of second-growth forest on a narrow, little-used road, in its lower reaches mostly an old railroad grade. Creeks enliven the route, and remnants of old trestles, and elk tracks, and gaudy volcanic rocks, and windows out to Enumclaw farms this way and Rainier glaciers that way. At the end, two (not one) smashing views.

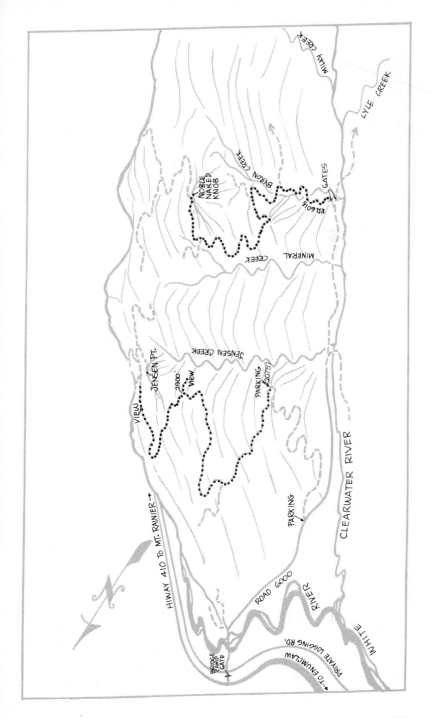

Drive Highway 410 past the Mud Mountain Dam turnoff 5¾ miles and turn right on a White River Tree Farm logging road signed "Bridge Camp Gate." (And also "Stop — Do Not Enter", but that's to alert you to the menace of logging trucks; the gate is usually open.) Descend to cross the White River. At the junction on the wide flat beyond, turn right, downvalley, on great big high-speed road 6000. At a scant 2 miles from the highway spot on the left a narrow woods road, elevation 1380 feet.

Whatever it is that turns on sport-drivers is lacking and thus this is a splendid footroad, uncommonly wheel-molested. Yet if begun here the walk is purely for long-leggitty beasties seeking a good stretch. The less-energetic would do best to take the next hike described in these pages. Alternatively, if they have a VW Beetle-size vehicle (anything larger feels crowded) and are willing to risk the disaster of encountering another car (turnouts are zero in number), they may drive the first 2¾ miles to the Big Switchback (turning around possible, parking very limited) at 2075 feet.

From the Switchback is a peek down to the Clearwater and up to Rainier. Windows become more frequent, with bitty views out to the Enumclaw plain and the Olympics, to Pete and Philip and Grass. At 1½ miles from the Big Switchback is a Y; go right. In 2 miles more is a T with a newer road, 2900 feet. Here, some 6¼ miles from road 6000, 3½ from Big Switchback, is a choice. If pooping out, turn right ⅓ mile to a recent clearcut with worthy views. For the full treatment turn left and proceed ¾ mile to the first Smashing View, from a leveled-off stretch of the ridgecrest at 3100 feet, down to the White River and across to the full length of Grass Mountain with its awesome clearcuts and brown-slash road network. Second-growth mostly screens the view from the other side of the crest so continue 1 mile to a 1975 clearcut and down the second of two sideroads ¼ mile to the jutting prow of 3200-foot Jensen Point and the second Smashing View.

Look across Jensen Creek and Mineral Creek to enormous brown clearcuts surrounding Noble Naked Knob and beyond to still-green headwaters of the Clearwater, least-known of Rainier's rivers because it doesn't quite start from The Mountain proper. Look past Hurricane Gap and Bearhead to the big ice cream cone, every detail close and clear from Curtis Ridge to Willis Wall to Liberty Ridge to Ptarmigan Ridge to the Mowich Face. Also see, across the Clearwater, 4960-foot Three Sisters, whose ascent is described in **Footsore 2.**

Round trip (from road 6000) 16 miles, allow 10 hours
High point 3300 feet, elevation gain 1900 feet
May-November

Clearwater Vista: Noble Naked Knob (Map - page 195)

In striking contrast to the long gradual ascent on old railroad grade through a green tunnel to Jensen Point, this is a short steep climb on modern truck roads through recent clearcuts to Noble Naked Knob, a scalped knoll on a point of a ridge thrust far out into valley air, commanding a view up and down the Clearwater. Look there and see cow-grazed pastures of the Enumclaw plain. Look there and, if The Mountain is in the mood, watch silent avalanches slide in slow-motion down Willis Wall.

Byron Creek

Drive road 6000 (see Jensen Point) up the narrowing Clearwater valley, crossing Jensen and Mineral Creeks. At 5½ miles from the highway is a Y, both forks gated. Whether or not the gate is open, park here, elevation 1520.

Take the left fork, road 6015, entering Byron Creek valley and steeply climbing beside the tumbling waters, passing from tall second-growth of the 1940s-50s to still-shrublike plantations of the 1960s. In ¾ mile cross Byron Creek to a Y at 2050 feet. Go left, recrossing the creek (and vowing to linger here on the descent, beside the white froth rushing down slabs from pool to pool) and switchbacking up the open ridge slopes. Pass a sideroad up the valley and continue to a promontory at 2400 feet. Wow. Tarry to goggle at the views, but not long because this is only the beginning. The road now swings into indecently-exposed Mineral Creek valley and ascends to a Y on the ridgecrest. Turn right the short bit along the crest to the 2900-foot summit of Noble Naked Knob.

Zounds. Up there beyond the still-wild headwaters of the Clearwater, beyond Hurricane Gap and Bearhead, stands The Mountain. And down there in the smog out the White River are Boise Ridge, fields of Enumclaw, and the Olympics. And all around are valleys and ridges stripped of trees in the 1970s, the seedlings still small (or not yet planted, since the logging continues). A maze of yellow-white roads, switchbacking and contouring and wiggling around, inscribes the red-brown slopes littered with bleached sticks.

It's enough. But there's more. Another 2 gently-climbing miles up the ridge road, views ever-growing, is the head of Mineral Creek and the foot of the final ridge, in a saddle at 3750 feet. And the bald summit of the ridge, 4560 feet, may very well urgently call those with sufficient energy.

Round trip to Knob 5 miles, allow 3 hours
High point 2900 feet, elevation gain 140 feet
May-November

Having done this and the previous trip and thus been introduced to the White River Tree Farm slopes of Rainier, a hiker can devise dozens more walks on his own, no need for a guidebook. Buy the appropriate USGS maps, write Weyerhaeuser (see chapter introduction) for a map of company roads, and go exploring.

For example, at the 2050-foot crossing of Byron Creek, go right instead of left, ascending to the ridge between Byron and Milky Creeks.

At the gates at 1520 feet, take the right fork, road 6000, cross the Clearwater, and climb the ridges around Lyle Creek that are so prominent from Noble Naked Knob.

At 1½ miles back down the valley from the gates, 4 miles from the highway, take road 6050 across the Clearwater and find miles and miles of high routes in Canyon Creek and Three Sisters country.

Just after crossing the White River, turn left, upvalley, to the logging roads of Camp Creek and Rocky Run.

Keep going to the West Fork White River, with road systems ascending high on both sides.

Grass Mountain — Main Peak (Map - page 193)

Grass Mountain is some 15 miles long, rising from the Green River at the Cascade front and extending far into the range, for most of its length forming the north side of the White River Valley. The only reason it's not longer is that at a certain point, for no apparent reason, the map gets tired of Grass and starts calling the ridge Huckleberry Mountain. This much mountain obviously provides material for any number of hikes, mostly in the stark landscapes of recent clearcutting, the views beginning early and growing and growing as elevation is gained. As representative examples on the highest or Main Peak, two hikes on the same route, one low, the other high, will be described. (For another summit see Grass Mountain — West Peak.)

Drive Highway 410 east 6 miles from the turnoff to Mud Mountain Dam. (Just beyond Mud Mountain ignore the "Grass Mountain" sign — see below.) Just after crossing Clay Creek (unsigned), note on the left a logging road

Fogbound snags on Grass Mountain

Fog streaming over a shoulder of Grass Mountain

making a reverse turn and climbing to a power transformer. For the first (lower) hike park near the highway, elevation 1500 feet.

Bad enough to scare off family sedans but not bad enough to much interest sport-drivers who in any event have thousands of miles of roads to razz hereabouts, the narrow, rough, steep road ascends Clay Creek valley, at ¾ mile, 1900 feet, swinging under a basalt cliff to splendid views down to the highway, Stink Lake, Philip, and Rainier. Now on a flat railroad grade in second-growth from the 1930s, the road contours east 1 mile to the edge of Cyclone Creek valley. Bending left, in ½ mile it comes to a Y, the right dropping to the creek; go left, climbing to a railroad grade that contours west at 2300 feet a scant 1 mile, then switchbacks east onto another flat grade for ½ mile to a series of view windows. Here, at 2500 feet, 3¾ miles from the highway, is a satisfying turnaround. (But if snow is deep, a party may well be satisfied with the viewpoint at 1900 feet.)

Round trip 7½ miles, allow 5 hours
High point 2500 feet, elevation gain 1000 feet
February-December

For the second (top-of-the-world) hike, drive to the windows at 2500 feet; otherwise it's a very long trip. Park here, where the road crosses a cutbank of rotten lava rubble-dirt on a steep sidehill and could be car-endangering.

Just past the dirt bank the road makes another switchback, west, and ascends to a T at 2650 feet. The right fork drops to Cyclone Creek; turn left on another railroad grade that goes on and on — and on — swinging into a number of creeklets feeding Clay Creek, each with its ghosts of old trestles. Windows open on Rainier. And now from nice young forest begin views to the scalped ridges of Grass, its summit marked by the lookout tower.

Approaching a Bonneville powerline which crosses Grass from the Green to the White, out in a flat of recent alder-logging on state land, pass a sideroad right to the powerline. Now climbing, pass a gravel pit and at 2¾ miles, 3100 feet, meet the Grass Mountain Truck Road (see below) at a point some 10 miles from Highway 410.

Turn right on the wider road (much-driven, more's the pity, by sports) and settle down to grind out altitude. During the first ½ mile keep right at two Ys; from then on simply forge ahead, passing many obviously deadending spurs. The road starts up across the steep final slopes of the mountain, clearcut in the 1960s, the new plantation a sprinkling of small shrubs. Views become continuous and overwhelming. At 4000 feet is a saddle; now there are views down to the basin of Lynn Lake and north to the Green River. The road ascends the ridge crest, on top of the stripped-naked world, to the summit at 4382 feet, 4¾ miles.

What a world! Out the White River to Enumclaw, Puget Sound, Seattle, the Olympics. Across the Forbidden Valley of the Green River to McDonald, Issaquah Alps, Si, Baker, Glacier, and beyond the Cascade Crest to Stuart. Let's see, there must be something else. Oh yes, The Mountain. Pow.

The summit is decorated not only by a batch of over-communication towers but by one of the last remaining of the state fire lookout towers. It's too airy and shaky for casual use, so stay off. Who needs it for a view, now all the trees are gone?

Round trip 9½ miles, allow 6 hours
High point 4382 feet, elevation gain 1900 feet
May-November

Grass can get to be a habit. Having attained this highest peak, one may aspire to only slightly lesser highs east and west.

From the Grass Mountain Truck Road, departing from Highway 410 just past the turnoff to Mud Mountain Dam, one can drive for miles, gaining access to western portions of Grass — and also the Main Peak, as described above. Indeed, for explorations of the peaks and basins neighboring Main Peak one does best to use this approach, saving time for the high rambles.

Up the White River valley from the Clay Creek logging road described here, several other roads take off before Federation Forest State Park is reached; all can be used for walks or drive-walks to eastern summits of Grass, some of which are still green.

Federation Forest State Park (Map - page 203)

A half-century ago leaders of the Washington State Federation of Women's Clubs realized there soon would be no low-elevation virgin forests of big trees except those protected in parks. Their efforts led to acquisition of this 612-acre preserve, part of it aptly called "Land of the Giants." Plantings by the Interpretive Center, plus identifying signs on the nature trails, provide a fine classroom

Trailside bench in Federation Forest State Park

in which to learn the native shrubs and trees, including centuries-old Douglas fir, western red cedar, western hemlock, grand fir, Sitka spruce (uncommon this far from the ocean), yew, and more.

Drive Highway 410 east from Enumclaw 17 miles to the Interpretive Center and parking area, elevation 1650 feet. Here begin the two Fred Cleator Interpretive Trails, both loops, the West Trail just short of 1 mile, the East under ½ mile. Together they introduce five distinct forest communities on a broad river terrace perched some 30 feet above the present level of the White River. Also preserved is a section of the Naches Wagon Road, or Naches Trail, over which the Longmire party came from the east in 1853.

Begin with a tour of the Center, open Wednesday through Sunday the year around; pick up a trail guidebook. If the Center is not open, study the plantings around it, all identified with tags, a living textbook. Then walk the interpretive trails, altogether totalling some 2 miles.

Now properly warmed up, take the new loop trail, 5 miles in length, that tours the whole park from one end to the other and on both sides of the highway. Start at the Interpretive Center and follow the path as it winds along the bench with views of the White River, dips into tall trees, crosses springs and marshes to the far west end of the park. Then cross to the north side of Highway 410 and loop back to the Interpretive Center.

Finally, the broad gravel swath of the glacier-fed White River is close at hand; hikers weary of ogling and gasping at forest giants can burst free from green twilight into bright day and wander the braided channels for miles.

Round trip 1-12 miles, allow 1-10 hours
High point 2000 feet, minor elevation gain
February-December

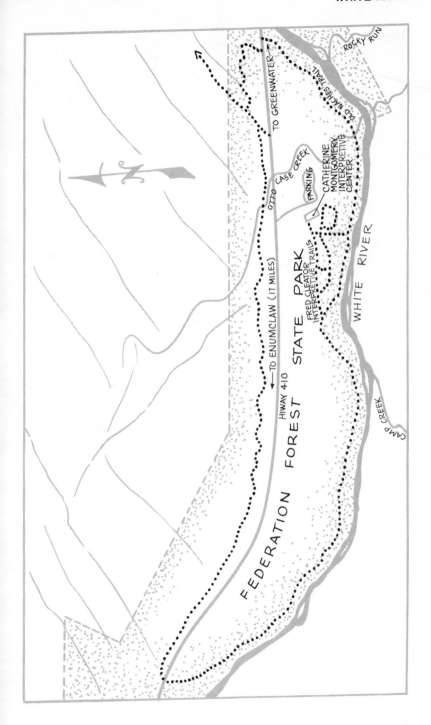

Greenwater River (Map - page 204)

Nice they surely are, but the Greenwater (Meeker) Lakes are the least attractions of this trail. First are the trees — groves of tall Douglas fir up to 5 feet in diameter, the more astonishing after the long drive up the denuded valley. Next are the basalt walls up to 200 feet high, moss-green and fern-decorated and waterfall-ribboned. And the river, now in greenwater pools lapping the feet of cliffs, now tumbling down bouldery gorges.

Drive Highway 410 east 2 miles from the hamlet of Greenwater and turn left on Greenwater River Road 197. Follow this 40mph logging freeway 8½ miles through numbing stumpland to the bridge over the Greenwater. A short bit beyond is a sign announcing "Greenwater Trail." Park here, elevation 2450 feet.

Note: These directions will not apply after logging starts, perhaps in 1979-81. Mt. Baker-Snoqualmie National Forest will attempt to maintain a trail but location of the start and the route may vary.

The immediate necessity (1977) is to cross Pyramid Creek, never dangerous but in possible absence of a footlog requiring over-the-ankles wading for a dozen feet. Proceed on a razzers' playroad over the bleak valley bottom. A Y soon presents itself. The track uphill left is the historic Naches Trail of the first wagon train to cross the Cascades to Puget Sound; considering what descendants of the wagon train folk did to Puget Sound, it's perhaps appropriate that the "Trail" has been dedicated by the Forest Service to ATVs. Go right (straight) here, threading through the maze of tracks in this playpen, entering the big trees, where the road narrows to trail — though still wide and flat enough that motorcycles snarl and fume along at speeds imperiling pedestrians. Splits in the trail may confuse; generally, where two equal paths are met, stay left, away from the river; but there is no real danger of losing the way.

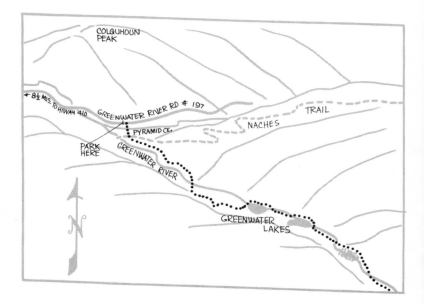

Greenwater River trail

Now, time to enjoy. Admire the trees. Pause to count rings on fallen specimens sawn through to clear the trail. Beyond the first of the lovely green basalt walls, 1 mile from the trailhead, is the first of the many picturesque footlog-bridges over the river — bridges unfortunately too big and easy to be wheelstops, though each noticeably thins the traffic.

At 1¾ miles, 2800 feet, is the first lake; the best part is the green pool at the outlet, crossed by the second bridge at the foot of a ferny wall. Twice more the river is crossed in the ½ mile to the second lake. Above its inlet, in a glorious cedar flat, big trees standing beside a tall basalt wall, are two nearly end-to-end footlogs — over Meadow Creek and over the Greenwater. In ¾ mile more, 3 miles from the car, 2950 feet, the trail crosses the outlet of the third "lake" — now a large alder marsh. Here, beneath a cliff of cordwood-stacked columnar basalt, beside a deep sand-bottomed pool that in season must stir thoughts of swimming, is a logical stopping place. But the trail goes on and so does the fun.

Round trip 6 miles, allow 4 hours
High point 2950 feet, elevation gain 500 feet
May-November

Snoquera Flats — Camp Sheppard (Map - page 207)

Along the Chinook Pass Highway on the approach to Mount Rainier lies the Mather Memorial Strip, dedicated to the first director of the National Park Service. In the portion outside the park, in Mt. Baker-Snoqualmie National Forest, the Forest Service is pledged to preserving the visual integrity of the White River valley as seen from the highway. Thus the valley floor and walls will remain forested — and beautifully so.

In this strip, on a flat alluvial terrace, during early New Deal days was located a camp of the ERA, older-folks version of the CCC, occupying a former campsite of the 1890s trail to the Starbo Mine on slopes of Rainier. From Snoqualmie minus almie plus ERA came the names, Snoquera Creek, Falls, Palisades, Flats, and Camp Snoquera, later renamed Camp Sheppard.

The site is now leased to the Chief Seattle Council of the Scouts of America. Under direction of Camp Ranger Max Eckenburg and support Ranger Ivan Kay, in the past dozen years the Scouts based at the camp have built 23 miles of trail, with another 29 miles on the master plan. The system ties into both the Cascade Crest Trail and the Wonderland Trail so the camp is a base for hikes in all directions. However, coverage in this book is restricted to trails in the immediate vicinity of camp, on and near Snoquera Flats.

"That's great for Scouts," you say, "But what about us?" When Ranger Max was asked if the trails might be used by the general public, he responded, "That's who they're for!"

Drive Highway 410 east 11 miles from the hamlet of Greenwater to the sign, "Camp Sheppard," and turn left into the large, marked parking area and picnic ground, elevation 2400 feet.

For openers take the Moss Lake Nature Trail. From the parking lot a path leading toward the valley wall comes in a scant ¼ mile to Campfire Circle in a stunning grove of forest giants. Here is the start-end of the nature trail loop of some ¾ mile. The way circles the marsh bottom of the "lake," whose amazing

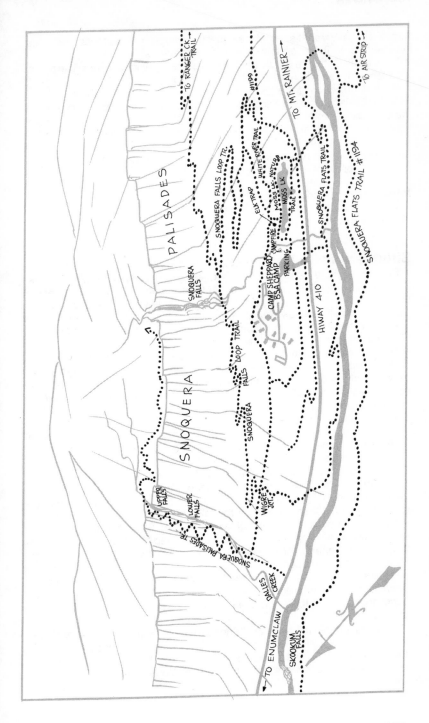

display of many varieties of moss usually climaxes in July. Moss and frogs here — and up there, on the valley wall, huge trees.

Back at the Campfire Circle, proceed on a trail to the inner camp. The public is welcomed; see where and how the Scouts live.

Back at the parking lot, walk the entrance road to near the highway and turn left on a paralleling trail. In a scant ¼ mile it leads to a highway crossing and on the other side to a Y. The left is to Skookum Flats across the White River; go right, downstream, on the Snoquera Flats Trail. In ½ mile is a Y. the left (straight ahead) fork proceeds along the river (and eventually, by taking appropriate right turns, back to camp in about 2 miles); for a shorter trip go right, in a scant ¼ mile recrossing the highway and returning to the parking lot.

Introductory round trips 3 miles, allow 2 hours
High point 2400 feet, minor elevation gain
April-December

Snoquera Falls Loop (Map - page 207)

Big-tree virgin forests. Intimidating looks up-up-up lava precipices of The Palisades of Dalles Ridge. Views down to the White River, whose greenery completely hides the highway. May is the best time to see the falls — in that season the meltwater-swollen torrent plunges into a 30-foot-deep heap of avalanche snow and spray clouds drench hikers. But the display of icicles hundreds of feet high is worth an early-winter visit.

Drive to the Camp Sheppard (which see) parking lot, 2400 feet. From there take the trail pointing at The Palisades — and up on that 500-foot near-overhang of a cliff see the thin ribbon of Snoquera Falls pluming down — or in spring see the Niagara flooding down — or at the right hour of a fall day see the mists windblown in a wavering rainbow. Walk to the start-end of the Moss Lake Nature Trail by the Campfire Circle; just beyond, intersect a road-wide trail. Turn right, uphill, to an elk trap maintained for research purposes. Here, ¼ mile from the parking lot, is the junction of a whole mess of trails, all clearly signed. Note the one going uphill right, signed "Snoquera Falls Loop Trail 1167, Snoquera Falls 1½" — that will be the route of the return.

Go left on White River Trail 1199, signed "Camp Sheppard ¼, Snoquera Loop Junction ¾." (The reason for doing the loop this way rather than the other is because it sneaks up on the falls, keeping the surprise to the last minute.) Proceed carefully through a profusion of crisscrossing paths to and from camp, whose roads and buildings are passed. At all unsigned junctions forge straight ahead. At all signed junctions stick with "Snoquera Loop." Passing mysterious open swaths on the hillside (they're for innertube sliding in snowtime), leave camp and proceed in continuously superb forest, in green twilight, on and near the valley floor. In ¾ miles from Elk Trap Junction is Wigre Junction, so called for a Scout leader who suffered an injury while building trail.

Turn right, again following the "Snoquera Loop" sign, and switchback up to the foot of the cliffs. Now the trail more or less contours, often close enough to the wall to reach out and put hands on. Look up the thrilling precipice. See the gorgeous fern-moss walls. See the monster Douglas firs growing from the rockslides — and marvel that they've survived the centuries of battering and gouging by falling rocks which have left every trunk a mass of impact wounds

A cedar grove on Moss Lake nature trail

— and these superimposed on burn scars from repeated fires over the ages.

Hark. What is that sound? Why does the earth tremble? What mystery is creating these clouds drifting through the forest? Turn a lava corner — and there are the falls! (This is an example of how the Sheppard trails are designed — not to get from here to there in a rush but to squeeze the maximum excitement from the country.) Even in season when the falls aren't falling, well may one cower, gazing up the beetling black walls. They do not have a permanent look. One imagines more substantial and fearful falls than mere water.

The loop trail now starts down, passing an unsigned junction and a signed one, and returning in constant grand forest to Elk Trap Junction.

Round trip 4½ miles, allow 3 hours
High point 3100 feet, elevation gain 700 feet
May-November

Footbridge over the White River

Snoquera Palisades (Map - page 207)

Having looked up-up-up the Palisades from the bottom, ascend a spooky little gorge via an impossible route and look down-down-down from the top.

At Wigre Junction (see Snoquera Falls Loop) continue straight ahead downvalley on trail signed "Dalles Creek Trail Jct ¼ mile." In that ¼ mile (1½ miles from the parking lot) reach a junction at the dropoff to Dalles Creek. Switchback right, uphill, on Dalles Creek trail 1198. (Ultimately signs will show the new name — "Snoquera Palisades Loop Trail 1198.") Switchback into the gorge and cross the creek in its dark, lush, big-tree depths, a place that in twilight is full of the oogalies that pad silently along behind lone hikers.

When Max and Ivan declared the Scouts were going to build a trail up this gorge, some Forest Service engineers burst into hysterical laughter. And truly, it's such a place as no trail has a right to be. Under drippy black-and-green-mossy Palisades walls, by pillars and clefts in the lava, amid big cedars anchored to rock, the trail switchbacks by a short spur to Lower Dalles Falls. Now, trapped in its idiot resolve to ascend this dank dark slot, the path writhes and wiggles between fern-garden cliffs and solemn great trees, trying to escape. The route is never dangerous, though looking up and down the switchbacks may give hikers the vertigo. Then, after some 30 switchbacks in ½ mile, the trail passes the Upper Falls, most of the year a small trickle, and incredibly breaks free of the gorge onto a forest shelf above the Palisades.

Now on gentle slopes, the trail turns southerly, traverses into a nice valley of a more relaxing Dalles Creek just below another falls hiding upstream in a little canyon. One has the suspicion that vast amounts of air are close by — and at 3350 feet the way emerges from trees onto the bald brink of a promontory. Be careful! Don't run to the edge! Cautiously step out on the viewpoint, look to nearby higher Palisades in stark profile, look down to forests of the valley, up to the 5270-foot summit of Sun Top.

Continue on, leaving the brink for more forest, ascend to the edge of the little Dalles Creek canyon just passed, then switchback out near the edge of the Palisades. At the turn of another switchback take the short sidepath to Point of

Springs, a thrilling viewpoint with the added embellishment of ice-cold springs. Return to the main trail and continue into a pole forest of an old burn and break out on the bald brink of North Snoquera Point, 4000 feet, 4 miles from the parking lot. This brink is not so giddy and invites cautious poking around in the rock garden of herbs and shrubs. Look down to Camp Sheppard, 1600 feet directly below; to leap off would seemingly risk being skewered by the camp flagpole. To previous views now are added Rainier.

Construction continues and by the time you arrive the tread may extend to a bridge over Snoquera Creek or onward to South Snoquera Point, 4800 feet. Eventually the trail will extend to other vista points and connect with a return down the cliffs to Sheppard, making a 16-mile loop suitable for older Scouts (and civilians) to do in a day.

Round trip 8 miles, allow 5 hours
High point 4000 feet, elevation gain 1600 feet
June-November

Skookum Flats (Map - page 207)

Machines speed along the highway on one side of the White River. On the other side, in big old trees of Mather Memorial Strip, between lava cliffs and river gravels, hikers can forget there are machines in the world.

From the 2400-foot parking lot at Camp Sheppard (which see) walk toward the highway on the entry road, find a trail paralleling the highway, and follow it upvalley a scant ¼ mile. At a sign pointing right to Skookum Flat Tail and Buck Creek Trail, cross the highway, jog left a hundred feet, and take the Buck Creek trail dropping into woods to the White River trail. Follow this upstream ½ mile to a footbridge, perfectly safe but likely to give acrophobes a thrill. On the far side, 1 mile from Sheppard, is a junction with the Skookum Flat Trail.

The trail upstream makes a pleasant 1¼-mile walk to the emergency airstrip. Downstream is the choice trip, however. Except at the very end, the 4½ miles to the Huckleberry Creek road are a constant delight, now on alluvial terraces, now beside the water, always in giant forest, here and there with looks across the valley to the Snoquera Palisades. At 2¼ miles from the junction are Skookum Falls, a satisfying turnaround. But just a bit farther are Skookum Springs Seeps, from whose 300 vertical feet of mossy basalt wall water droplets fall free. In any event, to avoid breaking the spell don't go all the way to the road; at 4 miles, when Dalles Campground is spotted across the river, turn back, thus avoiding the sight of logging, of which any user of this book can see a plenty on other trips.

The constant little ups and downs hardly raise a sweat. A bit of snow is a minor obstacle on the easy route — indeed, snow adds interest, since this unmachined side of the river is an animal highway and a hiker is likely to see tracks of coyote, bobcat, deer, rabbit, and a variety of little critters, raccoon-size, mouse-size, bird-size.

Round trip to Skookum Falls 6½ miles, allow 4 hours
High point 2500 feet, elevation gain 500 feet
March-December

Snoquera Falls

INDEX

OTHER BOOKS FROM THE MOUNTAINEERS

50 Hikes in Mount Rainier National Park
101 Hikes in the North Cascades
102 Hikes in the Alpine Lakes, South Cascades and Olympics
103 Hikes in Southwestern British Columbia
109 Walks in B.C.'s Lower Mainland
Trips and Trails, 1: Family Camps, Short Hikes and View Roads in the North Cascades
Trips and Trails, 2: Family Camps, Short Hikes and View Roads in the Olympics, Mt.
   Rainier and South Cascades
Bicycling the Backroads Around Puget Sound
Bicycling the Backroads of Northwest Washington
Discover Southeast Alaska with Pack and Paddle
55 Ways to the Wilderness in Southcentral Alaska
Hikers' Map to the North Cascades: Routes and Rocks in the Mt. Challenger Quadrangle
Guide to Leavenworth Rock Climbing Areas
Cascade Alpine Guide: Climbing and High Routes, Columbia River to Stevens Pass
Cascade Alpine Guide: Climbing and High Routes, Stevens Pass to Rainy Pass
Climbers' Guide to the Olympic Mountains
Darrington and Index: Rock Climbing Guide
Snow Trails: Ski and Snowshoe Routes in the Cascades
Mountaineering: The Freedom of the Hills
Medicine for Mountaineering
Mountaineering First Aid
Snowshoeing
The South Cascades: The Gifford Pinchot National Forest
Challenge of Mount Rainier
The Unknown Mountain
Fire and Ice: The Cascade Volcanoes
Across the Olympic Mountains: The Press Expedition
Men, Mules and Mountains: Lieutenant O'Neil's Olympic Expeditions
The Coffee Chased Us Up: Monte Cristo Memories
Challenge of the North Cascades
Bicycling Notes
Hiking Notes
Climbing Notes
Mountains of the World
The Mountaineer
Northwest Trees
The Ascent of Denali
Storm and Sorrow in the High Pamirs
Canoe Routes: Yukon Territory
Canoe Routes: British Columbia
The ABC of Avalanche Safety